Romulus founded Rome – but why does the myth give
him a twin brother Remus, who is killed at the moment of
the foundation? This mysterious legend has been oddly
neglected. Roman historians ignore it as irrelevant to real
history; students of myth concentrate on the more glamor-
ous mythology of Greece. In this book, Professor Wiseman
provides, for the first time, a detailed analysis of all the
variants of the story, and a historical explanation for its
origin and development. His conclusions offer important
new insights, both into the history and ideology of pre-
imperial Rome and into the methods and motives of
myth-creation in a non-literate society. In the richly
unfamiliar Rome of Pan, Hermes and Circe the witch-
goddess, where a general grows miraculous horns and
prophets demand human sacrifice, Remus stands for the
unequal struggle of the many against the powerful few.

REMUS

REMUS

A Roman myth

T. P. WISEMAN

Professor of Classics and Ancient History,
University of Exeter

CAMBRIDGE
UNIVERSITY PRESS

Published by the Press Syndicate of the University of Cambridge
The Pitt Building, Trumpington Street, Cambridge CB2 1RP
40 West 20th Street, New York, NY 10011-4211, USA
10 Stamford Road, Oakleigh, Melbourne 3166, Australia

First published 1995

Printed in Great Britain at the University Press, Cambridge

A catalogue for this book is available from the British Library

Library of Congress cataloguing in publication data

Wiseman, T. P. (Timothy Peter)
Remus: a Roman myth/T. P. Wiseman.
p.   cm.
Includes bibliographical references and index.
ISBN 0 521 41981 6 (hardback) – ISBN 0 521 48366 2 (paperback)
1. Remus (Twin of Romulus, King of Rome)
2. Mythology, Roman.
3. Rome – History – To 510 BC – Historiography.
1. Title.
BL805.W57   1995
398.2'0937'602–dc20   94-42523   CIP

ISBN 0 521 41981 6   hardback
ISBN 0 521 48366 2   paperback

CE

Roma fave, tibi surgit opus

Contents

Illustrations

xi

Preface

With the possible exception of the Trojan Horse, there is no scene in the whole iconography of classical myth more recognisable than that of the she-wolf and twins. And though few people today would be able to name even one of the Greek warriors hidden in the Horse, the she-wolf scene can still be relied on to evoke the formula 'Romulus 'n' Remus'. It takes a bit more knowledge to distinguish between them, and to put a story to the names. Fewer now than in our grandparents' generation know what happened to Remus.

Classicists know the story, of course, but they are astonishingly incurious about it. Dozens of books have been written about the Aeneas legend, its variants, its significance for Rome, its incorporation into the ideology of the Augustan principate. Nothing equivalent exists for the story of the twins. The specialist's equivalent of 'Romulus 'n' Remus' is the index entry that reads 'Remus, *see* Romulus'. In English at least, even those who should know better casually mispronounce the names; *Romulus* has a long 'o' (it is, after all, the eponym of Rome), *Remus* has a short 'e'. And even to put the names in that order is a solecism. For the Romans, the story of the twins was 'de Remo et Romulo'.

Remus in particular has suffered from this neglect. There are texts from antiquity which tell us that Remus was the elder twin; that Romulus was known as 'the other one'; that Remus outlived Romulus; and that *both* of them were demigods, celebrated in hymns and invoked in oaths. None of that makes sense if we assume that the story made canonical by Livy, Ovid and Plutarch is all there ever was. But there is no need to

xiii

assume that – and every reason *not* to, given the large number of variant versions detectable even in the ancient sources that survive.

The aim of this book is to look carefully at what the ancient sources tell us (and what they show us, for visual evidence is important too), paying particular attention to variants, contradictions and inconsistencies; and to apply it to what we know or can infer about archaic and republican Rome, in order to draw up a hypothetical reconstruction of the origin, development and exploitation of the legend.

I hope it will become clear in the course of the argument that in order to understand the process we must rid ourselves of preconceptions about 'the legalistic, authoritarian, and some-times pompous, if pragmatic, Romans' (to quote an agreeably pithy recent formulation of the standard view), and think ourselves back into a pre-imperial and perhaps less inhibited Rome, a community whose self-image was still evolving, in which openness to outside influences was not yet a matter for anxiety. It should never be forgotten that our picture of the Romans is almost wholly constructed from the works of authors writing – with the partial exception of Plautus – at a time when Rome was an imperial power which had defined itself as different from, and superior to, the peoples it had subjected.

> Let others better mould the running mass
> Of metals, and inform the breathing brass,
> And soften into flesh a marble face;
> Plead better at the bar; describe the skies,
> And when the stars descend, and when they rise.
> But, Rome! 'tis thine alone, with awful sway,
> To rule mankind, and make the world obey:
> Disposing peace and war thy own majestic way.
> To tame the proud, the fettered slave to free,
> These are imperial arts, and worthy thee.

The 'other Rome', as I call it in chapter 10 – the city in which and for which the Remus story was created – pre-dates this ideology. We shall have to do with a Rome which was not yet a paradigm of power.

Since I hope the book will be of interest not only to classicists and ancient historians but to anyone with a taste for myth, legend and story-telling, I have translated Greek and Latin quotations and done my best to avoid or explain technicalities. Even so, I am very conscious of the complexity of the argument. It could hardly be otherwise, when the subject is the elaboration of a legend over several centuries, in a society for which the sources of our knowledge are lamentably inadequate. I think some kind of sense can be made of it, but it does demand concentration.

It is a pleasure to record those who have helped in the writing of this book. I am grateful above all to the University of Exeter, for the two periods of study leave which enabled me to write it at all, and to the Institute for Advanced Study at Princeton, for providing me with ideal working conditions for three months in 1992. Sceptical but tolerant audiences at lectures and seminars in various places (from Finland to California), in the period 1988–93, helped to sharpen the argument, and my Exeter colleagues have been generous with ideas and suggestions. Tim Cornell and John North heroically read through and commented on the whole typescript; I am very grateful indeed for their advice, and hope I have profited from it even on the points where I have persisted in my own view. My thanks to Rodney Fry and Susan Rouillard, for drawing the maps and diagrams, and to Pauline Hire, for her confidence that my half-formed ideas would eventually make a book. Finally, I should like to repeat something I wrote twenty-four years ago, which is even more true today. My wife has been involved with this book and its vicissitudes to a degree well beyond the call of duty. For her patience and encouragement no thanks can be adequate.

TPW
Exeter 1994

CHAPTER I

A too familiar story

THE FABIAN NARRATIVE

The first history of Rome was written by Quintus Fabius Pictor, a senator from a very famous patrician family. He wrote in Greek, either during or just after the great war with Hannibal, in order to familiarise the civilised world, for whom Greek was the *lingua franca*, with the origins and achievements of the city on the Tiber which was now a major power in that world.

Greek readers of the history of a city expected to begin with a foundation story, including the genealogical association of the founder with the familiar world of heroic legend.[1] Fabius did not disappoint them. According to a library-catalogue inscription that happens to survive,[2] he related

Herakles' arrival in Italy and the return of Lanoios and his ally Aeneas and Ascanius; much later, the birth of Romulus and Remus and the founding of Rome by Romulus, who was the first king.

'Much later' covers the dynasty of the Silvii ('men of the forest'), descendants of Aeneas and rulers of Alba Longa, which Aeneas' son Ascanius had founded.[3] Eleven generations after Ascanius, the brothers Numitor and Amulius succeed to the Alban throne.

At that point began the story of Rome. Fabius' narrative does not survive, but it was followed in detail – with additions and variants – by two later Greek authors whose works do survive, Dionysius of Halicarnassus in the late first century BC (*Roman Antiquities* I 76–83) and Plutarch in the early second century AD (*Life of Romulus* 3–8). Plutarch, indeed, even cites

Fabius' source: 'The first to publish the story to the Greeks was Diocles of Peparethos, whom Fabius Pictor followed on most points.' But since it is impossible to tell which, if any, of Plutarch's items were in Diocles but not in Fabius (or even if he had access to Diocles' text at all), all we can do is combine Plutarch's narrative with that of Dionysius in order to reconstruct, at least provisionally, the Roman foundation-legend as it appeared in the first Roman history. It went something like this.

'DE REMO ET ROMULO'

Amulius offers his brother a choice between the kingship and the family fortune. Numitor takes the kingship, but Amulius then uses his wealth to depose him and seize the power himself. Fearing vengeance, he arranges to have Numitor's son killed, and appoints Numitor's daughter Ilia as a priestess of Vesta, supposedly as a mark of honour, but really to prevent her having children who might avenge their grandfather.[4]

Four years later, Ilia is in the sacred grove of Mars getting water from the spring. The sky is suddenly darkened, and a male figure of supernatural size and beauty appears and ravishes her. Afterwards he consoles her with the prospect of bearing the offspring of Mars himself – twin sons who will excel all men in warlike valour – and soars back to heaven on a cloud.[5] Ilia, unable to go on performing her duties as a Vestal Virgin, consults her mother and feigns sickness.

Amulius is suspicious, and in due course discovers her pregnancy. He complains to Numitor, who gets the whole story from his wife and reports it to the royal council. Is Ilia telling the truth? Evidently she is, for she gives birth to twins as the god foretold. Amulius refuses to believe it: one of the women must have smuggled in a second baby. As an unchaste Vestal, Ilia must die, and her offspring be thrown in the river. However, the first part of the sentence is commuted to imprisonment in solitary confinement, at the plea of Ilia's cousin, the daughter of Amulius.[6] (Plutarch gives the cousin's name – Antho, 'Flower' – and puts both sentence and intercession *after* the birth.)

The infant twins are put in a box and taken by Amulius' men[7] down from Alba to the Tiber, which is in flood. The men put the box down in the floodwater where it washes against the slope of the Palatine hill.[8] The water recedes, the box is grounded, the twins are tipped out crying into the mud beside a fig tree.[9] There now appears a she-wolf with swollen udders (for she has just whelped), who licks the babies clean and suckles them.

This miraculous scene is witnessed by Faustulus, the king's swineherd, who comes down from the hill and rescues the twins.[10] The she-wolf calmly retreats into a nearby cave, sacred to Pan,[11] and Faustulus takes the babies home to his wife. Now, Faustulus happens to know who they are: he was in Alba when Ilia's childbirth was made public, and even, by some heaven-sent chance, accompanied the king's servants on their errand to the Palatine. Not only that, but his wife Larentia has just given birth to a still-born child. So he and Larentia bring up the twins as their own, in secret,[12] and call them Romulus and Remus from *ruma* ('teat'), referring to their miraculous suckling.[13]

The boys grow up handsome, spirited and brave, as befits royal children supernaturally begotten.[14] Despising idleness, they pass their time in physical exercise and hunting, in 'driving off robbers, capturing thieves, and rescuing the oppressed from violence'.[15] But like their foster-father they are the king's herdsmen, grazing his beasts on the Palatine and frequently quarrelling with Numitor's herdsmen on the Aventine about the pastures between the two hills. One day, when the twins are about eighteen, Numitor's men take advantage of Romulus' absence at a sacrifice and make a full-scale attack. Remus leads the resistance, but is caught in an ambush and taken as a prisoner to Numitor.

Romulus, on his return, is all for mounting an immediate rescue attempt, but Faustulus dissuades him from his 'too frenzied haste'[16] and tells him the whole story of his birth and upbringing. Together they plan a greater strategy, to free all of Numitor's family from the tyranny of Amulius. Stage one is gradually to assemble as many supporters as possible in the *agora* at Alba without arousing suspicion.

Meanwhile, Remus is brought before the king, found guilty of the charges brought against him by Numitor's men, and sent to Numitor's house for punishment. Impressed by his physique and dignified bearing, Numitor questions him about his origin and from his reply is inspired to guess the truth.[17] He tells Remus the story, enlists his aid against Amulius, and sends a reliable messenger to summon Romulus. Romulus, in fact, is already close to the city, with his forces now in place. He joins Remus and Numitor and they plan the attack.[18]

Now the plot thickens. Faustulus comes to Alba bringing the conclusive evidence – the box in which the twins were cast away. He is stopped at the city gate by the king's guards and forced to show what he is trying to conceal. One of the guards recognises the box from his errand eighteen years ago, and Faustulus is hauled before the king and brutally interrogated. Forced to admit that the twins are alive, Faustulus nevertheless claims that they are minding their herds far from the city. (Amulius of course does not know the identity of the herdsman he has just turned over to Numitor.) He offers to go and find them and bring them to the king. As for the box, he is taking it to show Ilia, who he hears is in the king's custody.

Amulius sends Faustulus away with an escort of guards to find the twins, and despatches a messenger to summon Numitor, whom he wants to keep under surveillance while he deals with Ilia's long-lost sons. But the messenger changes his allegiance; he warns Numitor of Amulius' plot and urges immediate action. Under the leadership of the twins,[19] the combined forces of Numitor's retainers and the countrymen in the *agora* storm the citadel, put Amulius to death, and restore Numitor to his rightful throne.

CONCORD OR DISCORD?

This tightly constructed plot, well described by Plutarch as 'theatrical',[20] is a unity complete in itself, and clearly treated as such by both Plutarch and Dionysius. But Rome has still not been founded. It is not at all easy to see from the extant accounts how Fabius Pictor handled the rest of the foundation story. And that may not be an accident, for the subsequent episodes are not all as edifying as the tale of heroism and divine favour on which Fabius evidently lavished most of his art.

At first the story continues straightforwardly.[21] Numitor gives the twins and their followers permission to found a new city 'at the place where they were brought up' – that is, by Faustulus' hut on the Palatine hill.[22] But after that the surviving traditions differ.

Some authors say firmly that Rome was founded by both the twins together.[23] After that, *either* Romulus became tyrannical and killed his brother (with civil war resulting)[24] *or* Remus actually outlived Romulus.[25] Others betray a knowledge of that tradition without committing themselves to it. Valerius Maximus, for instance, gives an explanation of the Lupercalia which implies a joint foundation; John Tzetzes says evasively that the twins 'began' the foundation together, though he names only Romulus as the founder; the anonymous author of *De viris illustribus* attributes to both twins the foundation of the *civitas* before the building of the fatal walls.[26]

That last expedient can be traced back as far as Cassius Hemina in the second century BC, only a generation or two after Fabius Pictor. A fragment happens to survive from the second book of his *Histories*:[27]

Pastorum vulgus sine contentione consentiendo praefecerunt aequaliter imperio Remum et Romulum, ita ut de regno pararent inter se. Monstrum fit: sus parit porcos triginta, cuius rei fanum fecerunt Laribus Grundilibus.

The shepherd population, by consensus and without dispute, gave Remus and Romulus equal authority, on the understanding that they should arrange between themselves about the kingship. A portent followed: a sow gave birth to thirty piglets. To mark the event they founded a shrine to the *Lares Grundiles*.

The portent – more familiar in other legendary contexts[28] – is an aetiology independent of the foundation story; but the first sentence clearly implies that the herdsmen were meeting in assembly, essentially as a citizen body, to decide who should have authority over them. According to Diodorus, it was the

twins who had brought that about.[29] Very properly, therefore,
power is devolved on both, and they are invited to sort it out
between themselves. The author of the *Origo gentis Romanae*
describes the next stage:[30]

Cum igitur inter se Romulus ac Remus de condenda urbe tractarent
in qua ipsi pariter regnarent, . . .

Romulus and Remus were deliberating between themselves about
the foundation of a city in which they would rule equally.

The adverb *pariter*, like *aequaliter* in Cassius Hemina, is exactly
what one expects in a twin story, especially one in which
fraternal devotion has been so conspicuous up to now. Everything seems in place for a harmonious agreement, and the joint
foundation some authors report is exactly what we might
expect.

  But that is the minority tradition. According to Plutarch and
Dionysius (are they still following Fabius Pictor?), the snake
now enters the garden in the form of rivalry and discord.[31]
Two great stories follow – the augury contest and the death of
Remus – both of which appear in a striking variety of forms.

THE QUARREL

One of the few substantial surviving fragments of the great epic
poem of republican Rome, Quintus Ennius' *Annales* (written
not long after Fabius Pictor's history), concerns the twins'
competition for signs of divine approval.[32] The first few lines
are textually corrupt at a crucial point. I offer a deliberately
conservative text and translation:

>   curantis magna cum cura tum cupientes
>   regni dant operam simul auspicio augurioque.
>   †In monte Remus auspicio se devovet atque secundam†[33]
>   solus avem servat. at Romulus pulcer in alto
>   quaerit Aventino, servant genus altivolantum.
>   certabant urbem Romam Remoramne vocarent.
>   omnibus cura viris uter esset induperator.

Then, scrupulously taking great care in their eagerness for
kingly power, they apply themselves simultaneously to
auspicy and augury. On . . . Remus . . .[34] and watches

alone for a bird. But Romulus the fair on the high Aventine seeks and watches for the race of high-flying ones. They[35] were competing about whether to call the city Roma or Remora. The concern of all the men was about which of the two would be the commander.

Remora is important. It confirms, at an early stage in the tradition, the derivation of Remus' name from *remorari*, to delay.[36] Dionysius, Plutarch and the *Origo gentis Romanae* say that the dispute concerned not only the city's name but also its site: Romulus wanted it on the Palatine, Remus at a place called Remoria (Dionysius), Remonion (Plutarch) or Remuria (*Origo gentis Romanae = OGR*), which their sources identified as *either* the Aventine *or* a hill by the river 'about thirty *stadia* from Rome' (Dionysius), 'five miles from the Palatine' (*OGR*). According to this version, the twins will have watched for their omens each at his chosen site.[37] Ennius, however, had Romulus on the Aventine, and Remus evidently on the nearby *mons Murcus*.[38]

Who won the contest? Ennius seems to say, though the passage is desperately difficult,[39] that after the moon had set and the rays of the as yet invisible sun had shot across the sky, a single bird appeared on the left (the favourable side) at the very moment of sunrise;[40] that twelve birds then appeared, flying into the spaces defined as augurally propitious; and that 'from this Romulus perceived that it was to him that [the first signs?] had been given, the chair and throne of kingship, established by auspicy'.[41]

It is infuriating that the textual corruption prevents us from knowing whether Ennius made explicit the question of priority. The careful precision with which he identified the exact moments when the one bird and the twelve respectively appeared suggests to me that he expected his readers to understand that the auspicy was not unambiguous. However, we cannot be sure, and so this fragment of an early tradition, different in various ways from what the later authors say, remains tantalisingly uncertain.

The story most of our authors tell, with Remus on the Aventine and Romulus on the Palatine, is that Remus saw his birds first, but saw only six against Romulus' twelve. They then either announce Romulus the winner without argument,[42] or explain that the ambiguity between priority and majority led to a quarrel, and a fight between the rival twins' supporters.[43]

Dionysius, who tells the latter version at length, includes in it the startling information (known also to Plutarch) that Romulus *cheated*.[44] After they had taken up their positions, 'through haste and jealousy of his brother,[45] and perhaps also by divine direction', Romulus sent messengers to Remus falsely announcing that he had seen the birds. Remus, who in the meantime really *had* seen six vultures, went back with the messengers and demanded details from Romulus, who couldn't answer. At that point twelve 'auspicious vultures' were seen in flight, and Romulus brazened it out: 'Why ask what happened before, when you can see them with your own eyes?'

The *Origo gentis Romanae* tells the same story with a different slant and a little extra dialogue.[46] When Remus asks what Romulus has seen, and reports his own sighting of six vultures, Romulus replies 'I shall now show you twelve'; and they duly appear, with thunder and lightning from Jupiter. Remus can't argue with that, so in this version there is no quarrel and no fight. Instead, Remus yields with a speech of renunciation:

Multa, inquit, in hac urbe temere sperata atque praesumpta felicissime proventura sunt.

'In this city', he said, 'many things rashly hoped for and taken for granted will turn out very successfully.'

That is a remarkable prophecy, very uncharacteristic of the Rome we think we know. What about all those exemplary stories of rash commanders coming unstuck,[47] and the contrasting admiration of Fabius Maximus, 'who alone, by delaying, saved the situation for Rome'?[48] In this story, Remus the slow is beaten by Romulus the hasty.[49]

Remus evidently gave a very similar speech of renunciation in Diodorus Siculus' history in the middle of the first century BC, but the Greek author picked out a particular aspect of it. (In Roman augury, the left was the auspicious side; in Greek, as in everyday Latin, 'right' and 'left' connoted respectively 'lucky' and 'unlucky'.) In the Byzantine excerpt which is all that survives of Diodorus' narrative, we are told that Romulus' sign appeared on the right-hand side. Whereupon,[50]

Remus was astonished, and said to his brother: 'In this city it will often happen that *right* fortune follows *sinister* designs.' For Romulus had sent his messenger too hastily; he had been totally wrong for his own part, but his ignorance had been corrected by mere chance.

The Greek for 'too hasty' is *propetes*; the Latin technical term for 'auspicious birds' is *praepetes aves*.[51] It looks as if Diodorus' source was particularly interested in etymological explanations of augural terminology. One wonders whether he exploited the technical term for 'birds that prevent action'; they were called *remores aves*.[52]

THE DEATH OF REMUS

The same Byzantine excerptor allows us to follow Diodorus' narrative to its fatal conclusion. While Romulus is surrounding the Palatine with a trench (hastily, of course),[53] Remus nurses his resentment in jealousy of his brother's fortune. He tells the workmen that the trench is too narrow to keep enemies out. Romulus is furious, and orders all his 'citizens' to take vengeance on anyone who crosses it. Remus persists with his criticism. 'Enemies will have no trouble getting over it', he says; 'I can do it myself, easily.' And he does so. At which one of the workmen, called Celer, 'the swift' (*Keleros* in Diodorus' Greek), invokes Romulus' order, lifts his spade, and kills Remus with a blow to the head.[54]

Celer is an important character. Some authors say he was Etruscan, and fled to Etruria immediately after the murder.[55] That implies a guilty conscience and a disapproving Romulus.[56] Another version, however, makes Romulus reward him with the post of 'tribune of the knights' – that is, *tribunus celerum*, commander of the three hundred Celeres ('swift ones') who were the king's bodyguard.[57] Ovid tells us that Romulus had himself given Celer his significant name, and other sources say the Celeres were named after him.[58]

That perhaps gives an extra resonance to the speech Dionysius puts into Celer's mouth. In this version the inadequate
defence is a wall, not a trench. Remus says, '*This* wall any of
your enemies could easily cross, as I do.' And Celer insolently
replies, '*This* enemy any of us could easily punish', and hits him
with the spade.[59] Any of us Celeres, the king's strong-arm men,
does he mean?

If it is unexpected to find a member of this elite corps
wielding a spade, that is probably the result of disparate
elements being welded together in the story-telling process. It
evidently mattered that the murder weapon was a digging
implement. (Diodorus and Dionysius call it a *skapheion*, the
generic Greek word for a spade, mattock or hoe; in the *De viris
illustribus* it is a drag-hoe, in Ovid a shovel – respectively *rastrum*
and *rutrum*.[60]) St Jerome, who had access to an otherwise
unknown version of the story of the twins,[61] tells us that
'Remus was killed with a shepherd's shovel by Fabius,
Romulus' commander'; the Fabii derived their name from the
act of digging, being called after an ancestor who invented the
digging of pits to trap wolves and bears.[62]

Even leaving aside this remarkable variant, it is clear that
the versions of the Celer story differed according to their
authors' view of the responsibility for the murder. Did
Romulus give the order 'Kill anyone crossing the trench'?[63] If
he did, did Remus knowingly defy it?[64] Was Celer a thug, or a
loyal servant of his king?[65] Who was it who was too hasty this
time?[66] You could tell the story many different ways, and slant
it in Romulus' favour if that was your aim.[67]

If on the other hand you wanted to blame Romulus, there
was a better way of doing it than by using Celer. Livy does not
mention Celer at all. Of the two versions he tells, the better-
known one at the time was that Romulus killed the mocking
Remus with his own hand, uttering the splendid line 'So perish
all henceforth who cross my walls!'[68] Deservedly, perhaps, in
our own time this dramatic fratricide has overshadowed all the
other versions. But for Roman readers it was only one of many,
and not (for obvious reasons) necessarily the most acceptable.

Livy's alternative version, which we know was told by Licinius Macer in the seventies BC, left Remus' killer unidentified. The quarrel about the augury contest led to a general conflict between the twins' respective sets of supporters, in the course of which Remus was killed.[69] So too was Faustulus, who tried to stop the violence; failing, he went unarmed into the thick of the fighting to find a speedy death.[70] That version emphasised general conflict rather than individual jealousy and anger; Macer was a rationaliser,[71] for whom a realistic battle-scene was no doubt preferable to the somewhat childish confrontation over Romulus' trench.[72]

The most ruthless rationalising of the foundation story, however, is by Cicero in the *De republica*. He concentrates wholly on Romulus, mentioning Remus only once (as part of the *fabula* of Romulus' exposure and rescue), and attributes to Romulus alone the leadership of the shepherds, the attack on Alba Longa, and the killing of Amulius.[73]

Having achieved this glory, it is said that he first planned the foundation of a city under favourable auspices and the establishment of a *res publica*.

And with that Cicero changes the subject, launching into a long digression on the excellence of the founder's choice of site and the layout of the city walls. Only three pages later is the foundation itself briefly referred to as a *fait accompli*.[74]

It looks as if Cicero wanted to avoid entirely the morally contentious issue of Remus' death. Reasonably enough, in a work praising the traditional constitution of Rome as an ideal state, he would prefer his readers not even to think about the possibility of a fratricidal founder. In the *De officiis*, on the other hand, he faced the issue squarely:

cui cum visum esset utilius solum quam cum altero regnare, fratrem interemit.

When [Romulus] decided that it was more expedient for him to be king alone than with another, he killed his brother.

There is no defence for that, says Cicero; it was a crime.[75]

POST MORTEM

It does not seem to have been noticed that Cicero's phraseology in the *De officiis* passage makes better sense if the twins had already been ruling together for a time before Remus was murdered. (At the very least, the passage envisages their joint rule as a real possibility.) We noticed earlier that there was a tradition of a joint foundation, and that some – admittedly very late – authors made Romulus kill Remus after a period of joint rule.[76] Late authors, even Byzantine ones, sometimes had access to earlier traditions not otherwise attested, and it is not impossible that that version was known to Cicero.[77]

It had a sequel. Disaster followed the crime, in the form of civil war or an epidemic,[78] and the oracles Romulus consulted told him to place a curule chair next to his own, bearing Remus' sceptre and other royal insignia, and to rule in partnership with his absent colleague. (The Byzantine authors say he made a gold statue of Remus and placed it next to himself on the royal throne.) As Servius puts it, Romulus duplicated everything, 'acting in all things to appear his brother's colleague, so as not to judge himself his brother's murderer'.[79]

There were post-mortem sequels to other versions of the story, too. In Ovid's elegantly exculpatory narrative, the grieving Romulus gives Remus full funeral honours (with an allusion to Catullus' farewell to his beloved brother), and he and Faustulus and Acca Larentia and all the citizens of Rome weep around the pyre.[80] That night, Remus' unhappy ghost appears to Faustulus and his wife, and asks them to persuade Romulus to grant him an annual memorial day. Romulus gives the name *Remuria* to 'the day when worship is duly offered to buried ancestors' – that is, 9 May, the day of the ghosts (*lemures*), which in the Roman calendar was called *Lemuria*. Over the years, says Ovid, the name has got corrupted.[81] He has this explanation from Hermes himself, the guide of souls to the underworld, and he ought to know.[82]

Dionysius and Plutarch offer a different account of Remus' obsequies. Romulus buried him at Remoria, giving him six feet at least of the land he had wanted to occupy as king.[83] I think it would be anachronistic to see that as a generous gesture by the victor. It looks more like the ironic fulfilment of a vow or prophecy. There is a particular type of 'misleading oracle' story, of which two Italian examples date from the fourth and early third centuries BC:[84] the applicant is promised 'Yes, you will occupy such and such a place', and ends up buried there.

Oracles and premonitory dreams certainly featured in the story of the twins,[85] and it is possible, though no reference survives, that an apparently encouraging oracle was given to Remus. But perhaps we should remember Ennius' description of the augury contest: 'Remus *se devovet*', which if textually sound (and it is hard to see how it could be the result of a corruption) must mean 'vows himself to the gods below'.[86] Did Remus, in that version, make a deal with the gods of the underworld? If so, perhaps his burial at Remoria was their way of keeping their word.

THE PROBLEM

It may be helpful, at this point, to try to schematise the bewildering variety of foundation-story variants that can be detected in our surviving texts. The diagram on page 14 gives the essentials.

Why are there so many variants? The contrast with the Fabius Pictor story of the conception, birth and adolescence of the twins is very marked. There are variants in that narrative, but they are mainly rationalisations of the supernatural, reducing a 'poetic' narrative to a 'historical' one by removing the marvels.[87] Fabius' story, however, was ethically unproblematic. You could tell it with or without Mars and the she-wolf, and it was still something to be proud of.

Not so the story of the foundation. For a patriotic historian, the only safe thing to do was to say as little as possible, like Cicero in the *De republica*, and leave Remus out of it. 'The twins founded the city, and the gods chose Romulus to name it and rule it as king.'[88] Anything more than that, and you would be in trouble. The brute fact is that Remus had to be either

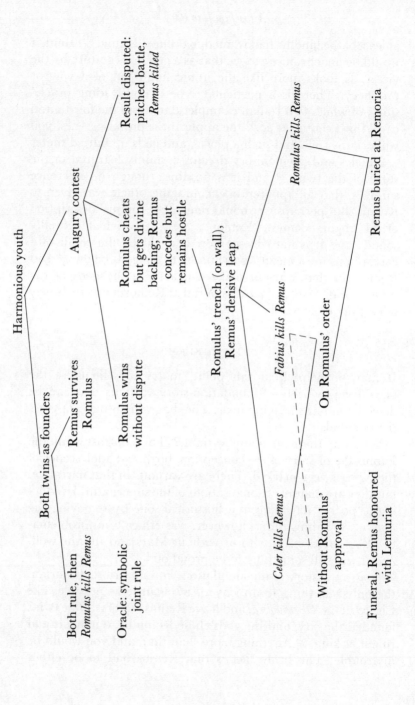

Harmonious youth

Both twins as founders

Remus survives Romulus

Augury contest

Both rule, then *Romulus kills Remus*

Oracle: symbolic joint rule

Romulus wins without dispute

Romulus cheats but gets divine backing; Remus concedes but remains hostile

Result disputed: pitched battle, *Remus killed*

Romulus' trench (or wall), Remus' derisive leap

Romulus kills Remus

Fabius kills Remus

Celer kills Remus

On Romulus' order

Without Romulus' approval

Remus buried at Remoria

Funeral, Remus honoured with Lemuria

forgotten or somehow written out of the script. Hence the proliferation of variant accounts.

An embarrassment for the patriotic is an opportunity for the hostile and the disaffected.

'What sort of people are the Romans? Why, mere herdsmen! Their land was taken by brigandage from its proper owners; they couldn't find wives because of their dishonourable origins, so they took them by a public rape; they even founded their city with a kin-murder, and soaked with a brother's blood the foundations of its walls.'

That, according to Justin, was how third-century BC Greeks reacted to the prospect of an alliance with Rome.[89] Six hundred years later St Augustine used the fratricide to denounce paganism, on two counts: the gods had failed to avenge Remus, and the 'city of men', thus inaugurated in envy and bloodshed, was clearly divided against itself. Augustine knew the texts, and he could see how embarrassed their authors were:[90]

It's of no significance to my case whether Romulus ordered the deed to be done or did it himself. Many brazenly deny it; many question it in shame; many find it too painful to admit.

In times of the greatest anguish and self-doubt, even the Romans themselves accepted the hostile view. There is a wonderful poem by the young Horace, written in the thirties BC after two generations of civil war, political strife, and civil war again:[91]

> Quo quo scelesti ruitis aut cur dexteris
>   aptantur enses conditi?
> parumne campis atque Neptuno super
>   fusum est Latini sanguinis,
> non ut superbas invidae Carthaginis
>   Romanus arcis ureret,
> intactus aut Britannus ut descenderet
>   sacra catenatus via,
> sed ut secundum vota Parthorum sua
>   urbs haec periret dextera?
> neque hic lupis mos nec fuit leonibus,
>   numquam nisi in dispar feris.
> furorne caecus an rapit vis acrior

> an culpa? responsum date!
> tacent, et albus ora pallor inficit
>   mentesque perculsae stupent.
> sic est: acerba fata Romanos agunt
>   scelusque fraternae necis,
> ut inmerentis fluxit in terram Remi
>   sacer nepotibus cruor.

Where, where are you stampeding, men of crime? Why do your hands feel the swords you have only just sheathed? Hasn't enough Latin blood been poured out over plains and ocean?

Not to enable Rome to burn the haughty citadels of envious Carthage, not to bring the unconquered British in chains down the Sacred Way, but to make the Parthians' prayers come true and cause this city to die by her own hand.

This isn't what wolves and lions do, savage only against what isn't themselves. What maddens you? Blind bloodlust, cruel violence, or guilt? Answer me! Not a word. Their faces are pallid, their minds struck numb.

That's how it is. What hounds the Romans is bitter fate and the crime of a brother's murder, ever since the blood of innocent Remus flowed into the earth, a curse to his descendants.

The death of Remus was a story that could only make sense as a symbol of strife and violence.

So why is Remus in the story at all? It would be much more straightforward without him. He has to be got rid of, at the cost of turning the foundation legend into a story of anxiety and guilt.[92]

The story is so familiar that that question is rarely asked. But it is fundamental. Twin stories, by their nature, are symmetrical. Jacob and Esau, Castor and Pollux, Zethus and Amphion, Eteocles and Polyneices – whether the twins are hostile or devoted, of similar character or different, they presuppose each other and their myths belong to both. I know of no twin story anywhere else in mythology where one of the twins is violently removed and the other goes on to a heroic career of his own.[93]

Moreover, twins in a foundation story ought to signify some

symmetry, duplication or twofold characteristic in the resulting community.[94] Why were there two kings and two royal
families at Sparta? Because Aristodemus, who led the 'Dorian
invaders' to Lacedaemon, had twin sons.[95] Why did two cities
share the fertile plain of Argos? Because the twin sons of Abas,
who quarrelled even in the womb, could not live together.[96]
There were such dualities at Rome, and the story could have
explained them. Instead, we have a murder, perhaps even the
murder of one twin by the other.[97]

That is the problem this book will try to solve. It consists of
three inter-related questions. First, why a twin in the first
place? Second, why call him Remus? Third, once you have
him, why kill him off?

CHAPTER 2

Multiform and manifold

The most recent solution to the problem is also the most spectacular. In the final chapter – indeed, the final phrase – of his book *Comparative Mythology*, the Professor of Classics and Indo-European Studies at the University of California, Los Angeles, identifies the murder of Remus as 'the primordial sacrifice of the Indo-European cosmic twin'.[1]

Jaan Puhvel's book is a very enjoyable combination of wide learning and lively presentation. He modestly calls it 'a compendium born of pedagogy', and one can see how his students at UCLA over the last thirty years or so must have been stimulated by his teaching. He defines his approach to mythology as 'tracing the mythical matter of disparate societies back to a common ancestry', and thus 'recapturing via the comparative method a piece of the onetime living religion of a hypothetical protosociety', that of the remote ancestors, in the third millennium BC, of the speakers of all the Indo-European languages from the Ganges to the Atlantic and beyond.[2]

It is a notoriously difficult field, and one in which the danger of uncontrolled speculation is particularly acute. Puhvel gives his students, and his readers, excellent advice:

Such an approach, to be fruitful, needs width and depth in several dimensions and enough similarity and variety to allow both positive conclusions and negative controls.

He attacks Lévi-Strauss's structuralism as

by nature generalist, universalizing, and ahistorical, thus the very opposite of text-oriented, philological, and time conscious. Overlaying known data with binaristic gimmickry in the name of greater 'understanding' is no substitute for a deeper probing of the records themselves as documents of a specific synchronic culture on the one hand and as outcomes of diachronic evolutionary processes on the other. In mythology, as in any other scholarly or scientific activity, it is important to recall that the datum itself is more important than any theory that may be applied to it.

That empirically reassuring message is emphasised by a description of his subject as

a study that is by definition historical, and more specifically philological, rooted in the minute and sensitive probing and comparison of primary written records.

Clearly we are in safe hands.[3]

One thing we have to take on trust from the start: along with Germanic myth and that of Vedic India, Roman material provides one of the three mainstays for the 'triangulation' by which the Indo-European source can be reconstructed. There is no Roman myth 'present as sacred lore in the native tradition'. But

Rome has ritual stripped of discernible myth on the one hand and quasi-historical epicized narrative on the other. Yet these remaining ingredients are so archaic and basic that Rome is nevertheless, paradoxically, crucial to Indo-European comparative mythology.

The aetiologies of rituals like the Lupercalia, closely associated with the foundation legend, 'in reality must go back to very archaic levels of religion, as shown by comparison with Old Indic parallels.'[4]

That's fair enough as a working hypothesis; how good are the results it produces? One conclusion that may raise classicists' eyebrows is the interpretation of the expulsion of the Tarquins and/or the Battle of Lake Regillus as the epicised version of an apocalyptic myth of the end of the world (the Old Norse Ragnarök).[5] If we are allowing 'variety' to provide 'negative controls', the differences do seem to be more substantial than the similarities. However, Puhvel offers that only as a passing thought. His conclusion on Remus is argued at much greater length, with a whole chapter to itself.[6] The essential elements are as follows.

First, the primordial giant Ymir in Norse mythology, from whose body Odin and his brothers shaped the world: his name is derived from an inferred proto-Germanic form *Yumiyáz*, meaning 'twin'. However, Ymir has no brother, nor even any parents, being formed from the interaction of primal entities.

Second, the earthborn god Tuisto reported by Tacitus from traditional German songs, whose son Mannus was the 'founder and origin' of the German race.[7] The name Tuisto, if correctly transmitted (the manuscript variants Tristo, Bisto etc. are probably not significant), certainly implies duality;[8] so it may well be that 'Tuisto means etymologically "Twin"'. But again, no brother; just a son.

Third, from Vedic India, Yama and his twin-sister Yamī, whose names are certainly from the Indo-European root meaning 'twin'. Yama was the first man to die and colonise the Otherworld; his half-brother Manu sacrificed his wife Manāvī and was the ancestor of mankind. Puhvel dismisses both Yamī and Manāvī and 'tries to restore the original myth':[9]

In the protoversion Yáma and Mánu were primal twins and Yáma was the sacrificed victim essential to the act of creation over which Mánu presided. In other words, 'Man' sacrificed his 'Twin'.

That seems a somewhat high-handed way to 'probe the primary written records'. However, let it be for the moment.

Fourth, the Iranian Yima, king of the Golden Age (Puhvel calls him Yama-Xšaēta). This is Jamshid, who 'gloried and drank deep' in Omar Khayyam; he too carries the twin name, but has no brother. In an earlier chapter, Puhvel contrived to turn his story into a myth of creation like that of his Vedic namesake.[10]

In the preface, Puhvel promises to give at the end of each chapter 'a selection of more specialized handbooks and detailed materials chosen with a view to reinforcing the presentations of the book itself'. For the twins chapter, however, no bibliography is offered, which is a bit unkind to Bruce Lincoln, on whose article 'The Indo-European myth of creation' it is clearly based. Lincoln in turn derived some of his material (particularly about Remus, to whom we shall come in a moment) from a paper by Puhvel himself in the same issue of *History of Religions*.[11] The two articles are interdependent, a single composite argument.

On the question of the Vedic Yama and Manu, they both refer back to an earlier Puhvel article of 1970, which in turn appeals to one by Herman Lommel twenty years earlier.[12] It was Lommel who suggested that Yama's twin sister and Manu's wife were later poetic inventions, and that Yama and Manu themselves could have been the primal twins. He called it, correctly, a conjecture (*Vermutung*), and described it as *nur hypothetische*. Puhvel in 1970 agreed that Yamī '*may* be merely a folkloristic foil to her brother', and that 'a primal relationship [of Yama and Manu] is thus *not excluded*'.[13] One gets accustomed, in comparative mythology, to the silent transformation of hypothetical conjectures into evidential data. Five years later Puhvel could take for granted the spuriousness of Yamī and Manāvī:[14]

restoring the original equation, we may conclude that Yama and Manu were primal twins and that Yama was the sacrificial victim essential to the act of creation over which Manu presided.

To recapitulate: the putative Indo-European creation myth, of primal twins called 'Twin' and 'Man', is inferred from (1) the Norse Ymir, who has no brother; (2) the Germanic Tuisto, who is the *father* of 'Man'; (3) the Vedic Yama, whose twin sister has to be replaced by his half-brother, and who himself has to replace the half-brother's wife as the sacrificial victim; and (4) the Iranian Yima, who has no brother, and whose story must be fundamentally reinterpreted to make it fit.[15]

But what the protagonists all have in common is a name that means 'double' or 'twin'. So argued Hermann Güntert in 1923, and it is endorsed in the *Indogermanisches Etymologisches Wörterbuch*.[16] 'Based on this phonological and semantic correspondence', writes Bruce Lincoln,[17] 'we *hypothesize* that there was originally a mythic correspondence and that all are derived from a figure in the Proto-Indo-European myth.'

As hypotheses go, it seems a little unsatisfactory. According to the surviving texts, three of the four so-called twins have no siblings at all; the fourth has a twin, but she is a sister, an embarrassment whom the interpreter must get rid of; the only 'primal twins' who can be conjecturally named (Yama and Manu) are presented in the texts as having different mothers, a fact which caused the original author of the hypothesis to explain that *yama* did not mean 'twin' in the physiological sense, but something more like 'Doppelgänger'.[18] One begins to see why Professor Puhvel offers no bibliography on the subject – and why, in an inconspicuous sentence earlier in the book, he describes his twins chapter as speculation.[19]

So far, however, we have not brought in the Roman material. Here, Puhvel himself is the originator of the hypothesis.[20] He begins with an assumption:[21]

A myth attested in India, Iran and Germania might well be assumed to be recoverable also from the remaining mainstay of Indo-European comparative mythology, namely, ancient Rome.

Where should we look for a Roman creation myth? Another assumption follows, with a great name attached to it:[22]

It is well known, especially from the works of such scholars as Mircea Eliade, that legendry surrounding urban beginnings tends to replicate myths of world creation. Therefore the traditions of Rome's founding are the most likely saga transpositions of Indo-European anthropogonic and cosmogonic lore.

'Such scholars as . . .'? The evasive phrase soon resolves itself into one scholar, Eliade himself, one work, *The Myth of the Eternal Return*, and indeed one sentence in that work: 'Every creation repeats the pre-eminent cosmogonic act, the Creation of the world.'[23] On the strength of that, Lincoln declares that 'the founding of a city is, in a very real sense, an action of creation', and Puhvel that 'the founding of Rome is quite literally a saga transposition of the act of creating the world, man, and society'. Then Eliade in his turn, citing the articles of Lincoln and Puhvel: 'As in so many other traditions [no evidence given], the founding of a city in fact represents a repetition of the cosmogony. The sacrifice of Remus reflects the primordial cosmogonic sacrifice . . .'[24]

In a very real sense, quite literally, in fact? When scholars validate each other so symmetrically, the phrases that should guarantee authenticity become devalued and begin to sound like bluff. But take it for the sake of argument. How do Remus and Romulus fit the pattern?

We need 'the twins "Twin" and "Man" and the sacrificing of "Twin" in the process of creation'.[25] Two points from an old-fashioned philologist's argument get us off to a good start: first, the traditional order of names *Remus et Romulus* may imply that Remus was the elder;[26] and second, Annaeus Florus' reference to Remus as a sacrificial victim suggests the idea of a human *Bauopfer* whose sacrifice would consecrate the foundation.[27] Then there is Remus' name. Suppose he was originally **Yemos*, like Yama, Yima and Ymir, a form of the Indo-European root from which the Latin *geminus* derives. Further suppose that attraction to the names Roma and Romulus, 'perhaps by alliterative versifying chroniclers', turned **Yemos* into *Remus*. That gives us Remus as 'Twin', the sacrificial victim.[28]

Romulus is a mere eponym of Rome, but he was deified as Quirinus. His original name, if it is to fit the pattern, ought to mean 'Man'. Puhvel suggests **Wiros* and/or **Wironos* – the former yielding *vir*, the latter, with a compound prefix, **Co-virinus* or *Quirinus*. QED. Even classical authors were aware of it, it seems: witness Propertius IV 1.31, *Ramnesque viri*, 'which formula may be translated as "the Romans of the Man", that is, the people of *the* Roman, Romulus'.[29] I should be astonished if any Latinist could be found who took *viri* there as a genitive singular.

But there is more. Romulus also provides the 'crude' version of the creation myth, 'surreptitiously preserved'. In the story of his murder and dismemberment by the senators we have in historicised form the slaughter of the primeval cosmogonic giant. But wasn't Remus the sacrificial victim? Yes, but he has been dealt with already:[30]

It attaches to Romulus rather than Remus because a man can be killed only once, as Remus already was in the preceding foundation episode; this is simply a consequence of the logic of storytelling.

It seems to me a tactical error for a comparativist to invoke the logic of story-telling. His business is with the abstract juxtaposition of 'mythologems', or at most the reconstruction of hypothetical origins for linguistic phenomena. Once focus on the here and now, on a story-teller with a real audience in a particular society, and the awkward questions begin to suggest themselves.

Why should a myth created for a different purpose, by unimaginable ancestors two millennia before and two thousand miles away, so impose itself that a community's account of its own identity must be perverted by it? Where is the cult or ritual that could have preserved it? If story-tellers were free to change the names to suit their own times, couldn't they change the plot as well? If they had to disguise a creation myth as a foundation story, why do it twice? And above all, why do it in such a way as to create stories by which their own community was embarrassed? What sort of a myth is it that provides what a society *doesn't* need?[31]

Here is Puhvel's answer:[32]

Rome was floundering in the backwash of its own suppressed mythical inheritance. It was trying to understand what had been sundered in the great Roman separation of myth and ritual. Ritual had lost its myth, which was of little concern in the peculiar atmosphere of Roman liturgical petrifaction. But the severed myth in its turn had become transposed to saga and history, thus purporting to be overtly understood. When this 'history' was no longer matched by the relevant ritual or theology, it had to make sense on its own terms. Coming to grips with primeval twins suddenly masquerading as city fathers was part of the price Rome had to pay for its peculiar tamperings with the normal workings of myth in societal thinking.

At that level of abstraction and metaphor, it may look like an explanation. But it doesn't work. The whole problem is precisely that the historicised story does *not* 'make sense on its own terms'. Clumsy story-tellers are not so much an answer as the evasion of one.

So even if tolerant readers allow the Germanic, Vedic and Iranian stories – suitably doctored, where necessary, by reinterpretation – to add up to a proto-Indo-European creation myth, all Jaan Puhvel's eloquence will hardly, I think, persuade them that the Roman foundation legend belongs to it.

DIOSCURISM

However, comparative mythology offers another answer – one that Puhvel mentions only to dismiss, though it is offered by the most distinguished of all practitioners of Indo-European studies, Georges Dumézil.[33]

Discussing Quirinus as the deified Romulus in his history of archaic Roman religion, Dumézil rightly insists on the particular historical context of the foundation of Quirinus' temple in 293 BC.[34] But he also keeps in mind the Indo-European inheritance:[35]

On the other hand, since the accounts of the earliest period of Rome are in large part humanized and historicized mythology, it must not be forgotten that Romulus, like a number of other personages in these accounts, may play a role which, among other Indo-European peoples of a more speculative nature, is attributed to one or to several gods. Until the foundation of Rome, when his character changes by becoming kingly, Romulus presents one dominant trait: he is a twin, inseparable from his brother; and both live as shepherds. How can we not be reminded of the Vedic and pre-Vedic theologem concerning the gods of the third function, which recognises in the pairing of the Nāsatya or Aśvin, the twin gods, a significance sufficiently representative for the canonical list of the gods of the three functions to be 'Mitra-Varuna, Indra, and the two Nāsatya'?

When he goes on to emphasise the significance of twins as representing abundance and fertility, and the correspondingly beneficent character of the Nāsatya as givers of life, youth and wealth,[36] one wants to ask why, in that case, the Roman 'humanising' of the pair required one of them to kill the other. But first Dumézil must be allowed to make his case. Seven arguments are offered for the essential similarity between the youth of Remus and Romulus and the nature of the Nāsatya.[37]

First, the Nāsatya were considered not quite proper gods because they mingled so much with men. 'This is how Romulus and his brother live. They are strangers to the established order . . .' For gods, read urban society; for men, read shepherds and fugitives. It doesn't seem compelling.

Second, the Nāsatya spent their time doing good and putting right injustice. Remus and Romulus could not do miracles, but 'they use every human means to protect their friends against brigands . . .' Again, a bit too general to be helpful.

Third, the Nāsatya rejuvenated old Cyavana; Remus and Romulus restored their grandfather to the throne of Alba. Hardly a close parallel, given the conventional nature of the whole 'sub-plot' of Amulius and Numitor in the Roman story.[38]

Fourth, one Vedic text alleges a difference between the Nāsatya: like the Greek Dioscuri, one of them had a mortal father. 'The inequality of the Roman twins is of another sort, but it is also considerable.' Indeed! It is well expressed by Dumézil in another context:[39]

Let us compare the deaths of these two twins: the wretched, irreversible end, without tomorrow or compensation, that Remus meets out on the boundary furrow, and the ascent into a divine world, the celestial and active immortality of Romulus–Quirinus.

This parallel is really an argument *against* comparability.

Fifth, the Nāsatya were asked to cure infertility in women. The Luperci, founded by Remus and Romulus, did that by flagellation. But as Dumézil fairly points out, the Roman aetiological legend is set after the death of Remus, under Romulus as king.[40]

Sixth, the Nāsatya once restored sight to a young man at the request of a *she-wolf*. 'The role of the "friendly" she-wolf in the legend of the Roman twins is well known.' But the Vedic example is exceptional, even paradoxical: 'throughout the *Ṛg Veda* the wolf is an evil creature, whose very name symbolically designates whatever is hostile and foreign'. That offers no parallel for the suckling she-wolf that became the symbol of Rome.

Finally, the Nāsatya once enabled a hero to survive in a

blazing furnace. 'One of the variants concerning the birth of Romulus and Remus has them born from the fire on the hearth . . .' Not quite right: it was from the hearth, not the fire itself, that the phantom phallus emerged in the story we shall look at in chapter 4.[41] It probably belonged to Genius, the god of generation, or to Lar, the hearth-god; but even if it was Vulcan, there is no sign that it gave the twins any power over fire.

Now, the Nāsatya – or the Aśvins, as they are more often called – are the Vedic manifestation of the Divine Twins, recognisably the Dioscuri of Graeco-Roman mythology and the Baltic *Dieva deli* (Sons of God).[42] Their traces have been identified also in Germanic myth by Donald Ward, whose book *The Divine Twins* is the standard work on the subject.

Ward lists fourteen defining characteristics of the Indo-European Divine Twins, namely:[43]

 1 Sons of the Sky-god.
 2 Brothers of the Sun-maiden.
 3 Associated with horses.
 4 Dual paternity.
 5 Saviours at sea.
 6 Astral nature.
 7 Magic healers.
 8 Providers of divine aid in battle.
 9 Divinities of fertility.
10 Differentiated as individuals.
11 Associated with swans.
12 Involved with mortals.
13 Aniconic idols.
14 Protectors of the oath.

Remus and Romulus score one (no. 10) out of fourteen. But in a fifteenth category, 'miscellaneous traits and functions', Ward has this:[44]

There is also evidence that the Divine Twins may traditionally have been associated with the founding of cities. The legend of the founding of Rome immediately comes to mind.

Why *should* it come to mind? In most versions of the story, the city is not founded until one of the twins is killed. Remus and Romulus are human, not divine, and share practically none of the defining characteristics Ward lists. Yet he assumes, without argument, that they form part of his subject.[45] Why?

I suspect the answer is that Ward, a less original thinker than Dumézil, was still influenced by the findings of an earlier generation of comparativists. His notes include references to a work neither Dumézil nor Puhvel ever mentions, *Mythologie universelle* by Alexandre Haggerty Krappe, published in Paris in 1930. Much of that ambitiously titled work is devoted to 'le Dioscurisme', of which Krappe identifies the Remus and Romulus story as a clear example.[46]

Krappe did not confine himself to Indo-European mythology. On the contrary, he made much use of ethnographic data from Africa, as does Ward himself (adding American parallels) in his chapter on 'universal Dioscurism'. One very widespread phenomenon is a taboo on twins, causing the mother to be exiled from the community.[47] Her place of exile, the 'twin-sanctuary', may attract fugitives and homeless people and in due course develop into an independent village. 'La légende de la fondation de Rome', observes Krappe, 'est peut-être l'example classique.'[48]

Really? Not just an example (that would be startling enough), but the *classic* example? The source of that judgement takes us back one stage further, to Krappe's mentor James Rendel Harris, who first discovered the phenomenon of Dioscurism (or 'Twin-lore', as he preferred to call it).[49]

Rendel Harris was an extraordinary man. Some idea of his character and reputation is conveyed by the homage (*Huldigung*) which prefaces his *Festschrift*:[50]

Traveller through four Worlds, Odysseus of the Oceans, Guest greatly beloved in the Tents of the Nations;

In Jesus Lane, in Fifth Avenue, and on the Caravan Routes of the East, ever the same: a Disciple of the Saviour;

Church Historian and Church Father, Patriarch of Bible Study, High Priest of the Parchments, Decipherer of the Palimpsests;

Author, Evangelist and Letter Writer, Master of British Humour;

Doctor doctorum and Amicus juventutis;

Polyglot and Polyhistor, knowing all things, acquainted with all things, save only Hate;

With hair of silver, still youthful at heart, a Virtuoso in Friendship . . .

He was immensely prolific (his publications took up more than a column of *Who's Who*), but a comment made by a colleague when he was in his thirties – 'it is a pity he does not allow himself time to think of more than one theoretical possibility at once' – became more and more true as he got older.[51] In 1927 (he was seventy-five), Harris published a pamphlet entitled *Was Rome a Twin-Town?*, expanding at length on a suggestion made more briefly in his earlier books on Dioscurism. That was what Krappe based his judgement on. As he wrote a few years later,[52]

On ne me demandera pas de répéter ici les faits ethnologiques: l'article de mon cher maître est sans doute à la portée de mes lecteurs. Que plus est, je les ai discutés longuement dans mon livre récent [i.e. *Mythologie universelle*]. Qu'il suffise de dire que j'accepte cette théorie dans l'ensemble.

It is worth looking back at Harris' earlier work to see how this particular theoretical possibility advanced to the status of a classic example. First, in *The Cult of the Heavenly Twins*:[53]

If reason should be brought forward for believing that Romulus and Remus escaped death by drowning in the Tiber, not by the kind offices of the she-wolf, but by being taken into sanctuary, we should at once be able to throw light on the tradition that one of the first things done by Romulus, when founding his city, was the establishment of an asylum for slaves and fugitives upon the Capitoline Hill.

Such reason evidently was brought forward, for in *Boanerges*, seven years later, the cautious conditional has vanished:[54]

We know that Rome is a twin-sanctuary; the traditions as to its foundation betray the fact; several layers of twin-tradition lie over one another, the destruction of the twins and their mother, the exile of the twins, the twins as creators of sanctuary; all of these can be easily made out. Curiously, the sanctuary is not where we should have expected it, on the island between the bridges, but on the

Capitoline Hill. No doubt, however, exists that Rome is a twin-town. The identification is multiform and manifold.

No one nowadays believes the theory, and Rendel Harris is a forgotten man; he does not even rate a mention in Puhvel's 'history of the subject' chapter.[55] But Harris's 'twin-lore' lives on,[56] in ever more exotic manifestations, and the apparently universal assumption that Remus and Romulus, one way or another, are part of some primeval mythic pattern must be ultimately due to him.

One thing that hasn't changed is the comparativists' ironical treatment of classical scholarship. Just as Harris and Krappe sniped at Mommsen, so Puhvel refers dismissively to 'those who deny the proper mythical heritage of ancient Rome'.[57] But their own solutions to the Remus problem are admittedly unsatisfactory,[58] and totally fail to account for the proliferation of variants noted in chapter 1. I think it is fair to conclude that Indo-European studies and comparative mythology offer no solution at all to the problem of the Remus myth.

We shall have to turn to old-fashioned classical scholarship after all, and see if that can do any better.[59] But first, since this will be a historical argument, we must understand where we are, in both time and place.

CHAPTER 3

When and where

ONE AND A HALF MILLENNIA

Like most areas of intellectual endeavour, the study of the ancient world has become specialised. No one person can master the whole of it. 'Pauly–Wissowa', the great encyclopaedia of *Altertumswissenschaft*, took ninety years to complete and consists of eighty-five fat volumes; but even that is not, and cannot be, the last word. Quite apart from the perennial process of reinterpretation, there is a constant stream of new information to be made sense of – not only artefacts, architectural remains and the other results of archaeological research, but also new documents, written on papyrus or inscribed on stone or metal. Inevitably, scholars concentrate their efforts on particular chronological periods, geographical areas, or types of data.

It takes a conscious effort to step back and look synoptically at the whole huge period of 'Graeco-Roman antiquity'. The time-chart (fig. 1) is designed to provide some sense of historical proportion, and to counter the telescoping effect by which past centuries become progressively shorter in the mind. It is not easy to remember that *every* century represents three or four generations of human life.

The time-chart covers a millennium and a half: from 900 BC, a conservative date for the earliest evidence of dwellings on the site of Rome, to AD 600, the pontificate of Gregory the Great,[1]

when the city, after having been more than once taken by storm, saw the remnant that the sword had spared wasting away by hunger and pestilence; when the senate and the old families that were still left

31

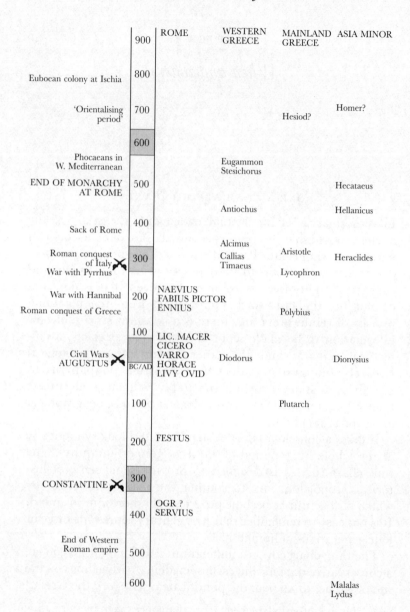

		ROME	WESTERN GREECE	MAINLAND GREECE	ASIA MINOR
	900				
Euboean colony at Ischia	800				
'Orientalising period'	700			Hesiod?	Homer?
	600				
Phocaeans in W. Mediterranean			Eugammon Stesichorus		
END OF MONARCHY AT ROME	500				Hecataeus
			Antiochus		Hellanicus
Sack of Rome	400				
			Alcimus		
Roman conquest of Italy	300		Callias	Aristotle	Heraclides
War with Pyrrhus			Timaeus	Lycophron	
War with Hannibal	200	NAEVIUS FABIUS PICTOR			
Roman conquest of Greece		ENNIUS		Polybius	
	100				
		LIC. MACER CICERO			
Civil Wars		VARRO	Diodorus		Dionysius
AUGUSTUS	BC/AD	HORACE LIVY OVID			
	100			Plutarch	
	200	FESTUS			
	300				
CONSTANTINE					
	400	OGR ? SERVIUS			
End of Western Roman empire	500				
	600				Malalas Lydus

Fig. 1. Time-chart, 900 BC – AD 600.

were exterminated by Totila, so that scarcely the name of senator and a shadow of a municipal constitution survived; when Rome was subjected to the degrading rule of an Eastern exarch who resided at a distance from her; when the old religion and along with it all hereditary usages were abolished, and a new religion was preaching other virtues and another kind of happiness exclusively, and was condemning sins unreproved by the old morality; when the ancient sciences and arts, all old memorials and monuments, were looked on as an abomination, the heroes of former ages as doomed to hopeless perdition; and Rome, for ever disarmed, was become the capital of a spiritual empire, which after the lapse of twelve centuries we have seen interrupted in our days.

That is, the end of ancient Rome and the beginning of papal Rome,[2] which was ended in its turn when the troops of united Italy breached the emperor Aurelian's walls at the Porta Pia on 20 September 1870.

Another page on the same scale would take the time-chart from AD 600 to AD 2100, from the dark age of Europe to the equally unimaginable world your great-grandchildren may live to inherit. 'Ancient history' is not all that ancient.

On the left, a selection of historical events and characters; on the right, the more important literary sources, from archaic to Byzantine, with which the argument will be concerned. In the dates column I have shaded four periods, each representing about two generations, which seem to me to be profoundly significant turning-points in the history of Rome. Three of them include battles – at Sentinum, Actium and the Milvian Bridge – which even at the time were recognised as epoch-making, and marked as such by quasi-mythic narrative.[3]

The first of these periods is known only archaeologically. It was when the valley between the Palatine and Capitoline hills was drained, gravelled, and turned into the common meeting-place (the *comitium* of the Roman Forum) for villages which had hitherto been separate. Public buildings, notably the *regia* ('king's house'), were constructed. They featured tiled roofs rather than thatch, and decorative terracotta plaques with scenes of men, gods and monsters; a bull-headed man on one surviving piece is recognisable as the Minotaur of Greek mythology.[4] This seems to be the moment when Rome becomes a 'city' in the proper sense – that is, a civic community, a *polis*.[5]

Three hundred years later comes the period of the Roman conquest of Italy south of the Apennines (338–267 BC), two generations of hard-won triumph which saw also the conclusion of the long internal power-struggle between the patricians and the plebeians, the beginnings of 'Roman representational art' in painting and sculpture, and the earliest evidence for the self-glorifying competitive ethos of Roman commanders and office-holders which in due course created the Roman empire, and then nearly destroyed it again.[6]

That near-destruction came in the third of our periods, the age of conflict and expansion from (say) the War of the Allies in 90–89 to the Augustan 'new era' introduced by the Secular Games (17 BC). Vast new territories were added to the empire (Asia Minor, Syria, Gaul, Egypt), but at the cost of bloody civil war and the loss of republican institutions in a disguised autocracy.[7]

The fourth turning-point has been described by a modern historian as 'the conversion of Europe'. The two generations from AD 270 to 330 saw the introduction of 'hard' government that insisted on taxation and the army; the building of a city-wall that was to serve Rome for 1,500 years; the Great Persecution, followed by the adoption of the persecuted cult as the official religion of the Empire; and the foundation of Rome's successor as imperial capital, the New Rome at Constantinople.[8]

I emphasise these revolutionary periods because two at least of them – where our evidence allows us to see it – provided a new mythology, a new way of making sense of Rome and her destiny in an era of cataclysmic change. From the third of them came Divus Iulius, Divus Augustus and the whole civic machinery of imperial cult;[9] from the fourth came Christian Rome and the eventual suppression of classical paganism. The first period is effectively beyond our knowledge, but the appearance of Greek mythological iconography may represent an analogous shift in mental attitudes; it is also quite possible that the name 'Rome' itself dates only from this period.[10] As for the second, it will be part of the argument of this book to suggest that it too was a period of cultic and mythological innovation, just as revolutionary, in its way, as the eras of Augustus and Constantine.

After chronology, geography. The map (fig. 2) makes clear the most important single characteristic of the site of Rome: it was between Etruria and Latium, on the Latin side of the river that always marked the boundary.[11]

It also shows the comparative proximity of Ischia, the earliest Greek settlement in the West, founded by Euboeans in the early eighth century. One of the colonists' main preoccupations was the exploitation of the iron workings at Elba, two days' sail to the north; about half-way (a convenient place to anchor or beach your ship overnight) was the outflow of the Tiber. The river was itself a thoroughfare into the interior, and at the lowest point where it could be forded – that is, at Rome, though it was probably not yet called that – an ancient trackway led off north-eastwards into the Apennines.[12] For Greeks and Phoenicians interested in trade, it was a place of some significance.

Our modern habit of thinking of 'Greek history' and 'Roman history' as two separate things is a real obstacle to understanding here. It is all too easy for even the most alert historians[13] to assert that 'Greek writers had only the haziest knowledge of Rome before the end of the fourth century', and that references to it in earlier authors 'tend to be mere passing references to an obscure and far-away place, about which they knew little beyond the mere name and probably cared less'. Does that mean that the Greeks in general knew nothing of Rome? It depends which Greeks one is talking about.

The Euboeans who settled on Ischia (and soon afterwards founded Cumae on the mainland) were the carriers of a powerful virus – the Ionian (and now panhellenic) epic tradition. Martin West's masterly analysis of 'the rise of the Greek epic' identifies five stages in its evolution: events in the late-

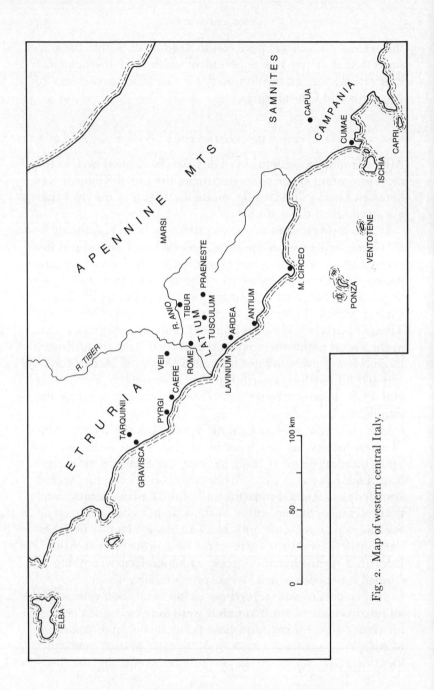

Fig. 2. Map of western central Italy.

Mycenaean world at Pylos, Iolcos and in Aetolia, about which epic saga-cycles developed; the combination in twelfth-century Thessaly of these sagas with a new one on the destruction of Troy; the elaboration of the Troy saga in Aeolian Lesbos; the development of the 'Homeric dialect' in its final form in tenth- and ninth-century Euboea, where prosperity and wealthy rulers offered a promising milieu for bards; and finally the incorporation of Near-Eastern elements, no doubt transmitted by such wide-ranging merchant venturers as the Euboeans who established their trading post at Al-Mina in Syria (fig. 3).[14]

The final stage probably involved Syrians and Phoenicians, in flight from the Assyrian domination of their homelands in the late eighth century, carrying not only their skills as metal-workers, ivory-carvers and jewellers, but also their stories of gods and men. What classical archaeologists call 'the orientalising period' was a time of excitement and spectacular opportunity. As West observes,[15] the epic tradition itself, conservative as it was in so many ways, manifests

a considerable degree of innovation and transformation, especially, I suggest, in the final Ionian phase that brought the epic to its astonishing acme in the eighth and seventh centuries.

That 'astonishing acme' is the *Iliad* and the *Odyssey*, for both of which our earliest evidence comes, in fact, from the west coast of Italy.[16]

At Caere, Tarquinii, Veii and Praeneste, the aristocrats of early seventh-century south Etruria and Latium acquired works of superb craftsmanship in precious metal and ivory from as far away as Syria and Egypt, and were buried with them in the 'princely tombs' which provide us with our evidence.[17] Nothing equivalent is known from Rome, but a Greek Kleiklos, 'he who is famed for his fame',[18] was evidently buried on the Esquiline about 640 BC, which confirms that the place by the river crossing was known to men who knew the tale of Troy.

In the next two generations, as we have seen (it is the first of the critical periods identified above), Rome became what a Greek might recognise as a city.[19] The Minotaur plaque is

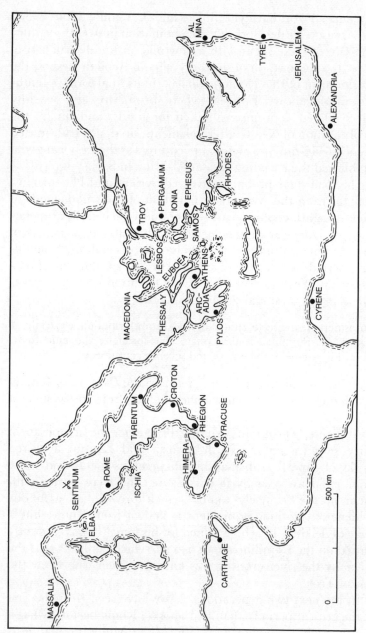

Fig. 3. Map of the central and eastern Mediterranean.

contemporary with a Greek settlement that flourished on the nearby Etruscan coast at Gravisca, one of the ports of Tarquinii; the surviving inscriptions from Gravisca suggest that many of those who made their dedications at the temple there were east Greeks from Ionia, especially Samos.[20] The Phocaeans from Asia Minor, neighbours to the Samians, were present in strength in the western Mediterranean in the sixth century, challenging Etruscan and Carthaginian sea power and successfully founding a distant colony with a great future, Massalia (Marseille).[21] They brought to their new city a wooden image of Artemis from the goddess's famous shrine at Ephesus; a replica of it was used in the sixth-century temple of Diana set up just outside Rome, on the Aventine.[22]

Another Roman temple of that period, built by the river harbour at the foot of the Capitoline hill, is known from excavation. The most spectacular of its remains is the terracotta *acroterion* which decorated the gable-end of the roof: it shows Herakles escorted by Pallas Athene, evidently being introduced to Olympus on his apotheosis (fig. 4).[23] The date 520 BC is a conservative one for this eloquent testimony to the 'reception' of Greek mythology in archaic Rome.

A TEST CASE

The story of Hercules at the site of Rome was a favourite with the sophisticated authors of the late first century BC. They told it – Livy in historical prose, Virgil in epic, Propertius and Ovid in elegant elegiacs – as an aetiological explanation for the Ara Maxima dedicated to Hercules in the Forum Bovarium.[24] The essential elements are as follows.

First, Hercules (Herakles) himself, driving the cattle of Geryon back from the far west after his tenth Labour. Pursuing, it was said, a runaway bullock, he made his way down the Italian peninsula, and called it *Vitulia* from the Latin for a bullock (*vitulus*). This story dates at least as far back as Hellanicus of Lesbos in the late fifth century.[25]

Secondly, Evander the Arcadian, son of Hermes and a prophetic nymph, in exile from his native Pallantion, now

Fig. 4. *Acroterion* from a temple in the Forum Bovarium. Rome, Antiquario comunale: photo by courtesy of the Archivio fotografico, Musei Capitolini, Rome.

settled by the Tiber at the Palatine hill.[26] As we shall see later, his main significance is as an aetiological explanation for the Palatine itself and the Lupercal below it.[27] The earliest known source for his migration to the site of Rome is Eratosthenes in the third century BC.[28]

Thirdly, Cacus, either a brigand or a fire-breathing monster, who terrorises Evander's colony. When Hercules arrives with the cattle, Cacus steals some of them, and Hercules kills him. An Etruscan Cacus is known from the late fourth century BC as a peaceful prophet; the villainous Cacus of the Augustan story (a calque on the Greek *kakos*, 'bad') is not attested before the second.[29]

Fourthly, Evander's mother, the prophetess, known in Greek as Nikostrate or Themis, in Latin as Carmenta or Carmentis.[30] After Hercules has rid her son's settlement of Cacus, she prophesies his apotheosis, and Evander (or Hercules himself) sets up the altar to the new god. The earliest known source for the prophetess, and for the altar with its Greek ritual, is C. Acilius in the first half of the second century BC.[31]

What we seem to have here is the characteristic mythologising of the Hellenistic age, with Hellanicus' Herakles narrative being elaborated by later authors for particular aetiological purposes. The cattle of Geryon, for instance, explain the name of the Forum Bovarium ('cattle market'). Carmenta provides a story for the 'Carmentalia' festival (11 and 15 January) and the shrine of Carmenta by the Porta Carmentalis.[32] A Roman patrician family attached its legendary genealogy to the story: Evander's daughter visited Hercules in his dug-out (*fovea*), and conceived the first of the Fabii.[33] The Latin city of Tibur, allied with Rome from 338 BC, gave its name to Carmenta in one version; according to Cato, the founder of Tibur was Evander's fleet commander, and the Tiburtines themselves believed that Hercules had personally set up the altar of Iuppiter Praestes there.[34] The natural assumption, from the texts we have, is that the whole nexus of stories is comparatively late.

Now, however, we know that the apotheosis of Herakles was celebrated at Rome already in the sixth century BC,[35] on an

archaic temple directly adjacent to the Carmenta shrine and
the later Porta Carmentalis, just across the Forum Bovarium
from the Ara Maxima itself. Of course there must have been
later elaboration, in plenty; but the essentials of the story – the
exploit, the prophecy, the altar – now seem to be much more
ancient than was previously thought.

Precisely in the sixth century BC, the tenth Labour of Herak-
les was made famous in one of the lost masterpieces of western
Greek poetry, the *Geryoneis* of Stesichorus of Himera.[36] We
know that the poem mentioned Arcadian Pallantion;[37] we
know too that there was a Pallantion near Rhegion at the toe of
Italy, in what the Greeks called Oenotria, and that Oenotria
supposedly took its name from an Arcadian Oenotros, son of
Lykaon.[38] It seems possible that the legendary association of
Arcadia with the southernmost part of Italy, exploited by
Stesichorus in his poem on Herakles, was transplanted at an
early stage to Rome,[39] and in particular to the 'cattle market',
close to the Palatine (*Pallantion*) and the Lupercal (*Lykaion*)
whose names were explained by the story of Evander.[40] It is a
reminder of how inadequate, and haphazard, our source-
material is, when a single new discovery can overturn our
presuppositions.

The particular lesson I want to draw from this salutary
example is that our sources – literary and visual alike – give us
no more than a *terminus ante quem* for the existence of the
traditions they attest. The argument from silence ('we do not
hear of this story, so it did not yet exist') is particularly
dangerous for such an ill-documented place and period as
archaic Rome.

But inadequacy of evidence is normal in ancient history. The
fact that we cannot hope to achieve certainty is no reason not
to do our best with what there is. Whatever conclusions we
arrive at are bound to be hypothetical; how good the hypotheses turn out to be will depend on how carefully we have
made our inferences from what evidence we *do* have.

CHAPTER 4

What the Greeks said

MATERIAL AND METHODOLOGY

'There is no time and no place', declared Arnaldo Momigliano, 'in which the Romans were free from Greek influences.'[1]

The nature of the influence, the eagerness with which it was accepted or the stubbornness with which it was resisted, varied according to the circumstances and necessities of each generation, from the origins of the Roman community right through to the world empire of Augustus and his successors, and beyond that to the Byzantine age. But at every stage, we see the myths of Rome's foundation predominantly through the eyes of Greeks.

The corollary of Momigliano's lapidary statement is almost equally true: there is hardly a time or a place in which Rome was not of interest to Greeks. Not, of course, to all Greeks all the time – but even from the very beginning, the place at the crossing-point of the Tiber must have had some significance for Euboean and Phoenician traders interested in penetrating the interior. By the late sixth century BC, Rome was a sufficiently substantial local power to be taken seriously by the Greeks of southern Italy and Sicily, and by their enemies the Carthaginians.[2] And from the late fourth century onwards she was a phenomenon of consuming interest to successive Greek cities and territories whose independence was ended in alliance with or conquest by Rome.

The shattering experience of 168–7 BC, when Rome defeated the kingdom of Macedon at the battle of Pydna, and Alexander the Great's successor walked in chains in a Roman triumph, prompted Polybius to write his great history of the rise of Rome, to explain to his fellow-Greeks 'how and under what system of government the Romans have succeeded in under fifty-three years [220–167] in bringing almost the whole inhabited world under them'.[3] That was just the most spectacular moment in a long development, from the alliance with the Greek cities of Campania in 338 BC to the conquest of Egypt, the last of the 'successor-kingdoms' of Alexander's empire, in 30 BC. At every stage, admiring or resentful Greeks had to try to make sense of Rome,[4] and her origins were a fruitful field for creative mythology.

I have listed in the Appendix (pp. 160–8 below) sixty surviving accounts of the foundation of Rome which differ from the Remus and Romulus story analysed in chapter 1. They are arranged in approximate chronological order of composition, from Lycophron (or pseudo-Lycophron) in the third (or second?) century BC[5] to John Tzetzes in the twelfth century AD. But in a sense the order is arbitrary. Most of these authors are explicitly quoting earlier authorities lost to us, of whom some are datable but most not (and many not even named). Moreover, just as the dates of our *surviving* sources are hardly relevant to the origins of the traditions they report, so too the dates of the lost authors offer us – or would offer us, if they were known – no more than a *terminus ante quem* for the traditions *they* reported.[6]

One of the latest of our sources, the Byzantine anthologist Constantinus Cephalus, is annotating an inscription from a temple in Cyzicus which we happen to know was put up about 160 BC, eleven hundred years before his own time;[7] on the other hand, the earliest source identifiable by name, Hellanicus of Lesbos in the late fifth century BC, offers an account of the foundation of Rome which is clearly a conflation of two separate versions already extant in his day.[8] What we have is a collection of stories which can only be dated on *a priori* grounds, controlled where possible by the date of the reporting authority as a lower limit.

This corpus of material has been a challenge to many historians in the last century and a half.[9] What follows in this chapter makes no claim to be anything more than another hypothetical reconstruction of the various traditions in particular historical contexts. The premise on which it is based was stated with firmness and clarity by Benedict Niese more than a century ago:[10]

Diese Sagenbildung entspricht einem wahrhaften, nie verlöschenden Bedürfnis der alten Welt. Sie ist der poetische Ausdruck für das Meinen, Denken und Verlangen der schaffenden Zeit, die sich darin eine Vergangenheit nach ihrem eigenen Bild setzt und sich in die Namen und Gestalten der Dichtung kleidet; nicht selten wird sie zu einer Art pseudonymer Zeitgeschichte . . . Derartige Geschichten gewinnen ein historisches Interesse, wenn es gelingt, die Gedanken und Zustände der Zeit, in der sie entstanden sind, aus ihnen heraus zu lesen.

This creation of [foundation-]legends corresponds to a real and permanent need in the ancient world. It is the poetic expression of the beliefs, thoughts and desires of the age that creates it, which thereby gives itself a past in its own image, and dresses itself in poetic names and manners. Quite often it turns into a sort of contemporary history under a different name . . . Stories of this type acquire historical interest when they make it possible to read from them the ideas and circumstances of the age in which they originated.

I assume for the sake of argument that each of the stories that have come down to us was created with some sort of contemporary situation in mind, and not as 'just some piece of nonsense'.[11]

THE FIRST CONTACT

The Homeric Odysseus' account of his visit to Aeaea, the island of Circe the witch-goddess, is part of a narrative that has no basis in real-life geography.[12] The only hint the poet gives is that Aeaea was where 'Dawn the early comer has her dwelling-place and her dancing-grounds, and the Sun himself has his risings',[13] which should mean somewhere far to the east. But he was probably concerned not so much to identify its location as to emphasise that Circe was the daughter of Helios, the Sun. At a very early stage, no doubt thanks to the Euboean settlers of Ischia and Cumae, the scene of Odysseus' fantastic adventures was identified as the Tyrrhenian coast of Italy. A poet in the Hesiodic tradition, perhaps identical with the sixth-century composer of the *Catalogue of Women*, produced a shorter catalogue of goddesses who bore children to mortal men.[14] It ends as follows:[15]

> And fair-crowned Cytherea bore Aeneas,
> having been united in sweet love with the hero Anchises
> on the peaks of Ida with its many wooded folds.
>
> And Circe, the daughter of Helios son of Hyperion,
> in love with the much-enduring Odysseus, bore
> Agrios and Latinos the blameless and strong,
> who far, far away in a recess of the holy islands
> were the rulers of all the famed Tyrsenians.
>
> And the divine goddess Calypso, united in sweet love
> with Odysseus, bore Nausithoos and Nausinoos.
>
> These are the goddesses who lay with mortal men
> though immortal, and bore children resembling gods.

It is possible that the juxtaposition of Aeneas and Odysseus reflects the poet's awareness of legends attributing to both heroes voyages to the western coast of Italy. Stesichorus in the sixth century seems to have brought Aeneas at least as far as Sicily, and probably to Italy as well; Hecataeus, at the end of the century, knows that Capua, a neighbour of the Greeks of Cumae, was founded by Capys the Trojan.[16]

However, it is the goddess mistresses of Odysseus who attract attention. Calypso's sons are a pallid pair,[17] but those of Circe are historically very important. Agrios, 'the wild man', and Latinos, eponym of the Latins, rule over the famous Etruscans (*Tyrsenoi*). The 'sacred islands' could be Capri, Ischia, Ventotene, Ponza and Monte Circeo – certainly Hesiod thought Circe's home was in the Tyrrhenian sea[18] – and the 'recess' could be the mainland behind them; but one can hardly ask for detailed geographical accuracy from a Boeotian poet. The main thing is that he has heard of Latins and Etruscans.

We know there was an Etruscan cult of the anthropomorphic sun-god in the sixth century, well before the Rhodians introduced the cult of Helios in Greece. It is natural to suppose that the local cult and the Homeric myth reinforced each other;[19] some such specific connection is necessary to explain the otherwise puzzling location of Circe in the west, against the indication in the *Odyssey* text itself. Another element may have been Italian skill in herb-lore: already in the fifth century Aeschylus knew that Circe had taught the Etruscans about herbs and poisons, and later authors attribute the toxicological skills of the Marsi (in the central Apennine highlands) to their descent from Circe.[20]

But who was Agrios, the wild man? At this point a digression is necessary.

Late in the fifth century AD, a certain Nonnos of Panopolis in Egypt wrote a huge mythological epic on Dionysus in forty-eight books. Unreadable as narrative, it is a wonderful store-house of over a thousand years' accumulated myths. Most of his story concerns Dionysus in India, and among the companions of the god is a son of Circe called Phaunos.

He is introduced at XIII 328–32:

> After these came Phaunos, leaving the fire-sealed
> Pelorian plain of rocky, three-crested Sicily,
> whom Circe bore, embraced by Cronion of the deep,
> Circe the sister of Aietas, witch of many poisons, who dwelt
> by the forest in the deep-shadowed circles of a rocky hill.

The first two lines allude to Hesiodic narratives. The plain sealed with fire is where the monster Typhoeus lies buried in the uneasy earth.[21] Peloris is the north-easternmost promontory of Sicily, on which there was a temple of Poseidon ('Cronion of the deep'). According to Hesiod, both promontory and temple were made by the great hunter Orion, who then went to live in Euboea before being immortalised as a constellation.[22] The combination of Sicily and Euboea pins down the context of these Hesiodic stories as the Chalcidian colonisation of the eighth century BC, before Circe was located further north, at Monte Circeo.[23] But Circe's *forest* is surely in Italy; Theophrastus in the late fourth century commented on the well-wooded nature of Latium, and referred in particular to Monte Circeo and its oaks.[24]

Phaunos next appears in book XXXVII, as (precisely) an expert on trees. He is in charge of the lumberjacks who go to the mountains to find timber for the funeral pyre of Opheltes; it is thanks to his mother Circe that he knows about timber and mountains.[25] Nonnos' epithet for him in this passage is *erēmonomos*, 'he who lives in the wilderness', a word the poet uses otherwise only for wild beasts and for divinities of the wild, such as Pan, the nymphs, or Dionysus himself.[26]

After the usual epic *ekphrasis* of wood-cutting and pyre-building, we see Phaunos in a different capacity, as the producer of fire (XXXVII 56–60):

> Fire was needed. So rock-loving Circe's son,
> Phaunos who lives in the wilderness, dweller in the land
> of Tyrsenia,
> who had learnt as a boy the skills of his wild mother,
> brought fire-breeding stones, the tools of mountain craft,
> from the rock . . .

Again that distinctive epithet; and now Phaunos is explicitly Etruscan, not Sicilian as he was before. Moreover, Circe is 'wild', *agroterē* – another adjective Nonnos uses elsewhere only for wild beasts and gods of the wild (Artemis in this case).[27] The combination of that very unexpected epithet with the place-name *Tyrsenia* must, I think, be another Hesiodic allusion – to the passage on *Agrios* and Latinos, rulers of the famed Tyrsenians.[28]

Nonnos' allusive erudition enables us to infer the identity of the Hesiodic 'wild man'. He is Faunus, the Latin god of the wild.[29] Nonnos, for his own purposes, humanises and transliterates him into Phaunos the hero, but still allows us to recognise him by that singular epithet and the un-Homeric wildness attributed to his mother Circe.

Phaunos does not give us a foundation legend, though we shall see that as Faunus he has a role in the native story of the twins. What I hope this digression has shown is that Nonnos offers a faint reflection, still just detectable more than a millennium later, of the earliest Greek reaction to the land of the Tiber valley. Dense woods, a wilderness, a formidable people ('the famed Tyrsenoi') – and ruling them, Latinos and the Wild Man.

THE DESCENDANTS OF CIRCE

It was easy to expand the Hesiodic genealogy to accommodate other Italian peoples: Auson, eponym of the Ausones of Campania, was identified as another son of Circe and Odysseus; Prainestos, founder of the Latin city of Praeneste, as a son of their son Latinos.[30] At least three different expansions claimed to explain Rome: Odysseus and Circe had yet another son, Rhomanos; or a daughter, Rhome, after whom her brother Latinos named the city; or three more sons, Rhomos, Anteias and Ardeias, eponyms of Rome, Antium and Ardea.[31]

The date of that last tradition is very controversial,[32] but two considerations suggest it is early. First, the three 'fraternal' cities represent what may have been a political reality in the late sixth century (to judge by the terms of the Carthage treaty), but not at any identifiable time thereafter.[33] Second, the triad is an archaic pattern in genealogy, more likely to represent the thinking of an early systematiser than that of a playful Hellenistic *littérateur*.[34]

The seventh and sixth centuries were a very creative period in mythography and genealogy. Some time in the middle of the sixth, roughly contemporary with the Hesiodic poet in Boeotia and Stesichorus in Sicily, Eugammon of Cyrene composed his *Telegony* as a sequel to the *Odyssey*. His hero is Telegonus, son of Odysseus and Circe, who goes to Ithaca in search of his father, and kills him by mistake; he then takes his father's body, with Penelope and Telemachus, to Aeaea, where Circe makes them immortal; in a spectacularly symmetrical conclusion, Telegonus marries Penelope (his father's widow) and Telemachus marries Circe (his father's ex-mistress).[35]

Why must Odysseus' body be transported to Circe's island? Perhaps there was a hero-cult of Odysseus that had to be explained; certainly there was a tomb at Monte Circeo, later identified as that of Elpenor, where consultation of the dead reputedly took place.[36] The plot of the *Telegony* evidently had more of an Italian slant than our surviving fragments reveal, for the offspring of those two symmetrical marriages were respectively *Italus* and *Latinus*.[37]

Like the Hesiodic tradition, the *Telegony* offered plenty of scope for elaboration. Telegonus founded the Latin city of Tusculum (his daughter Mamilia was the ancestress of one of the leading families there),[38] and Italus, Telegonus' son by Penelope, married Leukaria (daughter of Latinus), who bore him Rhomos, the founder of Rome.[39] 'Leukaria' is a bilingual eponym for Alba Longa (*leukē*, 'white' = *alba*), so what this genealogy expresses is the notion of Alba as the daughter of Latium, the wife of Italy, and the mother of Rome.[40]

All these versions are independent of the story of Aeneas and his Trojans, and therefore likely to be early.[41] But since Aeneas is probably already in the west in the sixth century, even association with him is not necessarily a proof of lateness. One version makes Rhome the daughter of Telemachus (and Circe?) and wife of Aeneas.[42]

ACHAEANS AND OTHERS

Late in the fifth century BC, when Rome had been a recognisable *polis* for five or six generations, the historian Hellanicus of Lesbos reported that it was founded by Aeneas, who came into Italy from the land of the Molossians with (or after) Odysseus;[43] he named the city after Rhome, who had persuaded the other Trojan women to put an end to their wearisome wanderings by burning the ships.[44]

The unnatural association of Aeneas and his enemy Odysseus clearly implies that Hellanicus was combining two inconsistent accounts; and comparison with other versions of the ship-burning story suggests that he was applying it to a context (Aeneas' flight from Troy) in which it did not originally belong.[45] Aristotle reports what looks like an older and more integral version of the story.[46] The Trojan women are slaves on *Achaean* ships, blown by the storms that afflicted so many of the Greeks on their return from Troy. They land and winter at Latinion (the land of the Hesiodic Latinos?), where the women burn the ships of their captors and force them to settle there rather than return to Greece. That makes better sense than Trojan women burning *Trojan* ships.

It is likely that Aristotle's story was originally located in southern Italy, at Siritis, where the river Nauaithos ('Shipblaze') offered an aetiological context.[47] So we should probably recognise three stages of development. First, the Trojan women burn their captors' ships in the far south of Italy; the likely context for that is the Greek colonisation of the eighth and seventh centuries (to explain a community of Greek men and non-Greek women?). Second, the same event is moved north to Latium, no doubt to express a conception of the Latins as at least half-Greek.[48] And third, Hellanicus the mythological systematiser, manipulating a tradition of creative ethnological genealogy that was already two centuries old,[49] transferred it to the story of the wanderings of Aeneas and his Trojan refugees. That was not a natural context, but Hellanicus' authority made it canonical.[50]

Hellanicus' combination of Aeneas and Odysseus reappears much later in the riddling prophecies of Lycophron's Cassandra, who stirs into her brew not only an allusion to the twins of the native Roman story but also the Etruscan founder heroes Tarchon and Tyrsenos, the sons of Herakles' son Telephus.[51] Plutarch reports a tradition that Rhome was the daughter of Telephus, and married to Aeneas; that must express a conception of Rome as an Etruscan city.[52]

Lycophron's description of Odysseus as *nanos* ('the dwarf') alludes to Hellanicus' account of the Pelasgian king Nanas: he and his people were driven out of Thessaly and eventually colonised 'Tyrrhenia' – hence the Etruscans were really Pelasgians.[53] But according to Herodotus, writing about the same time as Hellanicus, the Etruscans were really Lydians.[54] One of the Roman foundation legends seems to be an attempt to reconcile these two authorities: the Tyrrhenians originated in Thessaly, then went to Lydia, then went to Italy! They were driven out (of Latium?) by Rhomis, *tyrannos* of the Latins, after whom Rome was named. That looks like a version designed to insist that Rome was *not* an Etruscan city.[55]

It is striking that although Herakles, as hero and god, was known in Rome by the late sixth century, there is no Herculean foundation story. But there *is* a tradition which makes Latinos the son not of Odysseus and Circe but of Herakles and the daughter (or wife) of Faunus.[56] It was Evander the Arcadian, the other protagonist of the 'Herakles at Rome' story, who earned a foundation legend: Virgil alludes to the notion that Evander founded Rome, and named it either after his daughter or after the prophetess who told him where to settle.[57]

THE END OF INNOCENCE

What all these versions have in common is a sense of Greek *neutrality* towards Rome. There might be an issue about whether the city was Latin or Etruscan, but that was not something most Greeks would feel strongly about. From the fourth century onwards, however, and urgently in the third, Rome became a serious problem for the Greek cities of Italy and Sicily – no longer just an interesting neighbour but a dangerous and eventually dominant power. It may be possible to identify some new foundation stories which express this political reality.

The Sicilian historian Alcimus, in the second half of the fourth century, offers a genealogy quite unlike anything we have yet seen: Aeneas was married to Tyrrhenia; their son Rhomylos had a daughter, Alba; her son 'Rhodius' (textual corruption for Rhomos?) founded Rome.[58] This is the earliest datable evidence for Romulus, and the way Alcimus uses him shows what readjustments were becoming necessary. Alba is no doubt the same as 'Leukaria', mother of Rhomos in the old tradition; Alba Longa symbolised the Latins, but Rome's eponym as her *son* implied a power relation that the victory of 338 BC had reversed for ever.[59] So now Romulus must be her *father*, and Alcimus' genealogy combines old and new in revealing confusion.

Another Sicilian historian, Callias of Syracuse, was writing probably at the end of the fourth century. His account seems to have combined Trojan and Odyssean elements in the traditional way by making Rhome, the Trojan lady who burnt the ships, the wife of Latinos, identified as the son of Telemachus and Circe.[60] They had three sons: Rhomos, the usual Greek male eponym of Rome; Rhomylos, the native eponym Romulus; and Telegonus, now startlingly reidentified as the grandson, not the brother, of Telemachus, and the grandson, not the son, of Circe. Why? Perhaps because Tusculum, Telegonus' foundation, had lost its independence and acquired Roman citizenship in 381 BC; fraternal equality with Rome was the most that could be claimed for it now.[61]

An equally eccentric version, attributed by Dionysius to a Roman source, probably originates from post-338 Campania, now incorporated into the Roman state. Aeneas has three sons, Ascanius, Rhomylos and Rhomos (the same duplication of the Greek and the Roman eponyms that we find in Alcimus and Callias).[62] They divide up Latium between them: Ascanius founds Alba, as in the orthodox Aeneas story; Rhomos founds Capua, Anchisa (unknown), Aeneia (the Janiculum) and Rome. But Rome is then abandoned, and founded again fifteen generations later as a colony from Alba under 'Rhomylos and Rhomos' – who are presumably the twins of the Roman legend.[63]

We see again the forced combination of inconsistent versions. The second part of the story is late, after Eratosthenes' chronology compelled the invention of the Alban dynasty.[64] The first part reflects late-fourth-century realities, effecting a legendary 'demotion' of Capua from an independent Trojan foundation (as it was already for Hecataeus in the sixth century) to a level of merely fraternal equality with Rome.[65] Uneasy politics produce uneasy mythology.

An interesting variant on the Trojan story may also perhaps date from this period. Both Plutarch and Dionysius refer to a foundation of Rome by Rhomos son of Emathion, who was 'sent from Troy by Diomedes' – that is, presumably, allowed to escape from the fallen city. Emathion was the legendary first king of Macedonia.[66] Was this version invented at the time of Alexander the Great, when Rome was beginning her conquest of Italy?[67]

One effect of the Emathion story was to keep the Trojan origin of Rome without committing oneself to Aeneas. Some Greek historians, hostile to Roman claims, insisted that Aeneas never left the Troad, which is certainly what Homer implies.[68] Another way of saving both Homer and the Roman claim was to have Aeneas die in the Troad, but give him a son, Rhomos, who went to Italy and founded the city.[69]

The story of Aeneas in the west had probably been known since the sixth century,[70] but it was associated more with Lavinium, Aeneas' legendary landfall and the cult centre of Latium as a whole, than with Rome in particular.[71] In 338, however, Lavinium and the rest of Latium had come under Rome's control, and her cults and myths had become equally the cults and myths of Rome. The fourth century already saw Roman families claiming Trojan descent,[72] and the Aeneas story beginning its inexorable progress as the favoured – and in due course, the official – account of the origins of Rome.[73]

Some versions of it we have already looked at. Others can be quickly summarised: Aeneas himself as the founder (a rare variant, despite Hellanicus' precedent);[74] Rhomos and Rhomylos as the sons of Aeneas;[75] Rhomos as the son of Ascanius;[76] Rhome as the daughter of Ascanius.[77] We have an interesting expansion of that last version from Agathocles of Cyzicus: Aeneas leaves Troy with his granddaughter Rhome; they come to the Tiber, and Rhome dedicates a temple of Faith (*Pistis*, *Fides*) on the Palatine; later, when a city is founded on that hill (by whom?), it is named after her.[78] Roman Faith was a concept of some diplomatic significance; her temple – on the Capitol, not the Palatine – probably dates from 257, and was the scene of a strikingly archaic ritual.[79]

Some of the versions we know of must have had a significance which now escapes us. What did it mean, for instance, to give Aeneas four sons, Ascanius, Rhomylos, Rhomos, and *Euryleon*?[80] Or three sons, Rhomylos, Rhomos, and *Maylles*?[81] ('Maylles' may be textually corrupt as well as unintelligible.) Or a wife *Dexithea*, daughter of Phorbas?[82]

There were various mythological characters called Phorbas ('the shepherd'), but the one most likely to be relevant here was a son of Helios (brother, therefore, of Circe), whose daughter Ambrakia was the mother of Dexamenos. Both mother and son are eponyms: Dexamenai was a district in Ambracia in north-west Greece. Aeneas was said to have been received there by Dexamenos the father of Ambrax.[83] (Ambracia was the royal capital of king Pyrrhus, Rome's great adversary in the 270s BC, and was the scene of an epic siege by the Romans in 189.[84]) 'Dexithea', however, should mean 'she who receives the goddess' – and the story of how her sons Rhomylos and Rhomos were brought to the Tiber by ship, and there delivered to the site of Rome, has overtones of the reception of the Phrygian goddess, the Great Idaean Mother of the Gods, at Rome in 204 BC.[85]

That such events might have their effect on the foundation legend is strongly suggested by the very eccentric story reported by a late commentator on Virgil, that Rhome, who founded Rome, was the daughter of Aesculapius – i.e. Asklepios, the Greek god of healing. Aesculapius was brought to Rome from Epidauros, and installed in a temple on the Tiber island, just as the Great Mother was brought to Rome from Phrygia, and installed in a temple on the Palatine.[86] Aesculapius, 292 BC; Fides ('Faith'), 257; Magna Mater, 204. The establishment of Roman cults, and the stories told about their origins, were evidently part of the 'ideas and circumstances of the age' which could be reflected in foundation legend.[87]

WHERE ARE THE TWINS?

By the late fourth century, as we shall see in the next chapter, the Roman story of the twins and the she-wolf already existed. How did Greeks who wanted to make sense of Rome incorporate that story into their own elaborate mythology?

The Sicilian Alcimus knows of Romulus in the second half of the fourth century; but he is a Romulus without a brother, just another eponym of Rome like the 'Rhomos' and 'Rhome' of the Greek stories.[88] Callias of Syracuse, at the turn of the fourth and third centuries, has 'Rhomylos' as one of *three* brothers, which looks like the usual strategy for combining separate versions.[89] It is interesting that west Greek authors, comparatively close to Rome itself, are the first to register Romulus; but even they seem not to know he has a twin. For

Hegesianax, as late as the second century, 'Rhomylos' is just one of four brothers.[90]

We cannot even assume that those authors who refer to *two* brothers 'Rhomylos and Rhomos' were necessarily aware of the twins story.[91] Some of them very probably were: the Dexithea-author had Rhomylos and Rhomos tipped out on to the bank of the river in a manner very reminiscent of Fabius Pictor on Remus and Romulus; and the second part of an obviously composite anonymous version implies the dynasty of Alban kings which ends with the story of the twins. But both of those are clearly late, and Dionysius calls the second one 'Roman' anyway.[92]

Dionysius goes on to refer to a Roman tradition in which 'Rhomylos and Rhomos' were the sons of Aeneas' daughter by an unnamed father.[93] That could well be an early version of the twins story, before the chronological researches of Eratosthenes in the third century made necessary the invention of the Alban kings.[94] But it need not be. The divine parentage implicit in the 'unnamed father' story could be applied to a single founder, as it was by the third-century Greek author Antigonus ('Rhomos, son of Zeus').[95]

And who was the mother? Even when Aeneas' marriage to Lavinia had been accepted, there was still room for variety about the name of their daughter. Ilia, named after Troy? Rhea, named after the Phrygian goddess?[96] Or Aemilia, named after a great Roman family? Aemilia is identified as the mother of Romulus, but we are not told whether she bore the twins.[97]

It is clear that for some time after the appearance of the twins story, creative invention was still at work.[98] But gradually, as with Aeneas, an accepted version began to emerge. At some date in the late third or early second century, a pro-Roman benefactor at Chios instituted games in honour of the goddess Rhome, and dedicated an offering (probably a relief of the she-wolf and twins)[99]

comprising the story of the birth of Romulus the founder of Rome and his brother Remus. According to that story it came about that they were begotten by Ares himself, which one might well consider to be a true story because of the bravery of the Romans.

That seems to document the process of acceptance taking place.

At Cyzicus about 160 BC, the story of the twins and their mother was familiar enough to be used to decorate a dynastic temple of the royal house of Pergamum. But their mother's name was given as Servilia.[100] The Servilii, like the Aemilii, were a Roman family great enough to claim a part of the foundation story for themselves – not inappropriately, for they used 'Geminus' (twin) as part of their nomenclature.[101]

The twins story analysed in chapter I was told by a Greek, Diocles of Peparethos, probably in the third century BC, and after him by a Roman writing for a Greek audience, Q. Fabius Pictor. It did not immediately make all rival versions obsolete; but within a generation or so it had established its narrative of the ancestry, conception and birth of the eponymous founder of Rome beyond all serious challenge. Rhomos, Rhome and the other Greek etymologies, in all their bewildering variety of applications, were now just curiosities, material for learned lists.

THE PROMATHION VERSION

I have deliberately left for separate consideration the most curious of all the curiosities, marked as such in Plutarch's list.

It owes its place there to its very oddity. Plutarch's catalogue of reasons for the name of Rome begins with the common noun *rhōmē* ('strength'), and the name Rhome as variously applied by the mythographers; then, after a brief glance at other eponyms, he focuses on Romulus ('Rhomylos'), and gives the various accounts of his parentage. He concludes with a deliberate contrast between the 'utterly fabulous' version in Promathion's *Italika*, which he tells at some length, and the 'most credible and best attested', that of Diocles and Fabius Pictor, which he expands into a fully detailed narrative.[102]

Promathion set his scene at Alba, but the cruel king Tarchetios has a clearly Etruscan name. When the phantom phallus appears in the royal hearth, Tarchetios sends for advice to an Etruscan oracle. And at the end of the story, he is overthrown.

The only obvious context for that is the late sixth century, when there is good evidence for Etruscan attempts to control Latium.[103] On the other hand, the story seems to mix up the Penelope myth (unweaving the web), the birth of Servius Tullius (whose father Vulcan appeared as a phantom phallus),[104] and the familiar Fabian tale of the twins and the she-wolf. So is it an archaic survival, or the work of an irresponsible late compiler? Scholars are in deep disagreement.[105]

Tarchetios consults 'the oracle of Tethys in Tyrrhenia'. Why Tethys? Not to be confused with Thetis, the silver-footed Nereid who married Peleus and bore Achilles,[106] Tethys is a primordial power, daughter of Gaia and Ouranos, Earth and Sky, and consort of Okeanos, the river of Ocean that surrounds the world. Throughout antiquity, from Homer to Nonnos, Tethys is a symbol of the uttermost ends of the earth.[107] At what date could Etruria be thought of in those terms? Perhaps in the early fifth century BC, when the Athenians were told to flee 'to the ends of the earth' to avoid the invading Persians.[108] It was a practical suggestion: do what the Phocaeans did (and what the other Ionians were advised to do), take to your ships and colonise the western Mediterranean.[109]

Heraclides of Pontus, in the late fourth century, described Rome as 'a Greek city by the great sea', and the Gauls who sacked it in 387 as 'Hyperboreans'. That was an absurdity for his own time, but may be revealing for the world-picture of his sources.[110] For Heraclides was a Pythagorean, and his view of Rome may well be that of Pythagorean circles in Croton or Tarentum in the late sixth century BC. So great was Pythagoras' fame as a philosopher-magician that disciples came to him not only from the Greek colonies of southern Italy but also from Lucania and even Rome.[111]

The Hesiodic poet's realm of Latinos and Agrios, 'in a recess of the holy islands', was well known to the Ionians of Asia Minor in the sixth century BC. Most of the evidence is archaeological, and its cumulative impact is well expressed by Massimo Pallottino:[112]

The effect of the refined Ionian civilisation on the cities of Tyrrhenian Italy is widespread and deeply felt in the second half of the sixth

century. We could even say that there comes into being a genuine
cultural and artistic *koine* consisting equally of the Greek colonies and
the Campanian, Latin and Etruscan centres.

The greatest of all the Ionians in Italy was Pythagoras of
Samos, mystic and mathematician, who took up residence in
Croton about 530 BC. The alleged oracle foretelling his birth is
the closest known parallel to the oracle Tethys gave Tarchetios
in Promathion's story:[113]

[Response to Mnemarchos of Samos:] Your wife is already preg-
nant, and will bear a son who will excel all men ever in beauty and
wisdom . . .

[Response to Tarchetios of Alba:] A virgin must have intercourse
with the phantom; she will bear a son most famous for valour, who
will excel in good fortune and strength.

Note: 'a son', singular. In the story as we have it, twins are
born, thus rendering the oracle false. That inconsistency
cannot be original. The last part of the story looks like the
result of 'contamination' by an intermediate source, assimila-
ting an unfamiliar version to the familiar one.[114] In that case,
Plutarch knew of Promathion's *Italika* only from an author
who quoted it (perhaps in polemical disagreement), and from
whom he wrongly inferred that the phantom phallus begot
twin sons.

A brilliant suggestion for the identity of Promathion was
made by Santo Mazzarino, who pointed out a citation of
'Promathus of Samos' in an Aristotelian work which survives
only in a medieval Latin translation.[115] Aristotle's subject is
the source of the Nile, and he cites 'Promathus' for the view
that the Nile rises on the Silver Mountain, from where a
shorter river, the Chremetes, flows in the opposite direction
into the Ocean beyond the Pillars of Hercules.[116]

The Latin text is unreliable on proper names,[117] and 'Promathus' as a corruption of 'Promathion' is easy to accept. In
which case we have a Samian author interested in the ends of
the world, most naturally to be dated in the context of the great
Samian and Phocaean voyages of the sixth century BC. The
work of such an author might survive to the time of Aristotle,

but four centuries later Plutarch evidently knew him only at second hand, in a slightly garbled form.

There is nothing inherently improbable in the idea of a Roman foundation story of the late sixth or early fifth century BC – say, a generation after Stesichorus (*Geryoneis*) and Eugammon (*Telegony*), and contemporary with Hecataeus, who had Capua founded by the Trojan Capys. We have already had reason to suppose, earlier in this chapter, that some of the Greek accounts of Rome's origins may reflect political realities of the sixth and fifth centuries. The oracle's reference to the strength (*rhōmē*) of the future hero implies that he will be a Greek eponym, presumably Rhomos.[118]

What is extraordinary, however, is that this early Greek author evidently reported a native Roman story. The phantom phallus is a totally un-Greek concept. Greek gods do not manifest themselves in such a way. And it is not the king's daughter who conceives the wonder-child, but a slave girl. Both elements are present in the parallel myth of Servius Tullius, ruler of Rome at some time in the mid-sixth century.[119]

The power of generation was identified as *deus Genius*, and it is surely he who was thought of as the father of the founder in Promathion's tale.[120] Another wonder-child, the Etruscan Tages, was the son of Genius; he was 'born' from a ploughed field at Tarquinii, and taught Tarchon the *Etrusca disciplina*. It can hardly be a total coincidence that the miraculous conception in Promathion's story takes place in the house of Tarchetios.[121] As for the slave mother, that *might* derive from Greek myth (the Trojan slave women who burn the Achaeans' ships at Latinion), but it is more probably a native feature. Saturnus, the god of sowing, and thus of procreation,[122] was honoured in December at a festival when slaves were served by their masters; and on the last day of the Saturnalia, sacrifice was performed to the *di manes* of slaves at the supposed tomb of Larentia, foster-mother of Remus and Romulus in the Fabian version of the foundation legend.[123]

When Tarchetios discovers that the slave girl, and not his daughter, has coupled with the phallus, he proposes, in his rage, to kill them both. But he is dissuaded by Vesta, who appears to him in a dream. That too is surely a native Roman feature, reflecting the importance of the ancient cult of Vesta at the king's house (*regia*) below the Palatine. Later sources tell us that 'the prophecies of Tages' gave to the Vestals the responsibility for the fire in the sacred hearth, and that among the gods honoured in their cult was Fascinus, the male organ.[124]

So if Mazzarino is right about Promathion, and I think it more likely than not that he is, then Plutarch's choice of an 'utterly incredible' version, to set beside the Fabius Pictor story, has preserved for us a wonderful archaic fossil.

CONCLUSION

This long chapter has tried to deal with a bewildering mass of difficult and controversial material – fragments of lost and often undatable historians, to be interpreted against the shifting background of historical situations which are themselves very inadequately documented and incompletely understood. In such a case, no conclusion can hope to approach certainty; as was said at the outset, what is offered here is just hypothesis, subject always to replacement by better hypotheses when they come along. But if there is any validity in the arguments presented, we may draw some tentative conclusions from what the Greek authors said about the origins of Rome.

First, if we exclude Diocles, the undated source of Fabius Pictor, Remus is not named before the second half of the third century at the very earliest.[125]

Second, that date provides also the first evidence for knowledge of the story of the twins. Identification of Rhomylos as a brother of Rhomos does not in itself imply the twins story; it is more likely the mere juxtaposition of a Greek eponym with a Roman one.[126]

Third, when Romulus first appears, in Alcimus in the mid-fourth century, he appears alone.[127]

Fourth, what seems to be a Greek transcription of an archaic Roman legend implies that the founder hero was a single son, not one of twins.[128]

Fifth, though the tradition of Aeneas in the west was no doubt available from the mid-sixth century onwards, it did not become important in Rome till the late fourth. But it was then 'officially' adopted, and grafted on to the Romulus story.[129]

And sixth, the Odyssean legend of the offspring of Circe, daughter of the Sun, may have been of particular significance in archaic Latium and Etruria, as illustrating and explaining native cults.[130]

With those results in mind, limited and provisional as they are, we can now turn to the very different types of evidence that may help us to date the appearance of the Remus story at Rome itself.

CHAPTER 5

Italian evidence

SHE-WOLVES AND LIONESSES

When the young Theodor Mommsen first visited Rome in 1844, studying the antiquities in the Museo dei Conservatori, what made the greatest impression on him was not some masterpiece of classical art but an archaic bronze, probably Etruscan – the Capitoline she-wolf (fig. 5). 'Rugged and uncouth though it is, this statue moved my spirit more than all the beautiful images that surround it.'[1] Many another visitor has felt the same.

The origin of this wonderful piece is unknown. Perhaps from Caere or Veii in the late sixth or early fifth century BC? The experts are more or less agreed on the date, but the provenance remains a mystery.[2] The statue is first attested in the tenth century AD, as giving its name (*ad lupam*) to the place at the Lateran where the execution of papal justice was carried out; by the fifteenth century, at least, it was attached to the Torre degli Annibaldi. In 1471 it was one of the works of ancient art given to the city of Rome by Sixtus IV as the nucleus of the Capitoline collection. Bronze figures of the twins were added beneath it, possibly by Antonio Pollaiuolo and certainly before 1510. In 1586 it was mounted on the pedestal in the Stanza della Lupa where it has stood ever since, a magnificent symbol of eternal Rome.[3]

As her attitude makes clear, this she-wolf is not suckling. Her distended teats, as elsewhere in Etruscan art, explain her aggression and ferocity as a female defending her young,[4] but there is no reason to suppose that she was originally represented

Fig. 5. The Capitoline she-wolf. Rome, Palazzo dei Conservatori: photos by courtesy of the Deutsches Archaeologisches Institut, Rome (inst. negs. 70.652–3).

with cubs, much less with human infants. Four centuries later, a denarius of P. Satrienus (77 BC) shows a ferocious she-wolf, without the twins, as a symbol of Rome.[5] We cannot read that meaning back into the archaic period, although a statue of Mars with wolves is attested at the god's temple on the Via Appia in 217 BC, and a story of the battle of Sentinum in 295 may imply that already by then the wolf was thought of as the beast of Mars, and of Rome, *par excellence*.[6]

So the bronze in the Museo dei Conservatori offers us a she-wolf but no human sucklings; elsewhere in archaic Italy we find the reverse, a suckling but no she-wolf. At Bologna (Etruscan Felsina), a funerary *stele* of the late fifth century shows two scenes: above, a warrior in a chariot; below, a wild beast suckling a human child (fig. 6). Though sometimes described as a wolf, it is clearly a feline: perhaps a panther, possibly a lioness.[7] A contemporary document from Praeneste, the foot of a late fifth-century bronze *cista*, shows what is clearly a lioness suckling a child (fig. 7).[8] The motif of the new-born baby, abandoned to die but miraculously fed by wild beasts, is widespread in many mythologies; Telephus son of Herakles, Paris of Troy and Cyrus the Persian are among the most famous examples.[9] At least one version of it was evidently current among the Latins and Etruscans in the fifth century BC.

A ferocious she-wolf: wolves as the beasts of Mars: an infant suckled by a wild creature. The elements of the Remus and Romulus legend are demonstrably present in archaic Italy. But when were they combined into the Roman story?

THE MIRROR

Our earliest evidence for the she-wolf and twins is a document with a bizarre history (fig. 8). An engraved bronze mirror, supposedly found at Bolsena in Etruria, was sold in Florence in 1877 to the collector Alessandro Castellani. It was discussed at the Istituto di Corrispondenza Archeologica the following year, but doubts soon emerged about its authenticity, and the purchaser chose not to keep it. Evidently believing that it was of interest only to metallurgists, he presented it to the Kingdom

Fig. 7. Foot of a Praenestine *cista*, fifth century BC. Oxford, Ashmolean Museum: photo by courtesy of the Museum.

Fig. 6. Funerary *stele*, fifth century BC. Bologna, Museo civico: photo by courtesy of the Musum (neg. 1688/N12).

of Italy's new industrial museum, where it remained until 1939. In that year the Museo Artistico e Industriale was closed, and the mirror was passed to the Antiquario Comunale.[10]

It was widely assumed to be a fake. The principal editor of *Etruskische Spiegel*, the authoritative collection of Etruscan mirrors, had said so in 1897; eighty years later his judgement was endorsed by the author of the standard work on the iconography of the Roman she-wolf, Cécile Dulière.[11] But wrongly. In a long and detailed discussion in 1982, Richard Adam and Dominique Briquel demonstrated that there is no reason to doubt its authenticity; they were able to show that it is of Praenestine workmanship, approximately datable to the third quarter of the fourth century BC.[12] A hundred years late, the mirror now presents itself as a crucial document for the interpretation of the Roman foundation legend.

The scene it shows is a very strange one. The suckling she-wolf is on the side of a rocky hill; above, an owl and another bird (perhaps a raven?) perch on a dead tree; below lies a large lion, looking out genially at the spectator. There are four human figures, apart from the twins. (1) Above, lying nonchalantly on the rocks, is a young man, naked but for a cloak and hat. His left hand is raised in a gesture of refusal or farewell towards (2) a young woman, veiled and carrying a fan-like object. She has a sad expression, and looks intently at the young man. But he turns his head away, towards (3) a wild man, bearded and dishevelled, who stands to the left of the suckling scene, as one of the two witnesses of it. He is naked except for boots and a goatskin cloak loosely knotted round his neck by the forelegs; he carries a shepherd's throwing-stick. Opposite him, (4) another standing figure witnesses the suckling scene, and points at it with his right hand. He is bearded, wearing a belted tunic, and carrying a spear.

These four figures have been variously interpreted:[13]

1 The god of the Palatine (Klügmann, Jordan);
  a protective genius (Adam and Briquel);
  Hermes (Weigel, Wiseman);
  Faustus/Faustulus (Pairault Massa).

Fig. 8. Praenestine mirror, fourth century BC. Rome, Antiquario comunale:
photo by courtesy of the Deutsches Archaeologisches Institut, Rome
(inst. neg. 4409).

2 The shade of Rhea Silvia (Klügmann, Jordan, Rosenberg, Weigel, Wiseman 1991);
  Carmenta (Wiseman 1991);
  Acca Larentia, mother of the Lares (Pairault Massa);
  Lara/Tacita, mother of the Lares (Wiseman 1993).

3 A shepherd (Klügmann, Peter, Weigel);
  Faunus (Jordan, Wiseman 1991);
  a *lupercus* (Rosenberg, Adam and Briquel, Wiseman 1991);
  Faunus/Lupercus (Pairault Massa);
  Pan (Wiseman 1993).

4 Faustulus (Klügmann, Jordan, Peter, Rosenberg, Wiseman 1991);
  a shepherd (Weigel);
  Thybris/Tiberinus (Pairault Massa);
  Quirinus (Wiseman 1993).

It was natural to start from the 'known' – the she-wolf and twins – and interpret the rest on the premise that the mirror illustrates the foundation story. But some at least of the surrounding figures are very hard to explain on that assumption. As Adam and Briquel point out, with some understatement,[14]

on s'aperçoit ainsi que l'hypothèse courante, qui voit dans notre miroir la représentation de la légende romaine, ne va pas sans poser un certain nombre de problèmes.

Moreover, what should be a working hypothesis tends to become a preconception leading to forced interpretations. For example, Françoise-Hélène Pairault Massa takes it for granted that the scene represents the Lupercal cave with the fig-tree (Ficus Ruminalis), even though no cave is visible and the tree, portrayed as dead and leafless, is conspicuously *not* identifiable.[15] Similarly, Adam and Briquel ignore the iconographically compelling identification of the graceful young man in *chlamys* and *petasos* as Hermes, because 'he has no part in the legend'; and despite his conspicuous interaction with two of the other figures (his head turned to the wild man, his hand raised to the woman who looks at him), they blandly describe him as a purely decorative element, 'very vaguely justified by the context'.[16] Even more extraordinary is Dr Pairault Massa's identification of the figure on the right – standing upright, fully dressed, carrying a spear – as, of all things, a river god. That is what he *has* to be, despite everything about him, because 'the agent of destiny that drives the cradle of the twins to the predestined place (the Lupercal) is the Tiber'.[17]

If the premise results in conclusions like that, it is better to abandon it. My own second attempt at an explanation makes no assumptions about the wolf and twins, and tries to account for the four mysterious figures in their own terms. I think that the two standing figures are Pan Lykaios, identified by the goatskin and throwing-stick, and Quirinus, identified by the spear.[18] Their respective festivals at Rome were the Lupercalia and Quirinalia, on 15 and 17 February, during the nine days of *parentatio* for the dead (13–21 February). The only other named festival during that period was the Feralia (21 February), in honour of Tacita, or Muta, 'the silent goddess', whose story is told by Ovid in the *Fasti*.

She was a nymph called Lara – or Lala, 'the chatterbox' – who warned her sister Juturna to flee the approaches of amorous Jupiter; furious, Jupiter tore out her tongue and banished her to the underworld, with Mercury (Hermes) as her escort:[19]

On their way they entered a wood, where the guiding god is said to have taken a fancy to her. As he forced her, she vainly tried to speak through her dumb mouth, and begged with her expression instead of words. She conceived, and bore twins. They guard the crossroads, and always keep watch in our city: they are the Lares.

The Lares Praestites were the guardians of Rome. It seems to me likely that the story of their parentage explains the central 'panel' of the design on the mirror:[20] at the top, Hermes and Tacita; in the middle, their children, the twin Lares; at the bottom, a wild beast (*fera*) to symbolise the Feralia. In our literary sources, various implausible etymologies are offered to explain the name 'Feralia' and make it relevant to the cult of the dead,[21] but the natural meaning is surely the one implied here.

The Romans had two periods of the year for placating the dead. The other was the Lemuria (9, 11, 13 May), in Hermes' month, named after his mother Maia,[22] between the festival of the Lares Praestites on the Kalends and the festival of Hermes himself (Mercury) on the Ides.[23] To us, February is three months before May; for the Romans, whose year originally began in March, it was nine months *after* May. So the mirror scene can be combined with the tale in Ovid and the dates in the calendar to produce a coherent myth.

The date of Lara's mutilation, banishment and rape will have been 1 May, the day sacred to the Lares, who were conceived then, and to Bona Dea 'below the Rock', in whose grove the act no doubt took place.[24] The days of the Lemuria, when angry ghosts are placated,[25] perhaps represent her bitterness at the cruelty of her treatment. After nine months she gives birth in the underworld to the twin Lares; but now it is February, when the dead can again revisit the world above.[26] Hermes complacently meets his family at the Lupercal. The children will remain, suckled and protected by wild beasts, but their mother must return, the nymph of the infernal lake.[27] The twin Lares, protectors of the Roman state, are found by Pan, god of the wild (and of the Lupercal), and Quirinus, god of the Roman People (Quirites). Hence the adjacent festivals – Lupercalia, Quirinalia, Feralia, on 15, 17 and 21 February. The day after the Feralia, when the dangerous days of the dead are over, the grateful Romans offer sacrifice to the Lares.[28]

This reconstruction is of course hypothetical. But it does at least account for the data, including the body language of the figures on the mirror.[29] If it is right, then the mirror is no help for Remus and Romulus – or rather, it is of only negative help, as providing a *terminus post quem*. For if the twins suckled by the she-wolf could be recognised about 340 BC as the Lares Praestites, then it is hard to imagine that the Remus and Romulus story yet existed. As Albert Schwegler suggested long ago, that story may have been created out of the pre-existing myth of Lara and the Lares.[30]

THE OGULNIAN MONUMENT

So far, then, Italy has offered a sixth- or fifth-century she-wolf, but not suckling; two fifth-century wild beasts suckling human children, but not twins; and a fourth-century she-wolf suckling human twins, but evidently not Remus and Romulus. We seem to be closing in on our quarry, but have not yet found it.

The first clear sighting comes in 296 BC. Under that year, Livy has the following item:[31]

The curule aediles Cn. Ogulnius and Q. Ogulnius put several moneylenders on trial and confiscated their property. From this revenue to the public treasury they installed [i] bronze thresholds in the Capitoline temple, [ii] silver vessels for three tables in the shrine of Jupiter, [iii] Jupiter with a four-horse chariot on the roof, and [iv] statues at the Ficus Ruminalis of the founders of the city as infants beneath the she-wolf's teats; they also [v] paved with squared stone the way from the Porta Capena to the temple of Mars.

The translation is not quite certain: item (iv) could also be read as 'they placed beneath the she-wolf's teats statues of the founders of the city as infants', which has led some scholars to believe that the Ogulnii did what Antonio Pollaiuolo (if it was he) did eighteen centuries later, and added figures of the twins beneath an already existing she-wolf statue, whether the one in the Museo dei Conservatori or another.[32]

'*Beneath* the she-wolf's teats' (*sub uberibus lupae*) certainly seems to imply a standing animal. The mirror, on the other hand, showed the she-wolf lying down and offering her teats to the twins, with her head turned back to lick them, and that is the classic pose in literature for the suckling of Remus and Romulus.[33] It is likely that the Ogulnian monument combined the two approaches, showing her with her head turned back to the twins, but standing. That at any rate is how she appears on one of the earliest issues of Roman coinage, the didrachms issued about 269–268 BC showing the head of Hercules on the obverse and the wolf and twins with ROMANO on the reverse (fig. 17, p. 157 below).[34] Q. Ogulnius was one of the consuls of 269,[35] and it is likely in any case that the coin design represents the monument.

Whether they were added to an existing wolf statue, or part of a group created *ex novo*, it is clear that the twins are what mattered. They are not named, but the 'infant founders' are evidently the sons of Mars. The initiatives of the Ogulnii belong in a time of crisis and near-panic, as Rome's enemies to north and south, the Etruscans (and Umbrians) and the Samnites, joined forces with the dreaded Gauls in a coalition that threatened to repeat the sack of Rome a century before.[36] In that context, it was natural for the Ogulnii to use the resources of the public treasury on Jupiter Optimus Maximus, supreme god of the Roman state, and on Mars the war god. The first three of the offerings were to Jupiter in his Capitoline temple (fated to be 'the head of Italy');[37] the fifth was to Mars in *his* temple on the Via Appia. Mars had no temple in the city,[38] but the fourth offering honoured him through his offspring, founders of Rome, nurselings of his own symbolic beast.

That is clearly how Livy saw it. A few chapters later, reporting the great battle at Sentinum the following year, he makes much of 'the wolf of Mars' as a reminder of Rome's foundation story.[39] But what is the value of Livy's testimony? Did he have reliable information about 296–295 BC?

So far as the Ogulnian monument is concerned, the answer is probably yes. We know from Cicero that the pontifical college had archives (*commentarii*) going back to the third century BC, which could still be consulted in his time.[40] As long as the college was a patrician monopoly, its documents were secret; but that monopoly was broken in 300 BC, when the same Ogulnii, as tribunes of the *plebs*, successfully legislated to open up the college of *pontifices* and the college of augurs to joint patrician and plebeian membership.[41] It is a reasonable inference that from then on the pontifical *commentarii* were accessible; and that the newly constituted college approved, and recorded, the initiatives of the Ogulnii to procure the goodwill of Jupiter and Mars in the crisis of 296 BC. If that is so, then the ultimate source of Livy's report was contemporary and authoritative, and we can gratefully accept it as a reliable record.

For the story of Remus, one phrase is particularly interesting. Livy calls the twins 'the founders of the city', in the plural. As we saw in the first chapter, there were versions of the story in which Remus and Romulus ruled together.[42] Livy's formulation here is inconsistent with his own narrative of the foundation in book I, and therefore probably comes from his source; and his source, in turn, may have taken it from the pontifical records or from the inscription on the monument itself.[43]

The latter possibility may receive some support from an analogous monument erected six centuries later by the emperor Maxentius. The inscription was found in the Comitium, in front of the Curia Iulia. It is a statue-base, and bears the dedication date 21 April, the traditional date of the foundation of Rome. The statue-group, now lost, was dedicated 'To unconquered Father Mars, and to the founders of the eternal city'.[44] The use of the plural *conditores*, without naming the twins, is very reminiscent of Livy's account of the Ogulnian monument. In each case the context is religious, with the implication of a cult to the founder-heroes. Dionysius reports that hymns to the twins as the offspring of gods were sung by the Romans in his day, and an oath of loyalty quoted by Diodorus offers a precious glimpse of their place in the divine hierarchy of Rome:[45]

I swear by Capitoline Jupiter, by Vesta of Rome, by Rome's father Mars, by Sol the founder of the race, by Earth who favours animals and plants, and also by the demigods who were the founders of Rome, and the heroes who together increased her power, . . .

Demigods (*hēmitheoi*) and heroes are powers of the sublunary sphere, but still immortals.[46]

Maxentius' statue-group was in the Comitium; that of the Ogulnii was 'at the Ficus Ruminalis', the fig-tree under which the she-wolf suckled the twins.[47] Our sources give us two locations for the tree, either at the Lupercal, which is where one would expect, or in the Comitium (fig. 9). The double tradition was explained by a miracle: the wonder-working augur Attus Navius in the time of the Tarquins had caused the tree to move of its own accord from the Lupercal to the Comitium.[48] That ought to mean that the Ogulnian

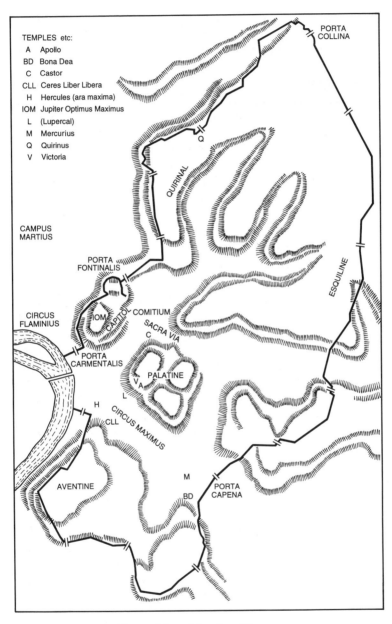

TEMPLES etc:
A Apollo
BD Bona Dea
C Castor
CLL Ceres Liber Libera
H Hercules (ara maxima)
IOM Jupiter Optimus Maximus
L (Lupercal)
M Mercurius
Q Quirinus
V Victoria

PORTA COLLINA

QUIRINAL

CAMPUS MARTIUS

PORTA FONTINALIS

ESQUILINE

CIRCUS FLAMINIUS

IOM
CAPITOL
COMITIUM
SACRA VIA
C

PORTA CARMENTALIS

V A
PALATINE
L

H
CIRCUS MAXIMUS
CLL

M
AVENTINE
BD
PORTA CAPENA

Fig. 9. Map of the city of Rome.

monument was in the Comitium, in which case Maxentius' may have been a replacement of it. But Dionysius reports a bronze statue group of the wolf and twins in a sacred enclosure (*temenos*) at the Lupercal. Since he describes it as 'of ancient workmanship', the most economical hypothesis is to identify it as the Ogulnian monument itself.[49]

Of the two places where the twin founders were evidently honoured, the symbolism of the Comitium is obvious enough: it was the meeting-place of the Roman citizen body.[50] But why should the Lupercal be, as Dionysius puts it, the 'holy place' of the story? At this point we approach the most complex and difficult part of the evidence for the foundation legend, namely its relationship with the annual ritual of the Lupercalia. Before addressing that, let us sum up what the Italian evidence has revealed.

Already in the fifth century BC, Etruscans and Latins were familiar with the she-wolf as a symbol of defiance, and with stories that involved wild beasts suckling human children. A story of a she-wolf suckling twins was known in fourth-century Praeneste, and evidently applied to her neighbour and successful rival, Rome. But Remus and Romulus are not yet identifiable, if our interpretation of the Praenestine mirror is right. (If it is not, then the scene on the mirror remains unexplained.) The first clear evidence for the she-wolf's sucklings as the twin sons of Mars, and therefore presumably Remus and Romulus, comes with the Ogulnian monument of 296 BC.

With a *terminus ante quem* of 296, and a probable *terminus post quem* between thirty and fifty years earlier (for the mirror cannot be more closely dated), the Italian evidence is consistent with the inferences drawn in the last chapter from the various Greek accounts of the origins of Rome. Provisionally, at least, it looks as if Remus and his twin brother are creations of the late fourth century BC. And if we can trust Livy's account of the Ogulnian monument, the story seems to have begun with both twins as the founders of the city.

CHAPTER 6

The Lupercalia

CERMALUS AND LUPERCAL

They were twins, and they were suckled by a she-wolf. Those are the basic data of the Remus and Romulus story; unlike all the other elements, they are immutable.[1] They correspond to three topographical items. The slope of the Palatine where the vessel grounded and tipped the twins out was called Cermalus or Germalus, from *germani*, 'brothers';[2] there was a fig-tree there called Ficus Ruminalis, from *rumis* or *ruma*, 'teat';[3] and the particular place on the slope where the miracle happened was called Lupercal, from *lupa*, 'she-wolf'.[4]

At least two, and probably all three, of these etymologies go back to Varro in the mid-first century BC. But other explanations, *not* involving the story of the twins, were available for all three names. Cermalus, for example, appears in a remarkable passage about Sibylline prophetesses written by Clement of Alexandria (about AD 200), whose source may have been the Greek scholar Eratosthenes:[5]

Heraclides of Pontus in his work *On Oracles* refers to these [the Phrygian and Erythraean Sibyls]. I say nothing of the Egyptian [Sibyl], nor of the Italian one, who dwelt at the *Karmalon* in Rome, and whose son Evander founded the cult-place of Pan in Rome which is called the *Luperkion*.

Evander's mother was the prophetic goddess whom the Romans called Carmenta or Carmentis, from *carmina*, 'songs' or 'prophecies'.[6] So Clement's reference evidently presupposes an etymology in which Cermalus was not 'Germalus, from *germani*', but 'Carmalus, from *carmina*', an item not in the

77

story of Remus and Romulus, but in that of Evander and Carmentis.

Similarly, the Ficus Ruminalis could be explained by reference either to the Tiber, of which 'Rumon' was supposed to be the ancient name,[7] or to the 'rumination' of flocks at midday in that shady place.[8] (Plutarch's description of the site of the Ficus Ruminalis owes something to both these ideas: 'a bank of the river, washing against a grassy meadow, shaded about with low trees'.[9]) High noon, when the flocks seek the shade, is when Pan is dangerously present,[10] so perhaps this 'pastoral' explanation of the fig-tree's name is another allusion to the cult of Pan, the herdsmen's god, at the Lupercal.

For the Lupercal, three etymologies are known which do not involve the she-wolf story. The first is a simple calque from the name of Pan Lykaios, whose home was on Mount Lykaion in Arcadia: as *lupus* (Latin) means the same as *lykos* (Greek), so Lupercal means Lykaion, the place of 'Lycaean' Pan.[11] The second is another pastoral reference: Lupercal from *lupi arcentur*, the place from which 'wolves are kept away' from the flocks.[12] The third is even more linguistically far-fetched: Lupercal from *luere per caprum*, 'to expiate through a goat', referring to the sacrifice of a goat at the Lupercal on the day of the Lupercalia (15 February).[13] That brings us to the final element in an amalgam of myth, topography and ritual performance.

About sixty years before the Trojan War (I summarise the narrative in Dionysius of Halicarnassus),[14] the young Evander left his native Pallantion in Arcadia, driven into exile by his political enemies. With two ship-loads of followers, he sailed to Italy to found a colony. Faunus, king of the Aborigines, gave them land, and on the advice of Evander's mother, the prophetess, they settled at a hill by the Tiber which they named after their home city. There they founded cults to their native divinities – to Lycaean Pan at the bottom of the hill and the goddess of Victory at the top. Pan's sacred precinct was the Lykaion, or Lupercal:

In ancient times, it is said, there was a large cave below the hill, roofed over with a dense thicket and with springs at the bottom beneath the rocks, and the dell adjoining the cliff was shaded by thick, tall trees. Here they set up an altar to the god and made their ancestral sacrifice, which the Romans still perform down to our own time in the month of February after the winter solstice, changing nothing of what was done at that time. The form of the sacrifice will be described in my subsequent narrative.

When he comes to the story of the she-wolf and twins, Dionysius carefully places it at the precinct of Pan, repeating his description of the landscape and referring back to the earlier passage: 'it was a holy place of the Arcadians, so the story goes, who founded it with Evander'.[15] But his account of the ritual is part of a later stage in the Remus and Romulus story, as he follows Aelius Tubero's version of the capture of Remus.[16] Numitor's men had quarrelled with the twins about their grazing land:

They knew in advance that the boys were going to celebrate the Lykaia [i.e. Lupercalia] in honour of Pan, the Arcadian festival as set up by Evander. So they laid an ambush for that moment in the ritual when the young men from the community around Pallantion [i.e. the Palatine] were required to leave the Lykaion [i.e. the Lupercal] after the sacrifice and go round the village at a run, naked except for loincloths made from the hides of the newly-sacrificed animals. This signified a kind of traditional purification of the villagers, as it is still performed even today.

The relationship of the Lupercalia ritual with the myth of the twins is a complex one. If the former is to be used to cast light on the latter, we have to deal with the ritual in its own terms and try to explain its nature without reference to the myth. That is not at all an easy task; the meaning of the Lupercalia was disputed even in ancient times, and it is even more controversial now, as the rival interpretations of comparativists and structural analysts compete to explain the fragments of information our sources provide.[17] I have tried to explain them myself, with what success it is too soon to say.[18] The next section sets out the evidence for what was done in Rome on 15 February, not in any vain aspiration to total objectivity, but at least with the intention of keeping conscious prejudice to a minimum.

THE RITUAL

'The third dawn after the Ides looks upon the naked Luperci.'[19] The Luperci were *sacerdotes*, a word for which the usual translation 'priests' is quite misleading.[20] They were not men of dignity and seniority like the augurs and *pontifices*; what characterised them was youth, nudity and vigorous activity. But they were responsible for carrying out the ritual on this occasion, just as the leaping Salii (also young and vigorous, though not naked) were responsible for *their* rituals in March.[21] The Luperci were organised as a *sodalitas* or *collegium*, with a *magister* in charge,[22] but it is not necessarily the case that all the members of it took part in the run each year; possibly the running was done by selected young men who thereafter became members of the college.[23]

What happened at 'the third dawn after the Ides' is described by Plutarch:[24]

They [the Luperci] slaughter goats; then, when two youths of noble birth have been brought to them, some of them touch [the youths] on the forehead with the bloody knife, the others bring wool soaked in milk and immediately wipe the blood off. After the wiping-off the youths must laugh.

The sacrificial victims were skinned, and the hide cut up into strips. We may assume that they were also butchered, and the meat cooked on spits, as was usual after a sacrifice.[25] That must have taken some time. A passage in Ovid describes the 'priests' (*sacerdotes*) cooking the entrails on the spits at midday; those who are invited have come to share the meat, and the young men are spending their time at exercise and sport.[26]

The Luperci were divided into two groups, the Fabiani and the Quinctiales, named after the patrician *gentes* of Fabii and Quinctii.[27] (It is disputed whether that was an original feature or a later development; a third group, the Iuliani, was added in 45 BC.) It is possible that the two 'youths of noble birth' in Plutarch's account were the leaders of the two groups. In that case, we should probably distinguish between the Luperci as a college, no doubt responsible for the sacrifice, the ceremony with the knife, the skinning of the goats and the preparation of the meat, and the two teams of naked young men – that year's *new* Luperci – whose representatives were ritually 'blooded' and cleansed, and who showed off their physical prowess as a spectacle to the public.[28]

When the meat was ready, it was shared out among those present, though the Quinctiales, for some reason, were evidently not allowed to have any.[29] After a cheerful meal with plenty of wine,[30] the young men took the strips of newly cut goat-hide, and ran about among the onlookers, using the thongs to whip anyone within reach. As Mommsen pointed out long ago, only the patrician Fabii and Quinctii, after whom the two groups of Luperci were named, used the *praenomen* 'Kaeso'; the implied etymology is from *caedere*, 'to strike'.[31] Other aspects of the performance are less clear: where did they run, what did they wear, at whom did they aim their lash?

The word most often used of the Luperci is *discurrere*, 'to run this way and that'; but some sources also imply that they ran *round* the settlement.[32] This apparent inconsistency appears even in our best-informed authority, Varro, who on the one hand described the Luperci running up and down the Sacra Via, and on the other calls the run a *lustratio* of the ancient Palatine city, which ought to imply an encirclement.[33] We know they started from the Lupercal; and it is possible, though far from certain, that the famous scene at the Lupercalia of 44 BC, when Antony offered Caesar the crown, implies that they ended in the Comitium.[34]

Varro's *lustratio* passage deserves a closer look:[35]

> ego magis arbitror Februarium a die februato, quod tum februatur populus, id est Lupercis nudis lustratur antiquum oppidum Palatinum gregibus humanis cinctum.

> I think rather that February was named after 'Purification Day', because that is when the populace is purified – that is, the ancient Palatine settlement is encircled by the naked Luperci, and girt with human flocks.

That strange final phrase may be explicable if we remember that the Luperci were called *crepi*; the feminine form *crepae* was a corruption of *caprae*, 'she-goats', so it is a reasonable inference that the Luperci were thought of as *capri*, 'he-goats'.[36] Since *grex* can in any case mean a group of people as well as a flock of goats or sheep, it would be a particularly appropriate word to apply to the Luperci, and Varro's *greges humanae* (plural) may well refer to the two groups into which the young men were divided. If so, then they 'girdled' the Palatine. Perhaps they spread out from the Lupercal and encircled the hill like beaters (an appropriate simile)? In that case the encirclement was not the route of the run, for there was no route. I think we should imagine them running about all round the Palatine, with the whole afternoon taken up by their exciting antics, and gravitating towards the Forum by the end of the day, with a final sacrifice at the Comitium.[37]

If the Palatine was girdled with quasi-goats, the Luperci were girdled with the goat itself. Or so at least they were in the first century BC, for it is evident that there were changes over time in the costume of the 'naked Luperci'. Pompeius Trogus, as excerpted by Justin, reports a statue of Pan Lykaios at the Lupercal, 'naked with a goatskin cape, the costume in which the running is done nowadays at the Lupercalia in Rome'.[38] Since Trogus was a Narbonensian, and may not have had first-hand experience of the Roman ritual, 'nowadays' probably refers to the time his source was writing, whenever that was. The statue of Pan in a goatskin cape sounds early: the iconography is that of the Pan-figure on the fourth-century BC mirror from Praeneste (fig. 8, p. 68 above). According to Trogus' contemporary Aelius Tubero, a Roman aristocrat who will certainly have known about the Lupercalia at first hand, the Luperci wore the skin of the sacrificed goat as a loincloth; Ovid and Plutarch confirm that all they had on was a *cinctus* or *perizōma*, the minimal covering used by young men at exercise.[39]

It is reasonable to infer a change in costume, no doubt for the sake of modesty, between the time of Trogus' source and the thirties BC, when Tubero was writing. Augustus may have taken it still further. He was certainly concerned about the moral dangers of the Lupercalia (he forbade boys before the age of puberty to take part in the run), and the visual evidence

Fig. 10. Funerary relief of Ti. Claudius Liberalis (*CIL* xiv 3624, Tibur), showing the young *eques* dressed as a Lupercus, carrying a whip and escorted by two attendants: second century AD (contrast Pan's 'Lupercus' costume in fig. 8). Vatican, Museo Chiaramonti: photo by courtesy of the Musei Vaticani (xxxii.38.31, inv. 9312).

for the Lupercalia in the second and third centuries AD shows the effects of that concern. We see young *equites* as Luperci, wearing substantial aprons clearly not of goatskin, and wielding not goatskin thongs but actual whips (fig. 10).[40] In these more puritanical times, the demands of equestrian dignity had clearly compromised even more the traditional nudity of the Luperci.

They ran (but where?), they were naked (but how naked?), and they hit people (but whom?). The short answer to the third question is 'anyone they met',[41] but there is a longer answer too.

In 276 BC Rome was afflicted by a disastrous epidemic of stillbirths and miscarriages, both animal and human. The healing god Aesculapius, imported from Epidaurus only sixteen years before, could do nothing. This was evidently the occasion when the flagellation of women in particular, in order to achieve fertility and a safe delivery, became an important part of the Lupercalia.[42] Some of our sources even imply that it was *only* women who were beaten by the Luperci,[43] but that cannot be right. Plutarch quotes an aetiology by the Hellenistic poet Butas (undatable, alas), which explains the wantonly aggressive behaviour of the Luperci as imitating the triumphant brandishing of weapons by the twins after the fall of Alba; Varro and Ovid, who accept the 'cathartic' nature of the ritual, specify the place itself – the Palatine settlement – as the object of the purification, and not just the women.[44] It seems clear that here too we have a development over time, in which a new significance was added to the existing ritual under the pressure of particular circumstances. But only the chance survival of a fragment of Livy enables us to see that. The sources that describe the Lupercalia for us did not think in diachronic terms; for them, all the phenomena were equally ancient and 'original', instituted once for all at the beginning and preserved unchanged.

Three other details are recorded about the ritual on 15 February. At some stage the Luperci sacrificed a dog; Plutarch was puzzled by that.[45] 'Hot salt' was carried, as an instrument of purification.[46] And the final batch of salt-meal cakes, ritually prepared by the Vestal Virgins from spelt gathered in May, was used at the Lupercalia; the other two had been offered to Vesta on 9 June (Vestalia) and to Jupiter Optimus Maximus on 15 September (the 'feast of Jove' during the *ludi Romani*).[47] That last item indicates how important the Lupercalia ritual was in the thought-world of archaic Rome – at the same level as the eternal flame and the *caput rerum*.[48]

The sophisticated Romans of a later time could see that it was a very ancient ritual, appropriate to a primitive community:[49]

fera quaedam sodalitas et plane pastoricia atque agrestis germano-
rum Lupercorum, quorum coitio illa silvestris ante est instituta quam
humanitas atque leges . . .

A quite savage brotherhood this, downright rustic and uncouth,
consisting of those genuine wolf-men whose famous woodland pack
was founded long before civilisation and law!

In this passage Cicero plays on the 'wolf' element in the word
Lupercus; his learned contemporary Varro thought that the
Luperci were originally transformed into wolves, like the initi-
ates in the Arcadian mysteries of Mount Lykaion.[50] That looks
like an erudite inference from the familiar equation of *Lupercus*
and *Lykaios*, with Varro's knowledge of the Arcadian cult
grafted on to the Roman one. But his idea comes close to the
explanation offered by modern comparativists, who very
plausibly infer an initiatory rite in which adolescents had to
live wild, like wolves, before returning and being accepted as
fully adult members of the community.[51]

As we saw in chapter 4, the first identifiable Greek reaction
to the peoples of Latium and Etruria was the naming of Agrios,
'the wild man', as a son of Circe and Odysseus and the brother
of Latinos. That is in a Hesiodic author of the sixth century BC,
or possibly even earlier; at some later stage, in an unknown
author exploited by Nonnos, Agrios was identified as
'Phaunos', a Greek transliteration of the Latin Faunus, prophetic god and mythical king of the Aborigines of Latium.[52]
Since Faunus in some Latin authors is the god of the Lupercal
cult,[53] wildness was evidently the cult's defining characteristic
at a very early date.

Two of Cicero's adjectives – *agrestis* and *silvestris* – correspond to the Greek word *agrios*. But he also calls the Lupercal
brotherhood *pastoricia*, 'appropriate to herdsmen', and it is to
this pastoral nature of the cult that practically all the details
known to us apply. The Luperci may have lived wild as wolves
once upon a time, but in the ritual as reported by our sources
they are thought of not as wolves but as goats.[54] Apart from the
name 'Lupercalia' itself, and the hint implicit in Hesiod's
Agrios, all our evidence seems to post-date the introduction of
Arcadian Pan, god of goats and herdsmen, as the divinity
presiding at the Lupercal.

The cult of Pan at Rome dates back at least to the third
century, since it was mentioned by Eratosthenes, and probably
to the fourth, if we are right to identify Pan as the wild man on
the Praenestine mirror.[55] The fifth century is also possible, but
before that it is unlikely that Pan was widely known outside
Arcadia. He probably came to Rome after the Dioscuri and
Apollo (484 and 431 BC) and before Asclepius (292 BC).[56] As
always, our sources are synchronic, unaware of development
over time. In Tibullus' picture of primeval Rome,[57]

cows grazed on the grassy Palatine, and lowly huts stood upon the
citadel of Jupiter. A Pan drenched with offerings of milk had his place
in the shade of a holm-oak, and there was a wooden Pales made by a
peasant's crook-knife. On a tree was hung the offering of a roving
shepherd, a trilling Pan-pipe consecrated to the woodland god . . .

In this learned and highly allusive passage, Pan in a Palatine
context must be a reference to the Lupercal.[58]

So the modern comparativist interpretation may be welcomed as a working hypothesis for the prehistoric *origins* of the
ritual; but the individual elements reported by our sources
could come from any of the various stages in its development,
either very ancient or comparatively recent phenomena. Thus,
the Pan cult is early but not 'original'; the flagellation of
women dates only from the third century BC; the nakedness of
the Luperci undergoes a progressive modification; their division into two named groups may be an innovation, as the
addition of a third group certainly was. What is clear from first
to last, however, is that the ritual never became obsolete. It
always *mattered* to the welfare of Rome.[59]

RITUAL AND MYTH

How much help can this necessarily provisional account of the
Lupercalia be for our enquiry into the Roman foundation
legend? Which (to put it crudely) came first, the ritual or the
myth?

To that question there can be only one answer. If the
Lupercalia ritual had been devised to explain or commemorate

a pre-existing she-wolf myth, it would be primarily concerned with wolves, not goats, and the pastoral god Pan would have no place in it. As it is, the canonical place-names for the wolf-and-twins story – Cermalus, Ficus Ruminalis, Lupercal – all have alternative etymologies,[60] and for the Lupercal in particular the derivation from the she-wolf is only one among many.[61] The myth was evidently not primeval.

In that case the ritual, in one form or another, was already there for the myth to be grafted on to it. But the ritual itself underwent changes over time, and it may be that the myth, once established, had some influence on the way the ritual changed. All we can do is identify the places in the story where the myth and the ritual evidently mattered to each other.

In one version of the divine conception of the twins, Numitor's daughter the Vestal Virgin is frightened by a wolf as she goes to collect water (presumably from the river). She takes refuge in a cave, where she is ravished by Mars.[62] Caves are appropriate for Pan, but less so for Mars; if the Lupercal is called Mars' cave by some of our sources, that may imply a reinterpretation made necessary by the attachment of the twins story to that particular place.[63]

The Lupercal was so called, in the first instance, probably because the Luperci were wild men, like wolves. When the Pan cult was introduced there, the name was explained as the Latin form of Arcadian Lykaion.[64] When the foundation story was developed, Mars' offspring were suckled at the 'wolf-place'; that is, the Lupercal provided a site for the myth, which in turn provided another explanation for its name. So when Varro reports a goddess Luperca, identified as the she-wolf by the etymology *lupa pepercit* ('the she-wolf spared them'),[65] I think we must take that as evidence for elaboration of the myth, not for any organic nexus of myth and ritual in archaic times.

The other point of contact between the ritual and the myth is at the stage of the twins' adolescence. Their story provides an aetiology for the naked run, and for the two groups of Luperci: the twins and their respective followers run in pursuit of thieves who have stolen their flocks; they are naked either to facilitate the pursuit or because they were exercising when the theft was reported.[66] Some authorities build this episode into the narrative of the foundation legend, to explain the capture of Remus by Numitor's herdsmen.[67] Others give the aetiology a looser connection with the narrative, explaining the running and the high spirits by reference either to the twins' victory over Amulius or to Numitor's allowing them to found their own city.[68] (Ovid's aetiology of the flagellation of women falls into that category; but it is attached to a later stage of Romulus' career, after the death of Remus.[69])

Since the twins' life as adolescents was that of herdsmen,[70] this part of the story was easily adaptable to the Lupercalia as a cult of Pan. But the Pan cult was supposedly introduced by Evander and his Arcadians long before Numitor's daughter gave birth to the twins, with the result that the foundation story had to be uneasily accommodated to a Palatine settlement that had already been founded once before. So when we find the suckling scene narrated at the holy place dedicated to Pan by Evander, and the grown twins portrayed as taking part in a ritual to Pan that Evander had brought from his native Arcadia,[71] we may take that as an indication that the story of Remus and Romulus evolved later than the story of Evander, and had to be adapted to it.

CHAPTER 7

The arguments

It is a reasonable inference from the evidence set out in the last three chapters that the story of Remus and Romulus, far from being the reflection of some primordial myth, probably originated in the fourth century BC. And if its origins do belong in historical time, then it is necessary to look for historically intelligible reasons for its creation. The three crucial questions were posed at the end of chapter 1: Why a twin in the first place? Why call him Remus? And once you have him, why kill him off?

Chapter 2 showed that comparative mythology provides no useful guidance. It is now time to explore a different tradition, and ask what answers to those three questions have been offered during the two centuries of modern classical scholarship.

NIEBUHR, SCHWEGLER AND MOMMSEN

In 1810, at the age of thirty-four, Barthold Georg Niebuhr left his post in the Prussian State Bank and turned to the profession of history at the newly founded University of Berlin. 'There in 1810–1811, in an extraordinary concentration of thought, he virtually created the modern study of Roman history.'[1] Nothing could better illustrate Niebuhr's critical method in the *Römische Geschichte* than his treatment of the Remus legend. He put his finger immediately on the two essentials: first, that the story must have been created by the Romans in order to explain their own community; and second, that a story of twins must imply some sort of double state.

Here is the passage, in Hare and Thirlwall's 1828 English translation:[2]

When the inhabitants of Rome, as their town began to rise out of insignificance, and they could utter the Roman name with joy, looked back upon their dark period, and retraced in thought the growth of their community, it was natural for them to call the founder of their nation Romus, or, with the inflexion so usual in their language, Romulus. If there was in their neighbourhood a town called Remuria, inhabited by a kindred race, which had been sometimes allied, sometimes hostile to them, and had sunk before their arms, they might consider its founder, Remus, as the twin brother of Romulus, slain by him in a fit of irritated passion: and in proportion as a double state, of peculiar character, established itself amongst them, the fiction which represented the city as founded by twins, became the more firmly fixed.

Remuria, in the story, is where Remus wanted the city to be founded, and where Romulus buried him after the fatal quarrel.[3] (Niebuhr identified it as the hill behind S. Paolo fuori le Mura, though that is neither 'five miles from the Palatine', as in the *Origo gentis Romanae*, nor 'thirty stades from Rome' – i.e. from the gate? – as in Dionysius.[4]) 'The conclusion which must be drawn from all this is, that in the earliest times there were two towns, Rome and Remuria, the latter being far distant from the city and from the Palatine . . . Thus we have a double kingdom which ends with the defeat of Remuria.'[5]

But that was not the whole story. Niebuhr believed, as have many after him, that Rome then 'united on terms of equality' with a Sabine village on the Quirinal, thus creating a new double state.[6] And later still there was the patrician–plebeian duality, as a result of which 'Remuria' was identified with the plebeian Aventine.[7] Niebuhr was untroubled by the explanatory overkill. He believed in a primitive poetic tradition which outlived its original stimulus:[8]

A double people the Romans certainly continue to be until low down in the historical age: this could not but be indicated symbolically on many occasions. The poem on the twin-brothers has no other meaning: and if it was first occasioned by the union of the Aborigines and the Pelasgians, or of Rome and Remuria, it was preserved by that of the Romans and the [Sabine] Quirites; and it gained the most vivid reality from the relation between the patricians and the plebeians.

Only the first stage of Niebuhr's reconstruction accounts for the *origin* of the story, for Remus' name, and for Remus' death. On the other hand, only the last stage – the patrician–plebeian conflict – would be regarded today as safely historical.

The next great historian of Rome, Albert Schwegler in Tübingen in 1853, took a quite different view. Dismissing as misguided what he called Niebuhr's allegorical or symbolical approach to the myth, he proposed instead a religious explanation. Schwegler noted that Rome's protecting gods, the Lares Praestites, were twins.[9] Which set of twins came first? Not Remus and Romulus: their story was too problematical to be original. The twin Lares must be very ancient, and the twin founders derived from them.

Schwegler appealed to the analogy of the Greek Dioscuri and the Vedic Aśvins, but supposed that the Romans developed the ancient motif in a particular way, with one twin cast as the envious and unlucky antagonist. The fratricide is merely aetiological: he dies who violates the sanctity of the walls.[10] As for Remus' name, that could be an expression of his unlucky status: *remores* in augury are birds that signify delay, and Remuria is the Aventine, the place of unsuccessful and ill-omened augury.[11] The Remuria that was five miles or thirty stades away is swept aside as a misunderstanding, a 'groundless doublet' of the Aventine Remuria.

The last point is clearly the weakest. Why should anyone ever have wanted to put Remuria anywhere else, if the Aventine was its necessary location? Nor is the explanation of 'Remus' convincing, since *remores* were delaying birds, not specifically unlucky ones.[12] But the ingenious idea that the twins story was derived from the twin Lares is confirmed, I think, by the Praenestine mirror (which turned up 24 years after Schwegler's history was published). Ironically, it was just that point that the third of the great Germans, Theodor Mommsen, explicitly rejected in his article on the Remus legend in 1881.[13]

For the creator of the *Römisches Staatsrecht*, the explanation of
the legend was naturally a constitutional one. Mommsen drew
attention to the phraseology of Cassius Hemina in the mid-
second century BC: both Remus and Romulus were invested
with *imperium*, 'on the understanding that they should arrange
between themselves about the kingship' – just like Roman
magistrates, whose powers were equal. So the story has nothing
to do with monarchy, but with double authority in a free state.
Remus, and the idea of twin founders, becomes necessary when
power is shared between two magistrates of equal status.[14]

According to Mommsen, then, Remus was added to an
existing foundation legend in order to justify a new concept of
constitutional collegiality. As a later addition, his name may
have been created 'by a simple but non-organic differentiation
from the main one [Romulus]'; it would have been Remulus,
except that by now the *-ulus* ending had come to carry a
diminutive sense.[15] That seems a less than compelling explanation; and Mommsen had even more trouble with Remus'
death, which he rightly described as 'out of harmony' with the
rest of the story as he understood it.[16] He offered two explanations – first, that the story of T. Tatius and the Sabines made
Remus unnecessary as a symbol of double authority (but that
should mean that Remus could be *forgotten*, not that a story of
his murder had to be invented), and second, that since the
Republic was the opposite of monarchy, the double-kingship
idea itself was less useful (but in that case, why was the story
invented in the first place?).

SCHULZE AND AFTER

Thanks to Mommsen's authority, that was how the state of the
question remained for more than twenty years.[17] Then, in
1904, Wilhelm Schulze of Göttingen published his systematic
researches into Roman nomenclature, *Zur Geschichte lateinischer
Eigennamen*. Of his 596 pages, 360 were devoted to Etruscan
name-formations and their survival in Latin; among the thou-
sands of examples were *remne* and *rumlnas*, Latinised
respectively as Remnius (or Remmius) and Romilius. Right at

the end of his disquisition, in the chapter on place-names, Schulze picked up these two items and modestly offered his answer to a big question – 'Was ist *Roma?*'[18] It added a new dimension to the investigation of the Remus legend.

T. Romilius (or Romulius) Vaticanus is named in the *fasti* as consul in 455 BC; the *tribus Romilia* (or Romulia), first of the 'rural tribes', which occupied land on the right bank of the Tiber, evidently took its name from the family.[19] Just as the Caecilii were named after Caeculus,[20] so, Schulze argued, Romulus was the eponym of the *gens Romilia*, who were originally *rumlnas*, from the Etruscan side of the river.[21] Their ancestor must have founded Rome and given it his own family name.[22] Not only that, but 'the memory of a hostile brother' clung to place-names like Remoria, which must have been the settlement of the *remne*; 'so Remus too turns out to be the eponym of an Etruscan *gens*'.

Schulze had shifted the argument on to the linguists' territory, and it is no accident that when the new journal *Glotta* appeared in 1909, the first number included a long article on 'Remus und Romulus' by one of the editors, Paul Kretschmer of Vienna. Kretschmer proposed to reverse Mommsen's reconstruction by making Remus the original founder and Romulus the later addition. He based this on a purely linguistic argument: the Greek sources normally call Remus 'Rhomos', the eponym of Rome, which implies a stage in the Roman tradition when Remus was the only founder.[23] Like Schulze, he accepted Remus and Romulus as real names; his argument was that each had been used as an eponym of Rome at successive stages in the creation of the tradition (though neither was satisfactory, since Remus had the wrong vowel, Romulus an extra syllable), and then joined as brothers in a single story. But the story became problematic, Remus' primacy was forgotten, and a motive had to be found to get rid of him. There was 'nothing historical or mythical, nothing symbolical or allegorical', just 'pure story-telling', the laws and techniques of which produced the development of the legend.[24]

That seems an inadequate explanation for a story involving the killing of a twin. Kretschmer's article is important not for its main argument, which is quite unconvincing, but for the attention he drew to two neglected facts. First, that Propertius treats Remus' death as a human sacrifice for the city's walls;[25] and second, that Festus preserves a tradition calling Romulus 'Altellus', the diminutive of *alter*, as if to make him 'just the second one'.[26]

Schulze's theory was dangerously seductive. Suppose, wrote Josef Mesk in *Wiener Studien* in 1914, suppose that the Romans, at some unknown date, were looking for an eponymous founder on the Greek model, and two important *gentes* with names similar to 'Rome' both claimed to supply one. This dispute of honour between the Romilii and the Remnii could have been solved by the expedient of making their respective eponyms *twin* founders. Splendid – except that the Remnii were never a *gens* at Rome, important or otherwise, as Schulze well knew.[27] But let it pass. The story, Mesk suggested, later became problematical, a second founder being not only super-fluous but extraordinary, and so the Romans got rid of the one whose name sounded less like 'Rome'.[28]

That marks a nadir of interpretative plausibility. But though his solution was so unconvincing, Mesk did at least understand the problem. As he pointed out, what one expects in a twins story is harmony and equality; the violent removal of one of them is a paradox. How different from Ettore Pais, whose *Storia critica di Roma* dismissed the death of Remus as 'an element of minor importance' in the legend![29]

A much more elaborate and ingenious variant on the Schulze hypothesis was produced by Arthur Rosenberg in his Pauly–Wissowa article on Romulus. He proposed, in the first place, the independent existence of an ancient indigenous story involving Romulus, ancestor of the inferred Etruscan *ruma* (whence *rumlnas* and the Romilii), and a Greek version which characteristically attributed the foundation of Rome to an eponymous Rhomos; the two were then linked, probably in the fifth century BC, by making Romulus and Rhomos twin brothers. Rosenberg followed Kretschmer in explaining Remus as a Latinisation of Rhomos; the Romans, having no personal name Romus, used the nearest-sounding name they

did know, namely Remus (from Schulze's Etruscan *remne*).
Rosenberg preferred Remmius to Remnius as the Latin form
of *remne*, but one still wants to ask what the evidence is for
their existence in fifth-century Rome.[30] Predictably, there is
no explanation for the death of Remus. Rosenberg offers
merely the truism that when it came to founding the city that
was named after Romulus, 'it now became important to the
narrators of the story to set Remus aside'.[31] So why was he
there to start with? Why create a character you will have to
get rid of?

Rosenberg's article appeared in the great encyclopaedia in
1914, summing up a formidable century of *Altertumswissenschaft*. What German scholarship had achieved seemed to be
definitive, and with one exception (to whom we shall turn in a
moment) serious historians left the foundation legend alone
for half a century. In *The Cambridge Ancient History* (1928),
Hugh Last accepted Rosenberg's explanation, complete with
Schulze's mysterious Remmii.[32] The ancient derivation of the
name Remus was still ignored.

BACK TO POLITICS

The exception mentioned above was Jérôme Carcopino,
whose book on 'the she-wolf of the Capitol' was published, to
great acclaim, in 1925. His argument was a complex one,
depending on the hypothesis of a Sabine take-over of Rome in
the mid-fifth century BC. That, thought Carcopino, was the
origin of the various double aspects of the Roman community,
such as the two groups of Luperci, which were reflected in the
twins story.[33] He suggested that the wolf was the 'totem
animal' of the Sabines, who therefore took the existing early-
fifth-century Etruscan bronze statue of the she-wolf, combined
it with two naked figures (like Luperci) to symbolise the two
peoples, Sabine and Latin; this group, placed at the Lupercal,
was later misinterpreted as the she-wolf suckling twins.[34] That
happened in the second half of the fourth century, at the time
of the 'Romano-Campanian federation' of 338 BC. The twins
symbolised the alliance of Rome and Capua, both 'sons of the

she-wolf', and the death of Remus was made necessary by the defection of Capua to Hannibal in 216.[35]

What matters here is not the improbable idea about the vicissitudes of the she-wolf statue, but the welcome return of political explanation for the legend of the twins. Schulze's etymologies are simply ignored; like Niebuhr and Mommsen, Carcopino assumes that the story must belong in some historically intelligible context, and explain some fundamental duality in the Romans' conception of their world at that time. Like Niebuhr (but unlike Mommsen), he even finds an intelligible motive for the removal of Remus. What he does not do is explain the name. Twins have to be equal, and according to Carcopino it would have privileged one over the other if either had been an eponym of Rome. So 'ils furent désignés tous deux par des vocables voisins', suggesting the identification without requiring it.[36] That is weak, not to say evasive: 'Romulus' just *is* an eponym of Rome. And what has 'Remus' to do with Capua?

After Carcopino, no one thought seriously about the twins story until the sixties, when an article by Joachim Classen and a brilliant but controversial monograph by Hermann Strasburger resumed the political theme,[37] with special reference to the death of Remus.

Classen insisted that the story of the twins was not, as Rosenberg had suggested, the awkward result of conflating different foundation stories. He saw it as a coherent whole, created in the republican period in order to illustrate the nature of kingship, from which the Romans were now free. Kings must rule alone; so if two men are equally entitled, murder must follow.[38] Mommsen, who also thought it a republican story, had seen it as symbolising the shared power of magistrates, and had failed to account for the murder. Classen's opposite theory explains the murder, but fails to account for Remus' presence in the story in the first place. Was he invented simply in order to provide a murder victim?

Yes he was, according to Strasburger. Here the death of Remus is one element in a much wider argument about the nature of the foundation story as a whole. Consider the following items in the biography of the founder of Rome:[39]

1 He was the son of a Vestal Virgin by an unknown father.
2 His foster-mother was a prostitute.
3 His youth was spent in banditry.
4 His followers were merely accumulated riff-raff.
5 He cheated his brother in the augury contest.
6 He killed his brother at the moment of founding his city.
7 He got women for his city by violently abducting them.

H. D. Jocelyn soon added another item:[40]

8 The birds that gave him victory in the augury contest were vultures – carrion eaters, portents of bloodshed.

How can this sequence of negative elements be explained? Only by assuming that the story of the twins took shape at a time when Rome's aggressive expansion was causing hostility, and that some at least of the episodes in it were created by Rome's enemies to discredit her.[41]

Strasburger's radical theory was widely attacked,[42] not always for good reasons. (It seems to me inadequate, for instance, merely to assert that 'the Romans took in their stride the idea that they were the descendants of robbers and had a fratricide in the foundation ritual of their city'.[43]) Though not all the elements in his argument are equally convincing,[44] the basic insight that discreditable episodes imply a complex origin for the story, at a time when the characteristics of the Romans were politically controversial, remains a plausible one. Strasburger assumed that the controversy was international – Greeks and Etruscans hostile to Rome – whereas Classen took it to be internal, a matter of Roman self-definition. Either would be appropriate to the fourth century BC.

This resumption of the political explanation of the twins story[45] provides possible answers to our third question, but not for the first two – why twins at all, and why 'Remus'? It is surely implausible to suppose that Remus was invented merely to be killed; and it must be significant that neither Classen nor Strasburger makes any attempt to account for his name.

ALFÖLDI AND AFTER

The nineteen-seventies opened unpromisingly for Remus. Both Michael Grant, in his book *Roman Myths*, and W. A. Schröder, in his commentary on the fragments of Cato *Origines* I, went back to Rosenberg, Schulze, and the Etruscan *remne*, supposedly Latinised as Remnii or Remmii. So too did Tim Cornell, in the first-ever detailed discussion in English of the foundation story, though he was a good enough historian at least to feel uneasy about 'the obscure Remmii'.[46]

As for the question 'why twins anyway?', Grant and Schröder saw no problem, merely referring to Greek influence: 'founders of Greek cities were often twins', wrote Grant airily, offering no examples.[47] Cornell gave a much more thoughtful answer, based on 'the evidence for a form of dual organisation in Rome' at a very early stage. He cited the two groups of Luperci, the two groups of Salii (*Palatini* and *Collini*, representing Palatine and Quirinal?), the two names for the citizen body (*Romani* and *Quirites*), and the twin Lares Praestites, guardian gods of the state.[48] 'The fact that the name Remus has no obvious mechanical explanation leads me to suspect that the concept of twins is an old feature of the tradition.'[49]

For the details of this idea of primordial duality Cornell referred to Andreas Alföldi's 'profound study' *Die Struktur des voretruskischen Römerstaates*, which had appeared the year before (1974). 'If Alföldi's thesis should turn out to be correct there would be no need of further discussion; but it is bound to prove controversial.'[50] It certainly did.

Andreas Alföldi was a man of immense learning, a giant of scholarship with few equals in the twentieth century. He also had some fixed ideas that were impervious to argument, one of which was that 'the original sacred story of the Roman twins and their foster-mother, the she-wolf, was not formed on Italian soil, but represents only the Latin variant of a mythological pattern distributed throughout Eurasia'.[51] The Turks, for instance, claimed descent from an ancestor who had been suckled by a she-wolf; and Alföldi convinced himself that a double organisation of the community (whence the twins) was equally ancient and widespread.[52]

Silvius, for instance, the founder of Alba Longa, was exposed and suckled by a wolf. No ancient evidence, but Alföldi refers us to his earlier book *Early Rome and the Latins* – where the reader is told that the detailed discussion will be given in the later book![53] Then there is the bronze she-wolf of the Capitol:[54]

This powerful and demonic beast belongs not to the aestheticising art-mythology of classical Greece, acclimatised in the middle Republic at Rome, but to the ancient religious stratum which first became known to us from the under-developed north of Eurasia.

Archaic art is not classical art, true; but the rest does not follow.

Much of Alföldi's argument depends on his interpretation of the Lupercalia festival, where he takes it as given that the two groups of Luperci were a primeval feature of the cult. Not only that, but they represented respectively the Palatine and the Quirinal, Mars and Quirinus, and they ran round the sacred boundary (*pomerium*) of the Palatine on 15 February (Lupercalia) and that of the Quirinal on 17 February (Quirinalia).[55] There is of course no evidence that the Quirinal was ever an independent community with its own *pomerium*; the two groups were named after *gentes*, not places (so the parallel with the Salii is inexact); that only one group could enjoy the sacrificial meat is *prima facie* evidence for the double structure being a secondary development; and the fact that a third group could be created in 45 BC may be thought to invalidate the whole argument (what did *they* represent?).[56]

Alföldi did not consider possible arguments against his hypothesis. For him, the comparative evidence put it beyond doubt, and he used it to explain the Remus story in a manner very reminiscent of the non-classical comparativists whose work we considered in chapter 2. Indo-European mythology knew of twins of whom one was immortal, the other not:

This polemical-antithetical element is perhaps partly responsible for the fact that in Rome the second twin-brother, misunderstood in his significance, gradually recedes behind the first and finally is almost forgotten.

That is an odd description of the fratricide story, but Alföldi goes on to explain that the Romans of the Republic had forgotten their (putative) original double monarchy, and remembered only single kings. So one of the twins in the supposedly ancient story had to be got out of the way, and the walls story was invented to achieve that.[57]

That is: the twins story is primordial because the double organisation of the state is primordial;[58] double kingship as an institution was subsequently forgotten, but the story that implied it was still current, and had to be embarrassingly altered. But why was the communal memory so selective? Why shouldn't the twin element drop out of the story when the double kingship dropped out of mind? At a later point in his argument, discussing *Zweiteilung und Doppelmonarchie*, Alföldi offered a simpler explanation: 'if the second leader got too powerful, he might easily share the fate of Bleda, who was killed by Attila as Remus was by Romulus in the Roman story'.[59] So much for one twin gradually receding behind the other.

The reviewers of Alföldi's book were respectful but unconvinced. Not many of them could match his erudition, but two who could deserve to be quoted. Arnaldo Momigliano's judgement was that Alföldi's book leaves us where we started as far as archaic Rome is concerned.[60] And the Dutch scholar H. S. Versnel, who announced in his long review article that 'in my opinion the main theses of this book cannot even lay claim to probability', took a very brisk line with Alföldi's account of the twins:[61]

Why had one brother to kill the other? Because later history knew only of a single kingship and so had to dispose of one of the first two kings? Was it in that case the most elegant solution to make the founder a fratricide? . . . Who will believe this presentation of facts?

The part of Alföldi's argument that seemed most plausible, though Versnel was sceptical about this as well, was the idea that the Lupercalia ritual reflected the primitive institution of the *Männerbund*, in which adolescent males had to live in the wild like bandits before being accepted as adults into the community, and that the story of the young Remus and Romulus and their followers was an example of this.[62] For the ritual, as we have seen in chapter 6, that may well be a fruitful idea; but how much help is it for the myth? Two recent writers who fully accept this anthropological perspective are Dominique Briquel and Jan Bremmer. Briquel sees Remus as a Lupercus who stays in the wild, who fails to pass through the initiation period into adult life; he represents the stage of chaos before civilisation, and his brother the hero-founder must surpass him, and get rid of him, 'pour édifier sa cité'.[63] Bremmer, unconvinced by Alföldi's 'dual organisation' theory, can only appeal to the universal 'special position' of twins; not surprisingly, he finds that the murder of Remus 'remains very much an enigma'.[64]

This survey of nearly two centuries of scholarship may conclude with Momigliano's chapter 'The origins of Rome' in the new edition of *The Cambridge Ancient History* – a suitably authoritative statement from one of the greatest historians of the ancient world in modern times. The foundation legend, he observes, 'represented in itself an ideological orientation':

Both Aeneas and Romulus had one divine parent . . . Both were leaders of migrant bands which in turn absorbed alien elements. The ultimate impression the Romans wanted to give of themselves was of a society with divine, but by no means pure, origins in which political order was created by the fusion of heterogeneous and often raffish elements, after a fratricide had marked the city's foundation.

The death of Remus was an 'element of guilt about their origins', like the story of the rape of the Sabine women.[65] No answer there, alas, to any of our three questions.

ARIADNE'S THREAD

How can we find our way through this labyrinth of argument and hypothesis? The first step, in my view, is to avoid the two paths marked 'Schulze' and 'Alföldi', for they lead only to dead ends. The archaic Remmii and the primeval dual monarchy of Rome are ideas that owe their existence not to evidence but to preconception. What evidence there is (reviewed in chapters 4–6) suggests that the legend of the twin founders was a comparatively late development – a republican story, as Mommsen and Classen insisted for opposite reasons, perhaps of the fourth century BC, as suggested for equally diverse reasons by Carcopino and Strasburger. The thread that may lead us through the maze is the insight offered by Benedict Niese in 1888: a foundation legend 'is the poetic expression of the beliefs, thoughts and desires of the age that creates it'.[66] What we should look for is not a linguistic or an anthropological explanation, but (in the broadest sense) a political one, for the foundation myth of a *polis*.

What is striking in the history of modern interpretations is the way some pieces of the evidence have been simply ignored. No one since Niebuhr, for example, has taken seriously the question of Remuria, the city Remus would have founded, 'five miles from the Palatine', 'thirty stades from Rome'.[67] No one since Kretschmer has bothered about Remus as a sacrifice in Propertius, or Romulus as 'the other one' in Festus.[68] And no one at all has tried to find a context for what the *Origo gentis Romanae* says about Remus, that he was named 'from slowness [*tarditas*], since people with that characteristic were called *remores* by the ancients'.[69]

CHAPTER 8

The life and death of Remus

EQUALS

First there were kings, then there were consuls. That sequence, enshrined in the lapidary opening sentence of Tacitus' *Annals*,[1] is the basic datum of the Roman historical tradition. Liberty and the Republic were defined as annual magistrates sharing equal power.[2] Much of the legend of the first year of the Republic turns on the question of the consuls' equal authority as a check to tyrannical behaviour.[3] The very name 'consul' connotes equality and collegiality.[4]

But it may not have been as simple as that. The authors who transmit the tradition were themselves aware of evidence that contradicted it. Livy, for instance, knows (though he does not act on the knowledge) that the magistrates of the early Republic were called not consuls but *praetores*, 'leaders' (from *praeire*, 'to go in front'), and that the annual ceremony of driving a nail into the wall of the Capitoline temple was entrusted to the 'chief leader', *praetor maximus*.[5] That terminology, and in particular the epithet *maximus*, does not suggest that equal authority was what mattered most. Livy also implies that early magistrate-lists might give *three* names for a given year, as in the 'linen books' for 440 and 439.[6]

Not only that, but the tradition itself admitted a whole series of exceptions to the consulship and its ideal of equal shared authority – the position of dictator, or *magister populi*, supposedly introduced only eight years after the expulsion of the kings;[7] the Board of Ten (*decemviri*) in 451–449 BC;[8] and the rule of the 'colonels', military tribunes with supreme authority, first resorted to in 444 and frequently thereafter, which effectively replaced the consulship from 426 to 367 BC.[9] Tacitus mentions these exceptions only to wave them away as brief interruptions in the reign of liberty,[10] but they are enough to invalidate the idea that from the start the Republic simply *was* the consulship.

The debate among modern historians on this matter seems to have resolved itself into a cautious acceptance of the essentials of the traditional version. That is the line taken, for instance, by Robert Ogilvie in his commentary on Livy, by Andrew Drummond in the new *Cambridge Ancient History*, and above all by Arnaldo Momigliano in a brilliant essay on the origins of the Roman Republic: 'I believe, as I said, that two annual magistrates replaced the life-kings exactly as tradition has it . . . We can go back to good old Livy, who thought that the two consuls replaced the kings.'[11] There are two main arguments for this position.

First, the existence by the first century BC of a consular list dating back to the beginning of the Republic. The question is, what is its status as a historical document? Drummond, representing the majority view, argues that 'there are . . . no solid grounds for disputing the general credibility of the core of the preserved consular list, and certain of its features taken together indicate that it is substantially reliable even for the fifth century'.[12] To call it a 'preserved' list, however, begs a big question. The list we have is probably the result of a century or more of historical research and conjecture, not necessarily any better founded than the tradition of literary historiography that developed in the same period.[13] Arguably, it is as much a part of that tradition as Livy and Dionysius, and can therefore hardly be used as an independent confirmation of their work. A detailed analysis of the variants in the consular lists between 444 and 342 BC came to a quite different conclusion:[14]

The Fasti of these years and the events associated with them existed in many different versions which can now be only partly reconstructed from the indications given in Livy and occasionally in Diodorus. The received tradition of these, as of most years in early Roman history, is to a very large extent an artificial construction, the conflation of a number of prior but equally artificial constructions, and it cannot be used directly as evidence for the actual events without thorough and radical criticism.

Roman history was always politically controversial, and a lot had happened in the three or four centuries between our sources (including the consular *fasti*) and the Rome they purport to describe. Not everyone is prepared to believe that historical accuracy was always a high priority.[15]

That consideration weighs equally against the second main argument in favour of the tradition. The question, as Momigliano puts it,[16] 'is how the Romans could have gone wrong over the most elementary facts of their constitutional history'. Momigliano dismisses the legends about Brutus and Lucretia,[17] but demands:

Why should the Romans say that two yearly *praetores* or *consules* replaced the king, if that was not the truth? How could they forget the character of the momentous change from monarchy to Republic? Did they have ulterior motives to conceal the truth? If so, what motives? These are questions which have never been satisfactorily answered by the modern historians who believe that the Roman historians either did not know the true facts about the creation of the consulship or concealed them.

It seems to me that this argument precisely misplaces the onus of proof. As Momigliano observes elsewhere in his essay, 'what we call Roman tradition about the origins of the Republic is in fact what we read in Diodorus, Dionysius and Livy'; that, in turn, 'is the result of two centuries of writing and rewriting Roman archaic history after Fabius Pictor'; and Fabius Pictor 'claimed by implication to know what had happened 300 years before him'.[18] The question, surely, is not how they could forget but how they could remember.

There is not, after all, a comfortable consensus on the reliability of Livy. We really do not know what form of 'republican' authority replaced that of the banished king. And even if we have faith in the tradition, it is clear that 'two men exercising equal power' was not a model that went unchallenged; according to Livy and the consular *fasti*, it applied to only nine out of the sixty years from 426 to 367 BC.[19]

The purpose of this long discussion has been to provide a context for Mommsen's 'constitutional' explanation of the story of the twins. If, as he suggested, Remus and Romulus are a legendary analogue of two magistrates with equal authority in a free state, then the circumstances which called them into being were probably the events not of 509 but of 367 BC.[20] *That* was the moment when the consulship (whatever its prehistory) became the essential supreme magistracy of the Republic.

It was also the moment when the equality of the two consuls was particularly at issue. The tribunes Licinius and Sextius were demanding that one consul should always be a plebeian:[21]

'Only the consulship is left for the plebeians to win. That is the pillar, the stronghold, of liberty. Gain that, and the Roman People will really believe that the kings have been driven out, and freedom established.'

In 367, after a long political struggle, they gained their point.[22]

So at least the tradition has it; but Livy goes on to report a patrician backlash, years with two patrician consuls, and then in 342 a law to enable *both* consuls to be plebeian.[23] It has long been recognised that the 'law of 342' is anachronistic (172 BC was the first year when two plebeians held the consulship), and that the tradition as we have it is unlikely to be historical. The most probable solution is that the legislation of 367 made it *possible* for one consul to be plebeian, while that of 342 laid it down that one consul *must* be plebeian.[24] Whatever the details, the general situation is clear enough: the patricians, self-defined as the ruling aristocracy of Rome, had been forced to share power with their plebeian rivals on exactly equal terms.

Here, I think, is the answer to our first question: why twins at all? As Mommsen rightly remarked, a double founder for a unitary institution is an internal contradiction.[25] Rome was not a double city like Budapest or Minneapolis–St Paul, though Niebuhr's desperate attempt to make it one – by inferring an ancient combination of Rome and Remuria – shows clearly enough what he thought the legend ought to mean. Mommsen's idea was better: not geographical but constitutional duality. However, two equal magistrates are not enough to require twin founders. The community itself must be, in some sense, a double one.

The establishment of explicit power-sharing between patricians and plebeians in the fourth century BC provides the necessary condition for the creation of the story of the twins. The point was made, as a modest suggestion, by Cécile Dulière in her discussion of the Ogulnian monument (p. 72 above):[26]

Etant donné le voisinage dans le temps de la consécration de la statue et du couronnement des efforts de la plèbe pour obtenir l'égalité complète avec les patriciens par la *lex Ogulnia* de 300, on pourra se demander si ce n'est pas cette nouvelle égalité des deux catégories de la population de la cité que les édiles ont voulu évoquer en plaçant les statues d'enfants jumeaux sous les mamelles de la louve.

The Ogulnian monument is our earliest evidence for the existence of the Remus story. I suggest that story and monument alike were created to celebrate that 'new equality'.

REMUS THE SLOW

Livy deals with the great reform of 367 BC in a curiously perfunctory manner. He has reported ten years of political confrontation, five of which were literally anarchy; he has given us a long speech by Appius Claudius, representing the responsible conservative's case against the reformers; he has brought the aged Camillus to the dictatorship in time for the crisis, after his final triumph over the Gauls.[27] But what comes next is close to bathos:[28]

[The dictator] had hardly disposed of that war before a more alarming commotion awaited him at home. After tremendous conflicts, the dictator and the Senate were worsted; consequently the proposals of the tribunes were carried, and in spite of the opposition of the nobility the elections were held for consuls. L. Sextius was the first consul to be elected out of the *plebs*.

Even that was not the end of the conflict. The patricians refused to confirm the appointment, and matters were approaching a secession of the *plebs* and other signs of appalling civic struggles. The dictator, however, quieted the disturbances by arranging a compromise.

Why does Livy not describe this *seditio*, these *ingentia certamina*, these *terribiles minae*? We are supposed to be at a turning-point in the history of Rome; so why doesn't he tell us what happened?

The answer, I think, is that he had no faith in the details presented by his source. We know he was using Licinius Macer for this period, and that he was well aware of Macer's habitual glorification of his own ancestors. Foremost among those ancestors was C. Licinius Stolo, joint leader of the plebeians' reform campaign and himself one of the first plebeian consuls.[29] Indeed, according to one version Stolo was the first plebeian consul of all; that presumably comes from Licinius Macer, but Livy did not accept it.[30]

We know that a good deal of late-republican political controversy went into the creation of the historiographical tradition on 367 BC. Following the concession of the consulship to the plebeians, Camillus the dictator is alleged to have founded a temple of Concordia on the slope of the Capitol, facing the Forum.[31] That is clearly a retrojection of the temple of Concordia founded by L. Opimius in 121, after the violent suppression of C. Gracchus and his followers.[32] Licinius Macer was himself a reforming tribune in the Gracchan tradition, and his historical work reflected his politics. (Dictators were of particular interest to him, given the recent grim example of Sulla.[33]) One of the recurring themes in his work was *concordia*,[34] the controlling concept in the late-republican elaboration of the events of 367. I think it is likely that Macer's narrative of that year was a great anachronistic set-piece of *popularis* politics and Licinian family pride, and that Livy, whose ruthless summary still reflects the idea of *concordia*,[35] could not bring himself to reproduce it in full.

Whatever really happened in 367 is lost to us – and in any case, as we have seen, the full achievement of power-sharing evidently did not come until L. Genucius' law in 342. Licinius Stolo is an important figure for the historiography of the first century BC, but for the history of the fourth century Genucius probably mattered more.[36]

According to Livy, the L. Genucius who was consul in 362

was the first plebeian to lead an army under his own auspices (with disastrous results). A different perspective, however, is implied by a strange story in Ovid and Valerius Maximus, of a Roman commander called Genucius Cipus, who discovered just outside the city gate that he had grown horns.[37] A *haruspex* was consulted, and reported that if Cipus entered the city, he would be king. So Cipus turned away into voluntary exile, never to return.

A very similar story was told of another praetor from a distinguished plebeian family, the Aelii (their first consulship was in 337). Since three different authors attribute it to three different members of the *gens*, and a fourth puts it in an impossible historical context,[38] its original form was probably as free-floating chronologically as the Cipus story. Aelius the praetor was giving judgement in the Forum when a woodpecker perched on his head. The *haruspices* announced that if he killed the bird it would be disastrous for himself and his family, but beneficial to the Republic, and vice versa if he did not. So he killed it.

The emphasis on haruspicy, an Etruscan art, is striking in both stories;[39] and in fact both the Genucii and the Aelii probably came from an Etruscan background.[40] An Aelius and a Genucius were among the first plebeian augurs, in the college created by the *lex Ogulnia* in 300 BC, at a time when the efficacy of Etruscan prophecy was evidently a significant issue.[41]

That is an aspect which will concern us later. What matters for the moment is the implied aetiology of each of these stories. On the face of it, their purpose is simple – to honour the self-denying patriotism of Genucius and Aelius, who sacrifice themselves for the Republic like M. Curtius in the chasm and the Decii Mures in battle.[42] But the stories are also explanations, by members of the new plebeian elite, that their *gentes* were as old and as honourable as those of the patricians, and absent from recent prominence in Roman public life only for the most admirable and patriotic of reasons. The praetors Genucius and Aelius are to be thought of as belonging to an undefined 'olden time', after which, as a consequence of their unselfishness, their descendants did not hold office until restored to their rightful status by the reforms of 367 and 342.

Two more famous stories, which unlike those of Aelius and Genucius were later incorporated into the annalistic tradition, did the same job for the plebeian Marcii and Iunii (first consulships in 357 and 317 respectively). Cn. Marcius, better known as Coriolanus, was a hero forced into exile by his ungrateful country, while L. Iunius Brutus, the fated ruler of Rome after Tarquin, died in the act of killing Tarquin's son, having already put his own sons to death for treason.[43] It clearly mattered, in the second half of the fourth century BC, to present the new plebeian elite as coming late to power, but with as old a tradition, and as just a claim, as the patrician families with whom they now shared it.

Hence 'Remus the slow'. We are told that his name derives from *remores*, a noun clearly related to the verb *remorari*, 'to delay'.[44] If the twins represent power-sharing equality, then Remus stands for the plebeians, whose share in the power was long delayed. When he was cheated by Romulus in the augury contest, Remus yielded to the gods' will with a riddling prophecy that was also a renunciation of power like that of Aelius and Genucius: 'In this city, many things rashly hoped for and taken for granted will turn out very successfully.'[45] As for instance the patricians' claim to a monopoly of power, now brought to an end by the long-delayed vindication of Remus and the Roman *plebs*.

REMURIA

'Romulus' must be an eponym of Rome. He is first attested – alone – in the Greek author Alcimus in the mid-fourth century, but he may well be older than that.[46] It is possible that the child prophesied to king Tarchetios of Alba in Promathion's archaic tale already bore the name of Romulus: certainly *rhōmē*, 'strength' or 'force', was among his defining characteristics.[47] If we are right in inferring that the twins story is a fourth-century innovation, then a single founder Romulus ('the Roman') was replaced by twin founders Remus and Romulus, the slow one and the forceful one, with Remus the elder and the more deserving.[48]

Romulus' name connotes strength and vigour,[49] but it is interpreted in a pejorative sense: hastiness and thoughtless action are what the various narrators of the foundation story associate with Romulus. In Dionysius, for instance, as soon as Remus is captured Romulus wants to rush off to Alba and rescue him; Faustulus has to dissuade him from his 'too frenzied haste' and plans a more careful strategy instead. In both Dionysius and Diodorus, Romulus anticipates the result of the augury contest and sends his messenger to Remus 'in haste'. In Diodorus, Romulus digs his trench round the Palatine 'hastily', and even Cicero's wholly demythologised version has Romulus found his city *perceleriter*. Ovid characteristically plays with the theme in his account of Remus' death: Remus himself was *male velox* in leaping over the trench, and met his death at the 'hasty hand' (*temeraria manus*) of the aptly-named Celer.[50]

This polarity of speed and slowness, haste and delay, seems to be associated with the art of augury. 'Delaying birds', that warn you to postpone your enterprise, are *aves remores*, from the same root as Remus' name; the other sort, that encourage you to act at once, are *aves praepetes*, from *praepetere* meaning *anteire*, 'to anticipate' or 'go first'. Ennius emphasises *praepetes* in his description of the augury contest, and Diodorus seems to allude to the same word, via a bilingual pun, in describing Romulus' hasty claim of victory.[51]

The creation of Remus, the significance of his name and the circumstances of his defeat in the augury contest all seem to belong together in a single integrated story. Its historical context can be guessed. In 300 BC the tribunes Cn. Ogulnius and Q. Ogulnius – the same who later put up at the Lupercal the statue group of the she-wolf and twins which is our earliest evidence for the Remus story – forced through a controversial bill giving plebeians equal representation in the colleges of the *pontifices* and augurs. Among the new augurs were a Marcius, a Genucius and an Aelius, all of them men for whose family histories the patient Remus would provide an appropriate analogue.[52]

Dionysius reports the augury contest:[53]

Fig. 11. Detail of a relief of the Circus Maximus, third or fourth century AD (Foligno). From J. Humphreys, *Roman Circuses: Arenas for Chariot Racing* (London, 1986), fig. 38: reproduced by permission of B. T. Batsford Ltd.

Romulus' observation post was the Palatine, where he intended to found his colony; that of Remus was the Aventine hill close to it, though some authorities say it was Remoria [i.e. Remus' proposed site for the city].

Plutarch and Festus identify Remoria with the Aventine; that looks like a conflation of two different versions, still separate in Dionysius and the *Origo gentis Romanae*. Festus also reports an *ager Remurinus*, which implies a site for Remus' city and observation point quite independent of the Aventine.[54]

The Aventine was famous for two things: Remus in the augury contest, and the secession of the *plebs*.[55] Those who had Remus on the Aventine pointed out the exact point where he watched for the birds, at 'The Rock' (*saxum*) above the temple and grove of the Bona Dea. The church of S. Balbina stands there now, on the height between the headquarters of the United Nations Food and Agriculture Organisation and the Baths of Caracalla. This part of the so-called 'lesser Aventine' was known as *mons Murcus*, after the goddess Murcia, whose shrine was in the Circus Maximus below.[56] That was appropriate for 'Remus the slow', since Murcia was the goddess of inaction, portrayed with her hand raised like a traffic policeman at the point where the chariots in the Circus had to slow down for the turn (fig. 11).[57]

It was also appropriate for the *plebs*, since the area known as *ad Murciae*, by the Porta Capena and the temple of Mercury, was always a crowded, downmarket part of town.[58] The reason for that was supposedly Ancus Marcius' wars against the Latins, which resulted in a huge influx to Rome, a rowdy new element that was settled on the Aventine and in the *ad Murciae* area below. The episode looks like a hostile aetiology for the existence of the *plebs* as a separate body within the state.[59]

The rivalry of plebeians and patricians was an idea associated with Murcia, in her capacity as the goddess of the myrtle grove (Venus Myrtea). The evidence is Pliny's description of the temple of Quirinus on the Quirinal:[60]

In it were two sacred myrtle trees, which for a long time grew in front of the temple itself. One was called 'patrician', the other 'plebeian'. For many years the patrician tree flourished more, luxuriant and vigorous. As long as the Senate was powerful, it too was huge, while the plebeian tree was shrivelled and neglected. But when the plebeian tree grew strong and the patrician one began to wither, from the Marsic war [90 BC] onwards the authority of the Senate was weakened and its majesty gradually withered away into barrenness. Not only that, but there was an ancient altar to Venus Myrtea, whom now they call Murcia.

So it seems that Remus' observation point in the augury contest was associated with the plebeians and their struggle for political equality.

The most famous episodes in that struggle were of course the secessions of 494 and 449 BC. For many Romans, those events (particularly the first) were vindications of liberty at least as important as the expulsion of the kings.[61] That was certainly true in the late Republic, and presumably also in earlier periods of political conflict. The 'struggle of the orders' itself lasted about two centuries, and in its final stages, in 287, there was a crisis leading to a secession;[62] no doubt already by then the tradition of the early secessions was being exploited and elaborated – perhaps even invented – for the needs of the moment.[63] So it is not surprising that the story as we have it in our surviving sources is confused and inconsistent.

The prevailing tradition about the first secession is that the plebeians marched out to a hill afterwards known as the Sacred Mount, just north of the Anio on the Via Nomentana (fig. 12).[64] Others, however, including Piso in the late second century BC, put the seceding plebeians on the Aventine; others again combined the two versions and had them occupy the Sacred Mount first and the Aventine afterwards.[65] A similar ambiguity applies to the second secession. One tradition puts it at the Aventine,[66] but Cicero names the Sacred Mount first and then the Aventine,[67] while Livy has the plebeians seize the Aventine first, then go to the Mount, and then back to the Aventine again.[68] It is obvious enough that variant versions have been conflated, but much less clear which ones are early; possibly the Aventine became the more attractive location in the late Republic, after C. Gracchus' last stand there in 121 BC.[69]

In the light of our previous argument, associating the creation of the Remus story with plebeian aspirations in the fourth century BC, it is natural to see a parallel between the variants in the secession traditions and the variants in the story of the augury contest. Where was Remuria, Remus' observation post and his site for the future city? Some said it was on the Aventine, some said it was 'another hill five miles distant from the Palatine', 'a place very suitable for a city, a hill about thirty stades from Rome'.[70]

Thirty stades would be 5.76 km, 3.89 Roman miles. But it is a general indication not to be pressed too exactly. (Strabo puts a place between the fifth and sixth milestones at 'thirty stades

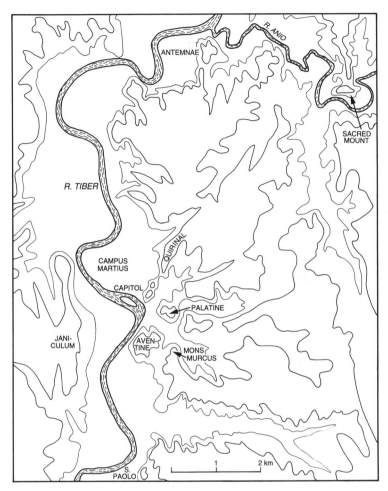

Fig. 12. The vicinity of Rome: suitable sites for a city. (The supposed site of Alba Longa was about 15 km off the map to the south-east, not far from Tusculum: see fig. 2.)

or a little more'; Dionysius has the same phrase for a site five miles out of Rome.[71]) Besides, 'from the city' should mean from the gate, so the distance from the Palatine would be greater than that.

How does the Sacred Mount measure up as a possible Remuria? It is certainly 'very suitable for a city'; the hill is larger than the Palatine, a promontory surrounded on three sides by the meandering course of the river Anio. It was just beyond the third milestone on the Via Nomentana,[72] say 4.5 km from the Porta Collina, which itself was about 2.2 km from the Palatine: just over four and a half Roman miles in total, which is not a bad fit for the distances our sources offer.

Antemnae on the Via Salaria (Monte Antenne in the Villa Ada) would also fit: just over four miles from the Palatine, and about 5.6 km – very close to thirty stades – from the Porta Fontinalis, if one went by the old Salaria. However, it was only 4 km from the Porta Collina, between the second and third milestones; and besides, Antemnae was one of the cities against whom Romulus fought,[73] so its site can hardly have been thought of as available for Remus' planned foundation. No other site fits the distance at all. The hill Niebuhr suggested, behind S. Paolo fuori le Mura, is much too close (as he himself realised), and no other suggestions have been offered.[74]

There is only one problem about identifying Remuria as the Sacred Mount. Dionysius says that Remus' chosen site was 'not far from the Tiber',[75] and the Sacred Mount is by the Anio. But if Antemnae and the hill by S. Paolo are ruled out, there simply are no suitable sites by the Tiber. It may be a confusion, by Dionysius or earlier in the tradition, with the more famous river taking the place of its tributary in the narrative. Something like that may have happened with the story of the mother of the twins, drowned (in one version) by order of the tyrant Amulius. She became the bride of the river god – but which one? The Anio in Ennius and Ovid, the Tiber in Horace and Statius.[76] It is easier to imagine the Tiber taking the Anio's place in the story than vice versa, and the Horatian version is rightly taken as a later variant. So too, perhaps, Dionysius on the site of Remuria.

Whatever the solution to that problem, the fact remains that the Aventine and the Sacred Mount are alternatives in the history of the secessions, just as the Aventine and Remuria are alternatives in the story of Remus. In one at least, and perhaps both, of the symbolic places of plebeian history, Remus planned to build his city, sat and watched for his sign, and in due course was buried at Romulus' order.[77]

A NECESSARY DEATH

For two of our three questions – why twins, and why 'Remus' – convincing answers can, I think, be found in the context of plebeian power-sharing in the fourth century BC. The difficult question is the last one – and necessarily so, since *any* reason for the existence of Remus is bound to be inconsistent with a need to kill him off. We must still look for a political explanation, but in the nature of things it must involve either changed circumstances or other and more imperative necessities. Or perhaps both at once.

The problem, as always, lies in our lack of contemporary evidence. How much of what we are told about the late fourth and early third centuries BC reflects with any accuracy the real political preoccupations of that time? The context I am going to suggest for the death of Remus depends on a passage in a Byzantine historian of the twelfth century AD, probably taken from the history of Cassius Dio, which was written in the early third century AD and therefore still five hundred years after the event. What Dio's source was we have no idea. But the story he told does not sound like anachronistic elaboration from the late Republic. It has some authentic-sounding archaic features, and its very oddity demands respect.

The date is 296 BC. Rome has been fighting the Samnites, on and off, for over forty years, and the Etruscans for fifteen. Evidence both for her success and for her claim to a permanent hegemony could be seen all over western central Italy, in the fifteen colonial settlements founded since 338, from Apulian Luceria in the south to Umbrian Narnia in the north, and in the purpose-built military roads that served them.[78] At the

western corner of the Palatine, above the Lupercal, a great
new temple precinct for the goddess Victory was nearing
completion after more than ten years.[79] But in 296 it was far
from clear that Victory and her temple would be any more
than a hollow irony. The Samnites and Etruscans had joined
forces with the Gauls in a common cause, to put a stop to
Rome's expansion for good.[80]

Livy's sources reported terror in Rome, and no doubt they
were right.[81] The goodwill of the gods had to be secured. One
of the ways of doing that we have already noticed in a different
context: the aediles Cn. Ogulnius and Q. Ogulnius used the
confiscated property of moneylenders to pay for costly embel-
lishments to the temple of Capitoline Jupiter, a paved
approach to the temple of Mars, and the bronze group of the
she-wolf and the twin founders at the Ficus Ruminalis.[82] (The
Ficus Ruminalis stood at the Lupercal, immediately below the
temple of Victory on the Palatine, with which it shared the
legend of foundation by Evander; according to the Arcadians,
Dionysius tells us, Victory was the daughter of Pallas son of
Lykaon, eponyms respectively of the Palatine and the
Lupercal.[83])

That is the context for the story in Zonaras. The news of the
Etruscan–Samnite–Gallic coalition gave rise to sinister portents:[84]

It is constantly stated, if anyone can believe it, that on the Capitol
blood issued from the altar of Jupiter for three days, milk for one day
and honey for another. In the Forum, a bronze statue of Victory on a
stone pedestal was found standing on the ground below, of its own
accord; and it happened to be facing in the direction from which the
Gauls were already approaching. The populace, frightened in any
case by these phenomena, were even more terrified by the ill-omened
decisions of the prophets.

Who were these prophets, and what did they say?

Four years earlier, the Ogulnii, as tribunes of the *plebs*, had
succeeded in opening the college of augurs to plebeian as well
as patrician members. In the late Republic, the college consisted of sober senators like Cicero and Hortensius, and what
they did had nothing to do with prophecy. But Cicero himself

makes it clear that in the past the augurs *had* been prophets, and the word is commonly used in Latin as a synonym for *vates*.[85] One of the first plebeian augurs was a Marcius, from a *gens* famous for prophecy and descended from Marsyas, who introduced the art into Italy; I think a similar case can be made for two of the other plebeians in the first joint augural college, but the Marcii alone suffice to make the point.[86] It evidently mattered, who was entitled to prophesy and whose prophecies would benefit the state.

It is possible, then, that the prophets who interpreted the portents of 296 BC were members of the reformed augural college. Whoever they were, their recommendations were 'ill-omened'. That translates *apaisios*, a very strong word in post-classical Greek, and one normally used of the portents and omens themselves.[87] Whether it was Zonaras' own word or taken from Cassius Dio, its meaning is abundantly clear from synonyms in Lucian and the scholiast to Oppian: 'foul', 'abominable', 'unrighteous', 'hateful', 'evil', 'terrible'.[88] That describes what the prophets decided, and what horrified the Roman people.

It doesn't take a genius of the mantic art to interpret blood on the altar followed by milk and honey. After a sacrifice, prosperity.[89] That is the inevitable response, and it was no doubt in order to elicit it that those particular portents were announced in the first place. Since an ordinary sacrifice would not be horrifying or abominable, it seems that the prophets were demanding what Calchas had demanded at Aulis, and what could still be demanded at moments of extreme crisis even in the fourth and third centuries BC.[90] It was the prospect of the Gauls that caused the terror in Rome,[91] and three times in the later history of the Republic the Romans resorted to human sacrifice to ward off a Gallic invasion.[92] On all three occasions the rite was ordered by the Sibylline Books, and a good case has been made for identifying a south-Italian episode of 330 BC as the origin of the Sibyl's remedy.[93] At any rate, there is no reason to suppose that the idea was unknown to the Romans in 296.

However, the story in Zonaras has a further twist:[94]

A certain Manius, Etruscan by birth, gave the people a more encouraging interpretation. True, Victory had come down [from her pedestal], but she had advanced and was on a firmer footing, which was an omen of their strength in the war. As for the altars, especially those on the Capitol where the Romans sacrifice in thanks for victory, they normally ran with blood in times of Roman success, not disaster. From those signs, therefore, he urged them to expect a good outcome. The honey, however, portended disease, because that is what sick people need; and the milk portended famine, for they were going to suffer so disastrous a crop failure that they would look even for food that was generated of its own accord. Such was Manius' interpretation of the portents; and he gained a reputation for wisdom and foreknowledge when subsequent events justified his prophecy.

The great battle at Sentinum in 295, though desperately close, was a Roman victory; but it was followed by three years of plague, so serious that in 292 the Romans had to summon Asclepius, god of healing, from his cult centre at Epidaurus.[95] (There is no confirmation of the famine in our surviving sources; but famine and plague go naturally together, as the Greeks and Romans were all too well aware.[96])

It is obvious that Zonaras' story represents a reinterpretation of the portents of 296, and their dreadful remedy, in the light of what happened later. That is, the 'prophets' had their way; the necessary sacrifice was performed, the battle was won, and the temple of Victory was duly dedicated in 294.[97] Only afterwards, when plague and famine persisted, were second thoughts required. The context of Manius' revisionist interpretation was probably the summons to Asclepius in 292, which was made on the advice of the Sibylline Books and 'the responses of prophets'.[98]

The temple and precinct of Victory, identified in 1981, have been thoroughly excavated by Patrizio Pensabene and his team from the University of Rome (figs. 13–15).[99] The area had already been explored by Vaglieri in the first decade of the century, and among his findings was a grave, covered by a heavy slab of carefully squared tufa, which extended underneath a wall in *opus quadratum* on which the precinct was supported. The terracing was evidently extended to a second wall (contemporary with the first, to judge by the quarry-marks); the first wall thus became obsolete, and blocks from it were reused for the erection of a monument of some sort above the site of the grave.[100] Since the grave contained a cup of fourth-century date (all that was left by tomb-robbers), and since the monument above it was where one would expect to find the altar of Victory (below and in front of the site of her temple, as near as practicable to a central alignment), it is natural to associate these mysterious remains with the events of 296–294 BC.[101]

Interpreting the archaeology is as uncertain as interpreting the fragments of the literary evidence, and any hypothesis must necessarily be very tentative. But one thing is clear: the grave is an anomaly. True, Vaglieri found other graves nearby, for both inhumation and cremation, but they were part of an archaic cemetery which had evidently not been used for at least two centuries.[102] As Vaglieri noted, the natural level of the rock had been artificially lowered, thus destroying much of the early graves; that is, the archaic cemetery must have been abandoned, and the ground cleared for other purposes, long before the grave beneath the wall was dug into the lower level.[103]

The other odd feature is the evident contemporaneity of the tufa blocks in the two walls. Furthermore, the inner wall (the one above the grave) was clearly designed to be an outer wall; the quality of its construction makes that absolutely clear.[104] What the data seem to suggest is that the wall built over the grave was very soon replaced by another wall, creating a terrace which buried both the grave and the first wall, and on which the monument, which may have been an altar, was placed. The positioning of the monument directly above the grave is not likely to be fortuitous.[105]

It is important to remember that the terracing walls of the Palatine were not there just to hold up the Victory precinct. They were also defensive – towering ramparts of squared tufa blocks which later generations identified as Romulus' citadel, Roma Quadrata.[106] In 296, when the construction programme was nearing completion, that aspect must have seemed particularly important.

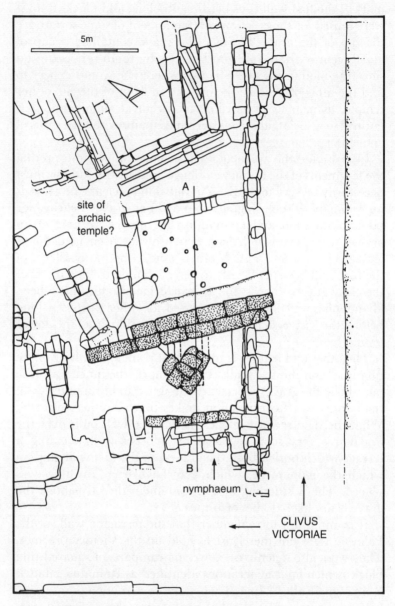

Fig. 13. Site plan of excavations in front of the temple of Victory. (After Pensabene 1990.88.)

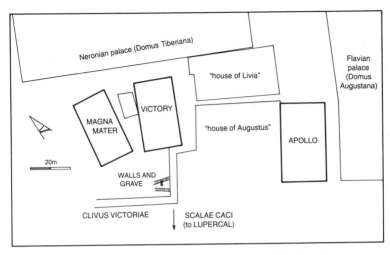

Fig. 14. Sketch-map of the western corner of the Palatine.

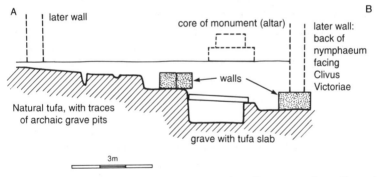

Fig. 15. Section through Vaglieri's excavation (fig. 13, A–B): walls and grave. (After Vaglieri 1907.187.)

But a defensive wall will only keep out the enemy if, at its building, proper sacrifice is made to the immortal gods.[107] What sort of sacrifice was made for these defences? They were below the temple of Victory, and Victory's statue provided one of the portents that resulted in the prophets' horrifying demand in 296. Nearly a century ago, the author of the standard work on foundation-sacrifice (*Bauopfer*) provided ample evidence for his contention that 'from all parts of the world, and even from recent times, the custom is frequently reported of consecrating the foundation of a city, the construction of a house, a bridge, a dyke or any other important building work, with the death of a human being. Usually this victim is inserted in some way into the foundation of the building.'[108]

Explicit examples from the Graeco-Roman world are not easy to come by. John Malalas alleges that a virgin was sacrificed at the foundation of Alexandria in 332, and another at the foundation of Antioch in 300.[109] How far back those stories go – as evidence for what was conceivable, not necessarily for what happened – is impossible to say; but there is clear archaeological evidence from Roman Britain that in the second century AD bodies of human victims were indeed sometimes buried below, or within, the foundations of buildings.[110] It could have happened in Rome in 296.

A related phenomenon, which was certainly part of the Romans' conceptual world at that time, is the talismanic hero-burial, the grave – often a secret grave – which protects the host city by supernatural means. That idea was familiar from Greek tragedy (Orestes in Aeschylus, Eurysthenes in Euripides, and above all Oedipus at Colonus in Sophocles),[111] and there is a hint of it in the Roman tradition. The *Argea*, or 'chapels of the Argives', to which ritual processions were made in March and May of each year, were so called because famous men of Argos were supposed to be buried there.[112] One of the *Argea*, the fifth in the fourth region, was at the Cermalus, 'by the house [or temple] of Romulus', and Pensabene has suggested that its site was that of the grave beneath the wall, which he interprets as a *hērōon*, or 'hero-shrine'.[113]

It will be obvious by now that my argument in this section is even more tenuous and conjectural than usual. That is a direct result of the nature of the subject. In addition to the normal difficulties involved in reconstructing late fourth- and early third-century attitudes, we have here to deal with an issue that even at the time must have been acutely sensitive, and perhaps not to be recorded except obliquely. Human sacrifice was something beyond normal experience, 'a most un-Roman rite', as Livy put it.[114] If it was necessary to carry it out in 296 BC, in the face of unprecedented danger to Rome, we might expect the memory of it to be disguised, if not obliterated, once the danger was past.

The literary and archaeological data, inadequate though they are, suggest that very thing. Zonaras' story offers a revised (and 'better') interpretation of the portents, with no horrific element involved; and Vaglieri's excavation below the Victory temple reveals *two* walls – the one built over the grave, and another one that concealed the first and supported the monument (or altar) beneath which it was now buried.[115]

I think the Remus legend may have undergone a similar development. Remus is killed at the foundation of Rome, as the trench is being dug or the wall constructed. As Propertius puts it, Rome's walls were firm thanks to the slaying of Remus; in Florus, we read of Remus as the first sacrificial victim, who consecrated with his blood the defences of the new city.[116] Those descriptions surely presuppose the notion of a foundation sacrifice. Most versions, however, turn the story of Remus' death into an exemplary tale: 'so perish all who cross my walls!' Like Brutus with his sons, so Romulus refuses to put even a brother's life before the safety of the city. That, I suggest, is an edifying reinterpretation, like Manius the Etruscan's reading of the portents in Zonaras.

It seems to me most likely that Propertius and Florus preserve the original version of the story of the death of Remus, created as a legendary analogue to the horrifying necessities of 296 BC; and that the more usual account was the result of the passing of the crisis, at a time when the Romans were happy to forget the body beneath the wall.

THE CREATION PERIOD

The argument in this chapter may be summed up as follows. Twin founders imply a double community in which both sides have equal status; that notion is meaningful at Rome only after the achievement of plebeian power-sharing between 367 and 342. Remus' name implies lateness, and the story of his renunciation of power parallels those of the ancestors of the plebeian Genucii and Aelii, whose first consulships are given as 365 and 337. The place where Remus would have built his city, and where he was buried, was either the Aventine or 'Remuria'; the site of the plebeian secessions was either the Aventine or the Sacred Mount; 'Remuria' may be the Sacred Mount, and the tradition of the secessions may have been formed in the final period of patrician–plebeian conflict leading up to 287. The story of the death of Remus involves the notion of a foundation sacrifice, for which the evidence for the crisis of 296 BC, and the building of the precinct of the temple of Victory, provides a unique historical context.

There may perhaps be a further item to add. One of the few episodes attributed to Remus and Romulus together is the aetiology of the two groups of Luperci: Remus led the Fabiani, Romulus the Quinctiales.[117] As Ovid tells the story, the twins and their followers rushed off in pursuit of cattle-thieves; 'Remus and the Fabii' caught them, and ate all the meat of the sacrificial feast as the prize of victory. It is obvious that this episode belongs to a stage in the development of the legend where Remus and Romulus are still joint founders, with Remus the senior partner, as the Fabiani were the senior group of Luperci.[118] It is equally obvious that Remus here has no plebeian significance, since each twin is equally associated with a patrician *gens*.

In 304 BC, Q. Fabius Maximus Rullianus as censor instituted the parade of the *equites* to the temple of Castor. Valerius Maximus, who reports this event, couples it with the running of the Luperci, as instituted by Remus and Romulus and their respective followers; the February run and the July parade, says Valerius, were the two occasions when the young men of the equestrian order could show themselves off to the city. I have suggested elsewhere that the occasion of the division of the Luperci into 'Fabian' and 'Quinctian' groups was probably the censorship of Fabius Rullianus, in the context of the introduction of an elite corps of light-armed cavalry.[119] If that is right, then the legendary aetiology of his innovation marks a stage in the development of the Remus legend.

Similar contexts can be found for episodes in the later history of Romulus as king. Take for example the story of the Sabine women. Ovid recounts that Romulus' purpose in abducting them was foiled by an epidemic of miscarriages, until an augur found a way to appease the gods by beating the women with goatskin thongs. In 276 BC a real epidemic of miscarriages led to the introduction of the flagellation rite at the Lupercalia.[120] After the abduction came Romulus' war against T. Tatius and the Sabines, who drove the Romans back to the very gate of the Palatine, and would have routed them but for Romulus' successful prayer (and promise of a temple) to Jupiter Stator. The Jupiter Stator temple next to the Porta Mugionia was vowed, and its construction begun, in 294 BC.[121] Tatius and Romulus made peace, and according to the prevailing tradition Romans and Sabines joined in a single body of common citizenship. One source, however, preserves a version in which the Sabines were given the lesser form of Roman citizenship, without the right to vote.[122] In real historical time, the lowland Sabines were given the citizenship 'without the vote' in 290 BC, and incorporated as full Roman citizens in 266.[123]

In due course Romulus became tyrannical, and surrounded himself with a bodyguard. These were the Celeres, the name given to the new elite corps of cavalry created in the late fourth century.[124] The final item is the death of Romulus – or rather, his mysterious disappearance, explained by the posthumous announcement that he was now an immortal, to be worshipped as Quirinus. The Quirinus temple, vowed in 325 BC, was dedicated in 293.[125]

Quirinus was honoured at the Quirinalia on 17 February, two days after the Lupercal festival. In Chapter 5 we identified him, along with Pan, the god of the Lupercalia, as a witness to the miraculous suckling of human twins by a she-wolf. Or rather, not human but divine: those twins were evidently the Lares Praestites, sons of Hermes and the silent goddess of the Feralia (21 February).[126] It seems to have been from the pre-existing myth of those protecting deities of Rome that the story of Remus and Romulus was first evolved. Effectively, therefore, the approximate date of that scene (third quarter of the fourth century BC, say the archaeologists) is the *terminus post quem* for the legend of the twin founders.[127]

The historical contexts we have identified in this chapter are all consistent with that. Between 342 and 266 BC, a period coterminous with the Roman conquest of Italy and the last stage of the 'struggle of the orders', a series of political events seems to have generated legendary analogues in the Remus and Romulus story, from the origin of the twins to the death of Remus and Romulus' rule as sole king. Not that the tale became immediately canonical. Greek foundation legends that ignored the twins could still be created in the third century BC.[128] But Fabius Pictor at the end of the third century gave it an authority that put all rival versions in the shade.

CHAPTER 9

The uses of a myth

PRE-LITERATE ROME

How is myth created? To put the question like that, with 'myth' as an abstract noun, is to ask for an unhistorical or even mystical answer in the idiom of Jungian archetypes or Dumézilian deep structures. Better to ask 'How are myths created?', or more precisely (since we are concerned with a foundation legend) 'How is a story that explains the origin of a community presented to, and accepted by, that community?'

Not by the written word. Although there is good evidence for literacy in Rome at least from the sixth century BC,[1] the documentary use of writing as attested in archaic inscriptions does not mean that Rome was a 'literate society'. As we know from the better-attested Greek world,[2] the exploitation of the alphabet takes a long time to affect the habits of an oral culture, where knowledge, understanding and the norms of behaviour are transmitted by word of mouth and memory. Literature, narrative and dramatic, came to Rome in the second half of the third century BC. From then on, there were written texts that could, and did, survive to be consulted long after the immediate context of their composition. That was a development of immense importance; but what preceded it was not mere barbarism and oblivion. It is ludicrous to imagine that during the previous half-millennium the Romans never reflected on the origins and nature of their community, and had no way of expressing their idea of themselves in narrative or dramatic performance.

By definition, written sources cannot provide first-hand evidence for a pre-literary culture. But we are not doomed to total ignorance. Inferences can be made from what our written sources do tell us, or what they imply, or what they presuppose. The nature of orality in archaic Rome is not completely beyond the scope of rational conjecture, and it is good to see that serious work on the subject is now at last being undertaken.[3]

At the very beginning of modern historical scholarship, Niebuhr put forward the theory that the legends and traditions of early Rome had been created in songs and ballads. He pointed out that Cato, in the second century BC, had known of an ancient custom at banquets, where the guests would rise in turn and sing the praises of famous men. That, thought Niebuhr, had created a body of heroic poetry which was later lost and forgotten.[4] Though brilliantly exploited by Macaulay in his *Lays of Ancient Rome*, the idea was rightly dismissed by serious scholars, and Cato's banquet songs were brushed aside as an irrelevance.[5]

Archaeological evidence has now provided a context for the custom Cato reported. In the 'orientalising' eighth and seventh centuries BC, the aristocratic *symposion* of archaic Greece was evidently adopted by local elites in Latium and Etruria.[6] The songs and stories at these all-male banquets effectively created the communal memory of the group, based on the celebration of the great deeds of past and present members of it.[7] In Greek, *hetairoi* at a *symposion*; in Latin, *sodales* at a *convivium*: in each culture, the rehearsal of the past reinforced the social cohesion of the present. That, it is reasonable to infer, is what was happening at the banquets Cato knew of, obsolete in his time but still within the range of memory.[8] But this new evidence does not mean that Niebuhr's theory can be revived. Banquet songs must have been comparatively short, unlike the elaborate heroic lays Niebuhr's model presupposes. And they must have celebrated the *mores* of an aristocratic elite, unlike the popular, community-based ballads imagined by Niebuhr and Macaulay.

What matters about Niebuhr's theory is the phenomenon which gave rise to it in the first place, and which still demands an explanation. Macaulay's is the classic exposition of it:[9]

The early history of Rome is indeed more poetical than anything else in Latin literature. The loves of the Vestal and the God of War, the cradle laid among the reeds of Tiber, the fig-tree, the she-wolf, the shepherd's cabin, the recognition, the fratricide, the rape of the Sabines, the death of Tarpeia, the fall of Hostus Hostilius, the struggle of Mettus Curtius through the marsh, the women rushing with torn raiment and dishevelled hair between their fathers and their husbands, the nightly meetings of Numa and the Nymph by the well in the sacred grove, the fight of the three Romans and the three Albans, the purchase of the Sibylline books, the crime of Tullia, the simulated madness of Brutus, the ambiguous reply of the Delphian oracle to the Tarquins, the wrongs of Lucretia, the heroic actions of Horatius Cocles, of Scaevola, and of Cloelia, the battle of Regillus won by the aid of Castor and Pollux, the defence of Cremera, the touching story of Coriolanus, the still more touching story of Virginia, the wild legend about the draining of the Alban lake, the combat between Valerius Corvus and the gigantic Gaul, are among the many instances which will at once suggest themselves to every reader.

It was rightly objected, against Niebuhr's ballad theory, that a poetic genre so important and so influential could hardly have been lost without any recollection of its existence. If we are to find an alternative explanation for the 'poetic' nature of the early Roman tradition, we need a genre, and a context of performance, with both a history and an afterlife.

The historians in whose works the tradition survives for us – above all Livy, Dionysius and Plutarch – were not wholly unaware of the unhistorical nature of much of their material. They comment on it less often than a modern historian would, but they do comment on it. And what they say is not 'this is what you'd expect from a ballad', but 'this is what you'd expect from a *play*'. Plutarch on the Remus and Romulus story, Dionysius on the duel of the Alban and Roman triplets, Livy on the crimes of the house of Tarquin, Dionysius on the Fabii at the Cremera, Livy on the fated fall of Veii – all of them in their different ways attest the power of the stage to turn history into melodrama, or rather (as we might prefer to put it) to create melodrama which masquerades as history.[10]

I think it is hard to overestimate the impact of theatrical performances in the Graeco-Roman world. Books were for the wealthy few, but the dramatic festivals were for everybody. As in democratic Athens, so in republican Rome, the audience in the theatre *was* the citizen body.[11] And (though it has sometimes been denied)[12] as in democratic Athens, so in republican Rome, the theatre was the arena for the 'making and remaking' of the community's myths.

There was a famous passage of Varro's *Divine Antiquities* – known to us mainly from St Augustine's lengthy discussion of it in book VI of the *City of God* – in which the great polymath distinguished three types of theology, dealing respectively with the gods of the poets, the gods of the philosophers, and the gods of the city.[13] The first type was the *genus fabulosum* or *mythicon*; Varro described it as 'particularly suited to the theatre', and Augustine's whole argument takes it for granted that the *fabulae* of what we would call mythology were acted, danced and sung on the stage at the *ludi scaenici*.[14] Varro was determined to distinguish all that from his third type, the *genus civicum*, because he wanted to distance the public religion of Rome from such 'unworthy' stories of the gods as the judgement of Paris, Leda and the swan, and Saturn devouring his children.[15] But Augustine (who of course had his own axe to grind) was quite justified in resisting that strategy. As he rightly pointed out, the theatres were put up by and for the Roman citizen body, and the *ludi scaenici* were public festivals in honour of the gods of the city.[16]

Varro's contemporary Cicero describes the stage as one of the main sources of information in late-republican Rome, and we know that at least from the time of Naevius in the third century BC there was a flourishing genre of Roman historical drama (*fabula praetexta*).[17] Ovid's reference to a play about the arrival of the Magna Mater at Rome in 204 BC (with the goddess's miraculous vindication of Q. Claudia's honour) shows clearly enough that Roman history and mythological tales of the gods were not mutually exclusive categories.[18]

No sources could be more literary – indeed, more 'bookish' – than Varro, Cicero and Ovid. They lived in the literate, sophisticated, multicultural world of late-republican and Augustan Rome; if the theatre in *their* day was where Roman citizens heard the stories of the doings of gods and men which made up their mental world, then I think we are entitled to infer, *a fortiori*, that the same is likely to be true of the pre-literate world of the fourth century BC.

Our earliest contemporary evidence for the Roman festival games (*ludi*) is a stray line from the dramatist Cn. Naevius in the late third century BC, preserved in the epitome of Festus' encyclopaedia:[19]

Liberalia Liberi festa, quae apud Graecos dicuntur Διονύσια. Naevius: libera lingua loquimur ludis Liberalibus.

Liberalia: festival of Liber, called by the Greeks *Dionysia*. E.g. Naevius: 'We speak without inhibition at the Liberalia games.'

The Liberalia festival was on 17 March. The games on that day were later transferred to the Cerealia (12–19 April),[20] perhaps as a result of the suppression of the Bacchic cult in 186 BC; but that did not last. By the second century AD, at least, Liber had his *ludi* back on his own day, and their name could even be used to signify *ludi scaenici* in general.[21]

The temple of Ceres, Liber and Libera (identified as Demeter, Dionysus and Kore) was an important feature of archaic Rome, standing on the slope of the Aventine above the starting gates of the Circus Maximus (fig. 9, p. 75 above). It was supposedly vowed by the dictator A. Postumius in 496 – either because of a famine, or to gain victory in the battle of Lake Regillus – and dedicated by the consul Sp. Cassius in 493.[22] Annual *ludi* were part of the vow, and according to one tradition the resulting games in honour of Ceres and Liber were the first ever *ludi scaenici* at Rome.[23] Both the temple and the cult were conspicuously Greek, so it is not surprising that the games at the Liberalia were identified with the Dionysia, the Athenian dramatic festival *par excellence*.[24]

The main context for Attic drama was the City, or Great, Dionysia, in honour of Dionysus *Eleuthereus*. The god's title refers to liberty (Greek *eleutheros* = Latin *liber*, 'free'); Liber personified *libertas,* and as Naevius remarked, the Liberalia games were a time for freedom of speech. So it looks as if the Romans deliberately chose that particular Athenian Dionysus – the recipient of honour by dramatic performance – to identify as Liber.[25]

Whether that association goes right back to the foundation of the cult in the early fifth century, it is impossible to say; the Liberalia–Dionysia could be a fourth-century phenomenon, from a time when the evidence of vase-painting reveals strong influence from the genres of Attic drama in the Greek cities of Italy and among their hellenised neighbours.[26]

It may not be accidental that the foundation of the Ceres–Liber–Libera temple is attributed to the year of the first plebeian secession, and that one of the alleged results of the second secession (in 449) was that the temple should serve as an archive where decrees of the Senate were deposited in the care of the plebeian aediles. As we noted in the last chapter, the traditions on the early stages of the 'struggle of the orders' may well have taken shape in its later stages, in the fourth or early third century BC.[27] One of the symbols of the plebeian cause was Marsyas, the wise satyr who brought the science of augury to Italy, whom the great plebeian house of the Marcii honoured as their ancestor, and whose statue was set up in the Comitium at Rome, probably in 294 BC; he was in the service of 'Father Liber', and his statue symbolised a free city.[28]

Particularly important in this context are the Plebeian Games (*ludi plebeii*) in November. Their format, as known from the early-imperial calendars, was conspicuously parallel to that of the Roman Games (*ludi Romani*) in September, and the natural assumption is that they were created by the plebeians as an indication of the separate identity of the *plebs*, presumably in the fifth or fourth century BC.[29] The *ludi Romani* were centred on the Ides of September, the 'feast of Jupiter' on the dedication date of the temple of Jupiter Optimus Maximus on the Capitol; the days before that date (probably beginning on the 7th) were *ludi scaenici*, the days after it were *ludi circenses*, for chariot races in the Circus Maximus. The *ludi plebeii* were centred on the Ides of November, when another 'feast of

Jupiter' was held (the Ides of every month were sacred to him), and the *ludi scaenici* and *circenses* were distributed before and after in the same way.[30]

The Capitoline temple was vowed, it was said, by Tarquinius Priscus, the fifth king of Rome, who also instituted the *ludi Romani* and laid out the Circus Maximus for their performance.[31] But the temple was not dedicated until after the expulsion of the kings, in the first year of *libertas*. According to one tradition, the *ludi plebeii* were started then; another version dated them to the reconciliation after one or other of the plebeian secessions.[32] The history and significance of these great festivals were clearly a matter of some ideological importance. Not surprisingly, they were involved in the story of the plebeians' power-sharing victory in 367 BC.

Once again, Livy's ruthless way with his sources makes it difficult to see what sort of story they were telling. Just after the passage quoted in the last chapter, with its perfunctory account of the historic compromise, Livy has this:[33]

The Senate decided that this event deserved to be commemorated – and if ever the immortal gods merited men's gratitude, they merited it then – by the celebration of the Great Games, and a fourth day was added to the three hitherto devoted to them. The plebeian aediles refused to superintend them, whereupon the younger patricians were unanimous in declaring that they would gladly allow themselves to be appointed aediles for the honour of the immortal gods. They were universally thanked, and the Senate made a degree that the Dictator should ask the people to elect two aediles from amongst the patricians, and that the Senate should confirm all the elections that year.

So ends Livy's sixth book, and his seventh opens with the comment that the first curule aediles – the magistrates responsible for looking after the *ludi Romani* – held office in the year of the first plebeian consul. Now Licinius Macer, whose account of these proceedings Livy evidently had in front of him, seems to have named the first plebeian consul as his own ancestor C. Licinius Stolo.[34] Livy used a different consular list, which put Stolo's year of office in 364, and under that year he reports the introduction of *ludi scaenici* to Rome.[35] I think it is possible that he has separated two items that belonged together in his source; that Licinius Macer reported the introduction of stage performances as one of the acts of the first plebeian consul; and that the refusal of the plebeian aediles to put on the *ludi Romani* (with the consequent creation of patrician curule aediles to do it instead) is all that survives of a partisan narrative, suppressed by Livy, on the origins of the *ludi plebeii*.

That, of course, can be no more than a hypothesis. But what is clear from the scattered evidence that survives is that the dramatic festivals of the early Republic – whatever form they took in that profoundly obscure period – were intimately bound up with the same issues of plebeian self-consciousness that we have inferred as the creative stimulus for the story of the twins. What does it mean, for instance, that John Lydus marks 8 November, perhaps the first day of the *ludi plebeii*, as a 'memorial of Remus and Romulus'?[36] It must mean something; it must come from somewhere. What, and from where, we cannot tell, but the fourth century BC does at least offer a plausible context.

Among the very few pieces of contemporary literary evidence for fourth-century Rome is a comment by the philosopher Theophrastus (friend and successor of Aristotle) about the Roman colonists at Circeii. This promontory on the Volscian coast was identified as Circe's island, and according to Theophrastus the colonists pointed out the grave of Odysseus' young companion Elpenor, who fell off the roof of the witchgoddess's palace in the tenth book of the *Odyssey*.[37] It was probably in the sixth century BC that the Hesiodic poet named the sons of Circe and Odysseus as Agrios and Latinos, rulers over the famed Etruscans. Ever since then, Circe had been a significant presence in the communities of Latium and Etruria.[38] At Rome she manifested herself as the founder and eponym of the *ludi circenses*: she invented the games as an honour to her father Helios, the Sun, and the Circus Maximus in which they were held was named after her.[39]

The canonical form of the Circus Maximus as a building, a huge elongated arena with permanent terraces of seats all round, dates back only as far as Julius Caesar. The original Circus was simply the valley between the Aventine and the

Palatine, 'marked out' for use at the games.[40] The starting-point for the chariot races was immediately below the temple of Ceres, Liber and Libera; the turn was at the shrine of Murcia.[41] Those two poles represented two contrasting concepts, each with its tutelary goddess: the urge to speed, and the need to slow down.

Stimula, the 'goad' personified, was the power that urged men to intense activity, precisely the opposite of Murcia.[42] There was a grove of Stimula between the Tiber and the Aventine; since her name was interpreted as Semele, the mother of Dionysus, and the grove was a centre of Bacchic worship, it must have been adjacent to the temple of Ceres, Liber and Libera.[43]

There was also a grove near the shrine of Murcia. It was the grove of the Bona Dea below 'the Rock' on the *mons Murcus* where Remus watched for his sign.[44] The Good Goddess was identified as the daughter (or the sister and wife) of Faunus, and Faunus was thought by some to be a son of Circe.[45] A final item in this dimly-perceived mythology comes in Martianus Capella (fifth century AD), whose source was evidently learned in both Hellenistic and Etruscan theology. In the sixth of the sixteen regions of the sky lives Celeritas, the daughter of the Sun, along with two sons of Jupiter, Pales and Favor.[46] That is, Circe has become 'speed' personified, and her companions are the eponym of the Palatine and a god whose name alludes etymologically to Faunus.[47]

In Ennius' narrative of the augury contest, Romulus is on the Aventine proper, and Remus on the *mons Murcus*.[48] That means, I think, that Romulus the hasty was above the starting-line of the Circus and the grove of Stimula, and Remus the slow was above the turning-point of the Circus and the shrine of Murcia. The ideology of speed and slowness detectable in the story of the twins, a symbol of the respective natures of the patriciate and the *plebs*,[49] is also an expression of the topography of the Roman games.

Ludi circenses, ludi scaenici: Liberalia in March, Cerealia in April, Roman Games in September, Plebeian Games in November. These, and no doubt other festivals too,[50] are likely to have been the occasions in which the Roman citizen body created and recreated its own mythology. The *ad hoc* wooden theatres put up each year for the *ludi scaenici* fell far short of the great theatre of Dionysus at Athens (itself a fourth-century phenomenon) – but they probably played a similar role in the life of their community.[51]

MAKING A STORY

It is important to try to imagine the effect of stage performances on a largely non-literate audience. What you see performed *is* what happened; you have no books to refute or confirm it; your only other source of information is what other people (parents, nurse, teacher etc.) have told you in a far less vividly authoritative way. Even those who do have access to written sources can still accept drama as fact – like Plutarch, who believed Euripides on Phaedra and Hippolytus, or the Duke of Marlborough, whose knowledge of history was all from Shakespeare.[52]

What has to be remembered above all is the immediacy of the impact. Once a story has been presented to an audience and accepted, it exists in their minds from that moment. If you don't like the story, that's too bad; you can't just say 'it isn't true'. (Or rather, you can try, as Stesichorus did with Helen of Troy,[53] but it will make no difference.) You have to present another story, and get *that* one accepted in the same way. Once this basic principle is understood, the crux of the Remus and Romulus legend – 'If you need Remus, why kill him? If you have to kill him, why do you need him?' – becomes an irrelevance, a problem only for a different sort of narrative. It seems to me likely that the story as we have it is an accumulation, built up by the presentation of tendentious dramatic tales at successive *ludi scaenici* in a politically polarised community.

Let us suppose, for instance, that after the achievement of power-sharing in 367 it became important for the plebeians to express the idea of Rome as a double community. Their first attempt was via the Lares Praestites, the divine protectors of Rome. The story as told in Ovid and on the Praenestine mirror (pp. 65–71 above) could be a two-act performance at the far end of the Circus Maximus in front of the temple of Mercury (Hermes),[54] with the god coming out of his own temple and escorting Lara to the underworld via the nearby grove of the Bona Dea.[55]

Let us further suppose that during the constant wars of the later fourth century, Mars rather than Mercury came to seem the appropriate father of the Roman race. A new version of the she-wolf story was offered to the citizen body: the twins were human, though the sons of Mars, and they were the joint founders of Rome. This new story, like the previous one, was associated with the Lupercalia, but now the Lupercalia festival itself was being reinterpreted in a martial idiom.[56] The story caught on, and from this stage of its development survive the references to both twins as founders, and even as demigods, to whom hymns were sung and by whom oaths were sworn.[57]

Still further, let us suppose that the ideological conflict continued, focused now on the patricians' continued monopoly of the pontificate and the college of augurs; that the plebeians were now evolving and elaborating their own history of unjust deprivation, heroic secession and eventual vindication; and that the next scenario to be presented at the Plebeian Games or the Liberalia was the tale of the augury contest, and the cheating of the slow and honest twin by the fast and unscrupulous one.[58] There they were, visible from the Circus: Remus watching above Murcia, Romulus above Stimula.

Once created, once received into the Romans' consciousness, Remus could not be waved away. He existed. No doubt the patricians didn't like him, but they couldn't ignore him. But they too had their *ludi scaenici*, the Roman Games put on by the curule aediles. Let us now suppose that they developed the story in their own way, first by exploiting Remus and then by creating his death.

One of the recurring issues in the bellicose Rome of the late fourth century was that of military discipline: which is more important, obedience to orders or opportunistic brilliance? The latter was a particularly patrician trait, symbolised by that dashing general Q. Fabius Rullianus, who began his astonishingly successful career (three triumphs, consul five times, dictator, censor) with a victorious engagement against the orders of his commanding officer for which he narrowly escaped execution.[59] Flair, gallantry and glamour were qualities that could equally be described as rashness, arrogance and exhibitionism. But they were publicly celebrated in the late fourth century, when Delphi instructed the Romans to put up a statue to the bravest of the Greeks.[60] The man they chose was Alcibiades – rich, young, aristocratic and famous for his charioteering; a great general, but a charismatic maverick rather than a team player. That must have been a consciously ideological decision.

So too, I imagine, was the creation of an elite corps of aristocratic cavalry, trained for speed and known as the *Celeres*, for whom Fabius Rullianus as censor in 304 introduced the annual parade from the temple of Mars on the Via Appia to the temple of Castor in the Forum. I think it is likely that Fabius also introduced the duplication of the Luperci, whose youth, vigour and equestrian status advertised the same aristocratic value-system.[61] That Remus was the first leader of the *Luperci Fabiani*, and the victor in the aetiological pursuit of cattle-thieves,[62] surely implies a patrician narrative exploiting him for the other side in the partisan dialogue.

Changed circumstances demand new myths to comprehend them. In the terrible crisis of 296–295 BC, the ideological tensions were still there, personified in the two consuls who fought the battle of Sentinum: Fabius Rullianus, the victor, and the plebeian Decius Mus, whose self-sacrifice allegedly turned the tide of battle. Perhaps it was at the dedication of the temple of Victory in 294 that the great story of the death of Remus was first presented.[63] For the security of the city wall, even a brother must be sacrificed – and the name of Romulus' agent was either Celer or Fabius.[64]

Remus had been removed from the story, but its development went on. Let us now suppose that in the late 290s, for the dedication of the temples of Jupiter Stator and Quirinus,[65] the myth-making producers of the *ludi scaenici* created first the story of the rape of the Sabines and the battle in the Forum, and then the miraculous disappearance and revealed apotheosis of Romulus.[66] Thus, in the space of about one generation or even less, the essential narrative structure of the foundation legend would have been completed.

But there was still plenty of room for interpretation. The 280s are a hopelessly ill-documented decade, but what hints survive imply a period of acute tension, both internally and in foreign affairs: a secession of the plebeians to the Janiculum in 287, a bloody defeat by Gauls and Etruscans in 283, undiplomatic insults from the Greeks of Tarentum in 282, the execution of rebellious Praenestines in 280, and so on.[67] The story of the death of Remus may have been a patriotic one in 295, but in the next few years there were surely plenty of people, within Rome and outside, who preferred to see it as an ill-omened act of fratricide.[68] Let us suppose that the story was still being recycled, and elaborated, for topical consumption at the *ludi plebeii*.

Of course, it may not have happened like that. By definition, non-literary story-telling (dramatic or otherwise) leaves no textual evidence behind. But I think this hypothesis does at least provide an explanation – perhaps the only explanation – for the complexities of the tradition as we have it. When everything is done orally, with no texts to be consulted long after the event, stories can be invented or forgotten, developed or travestied, in quite short periods of time; and a politically conscious drama, if it existed in something like the form suggested above, would have provided both the motive and the medium for creative myth-making.

INTO LITERATURE

When L. Scipio Barbatus, consul in 298 and censor (probably) in 280, was buried in the new family tomb on the Via Appia, an eight-line verse *elogium* was inscribed on his coffin. It took the form of an address to an audience, and is plausibly interpreted as having been originally composed for the funeral.[69] That is our earliest certain evidence for the use of written narrative in Rome. If we assume a date in the range 270–250

BC for Barbatus' death, it belongs a generation or two before
the first Latin literary texts – plays and a translation of the
Odyssey by Livius Andronicus, plays and an epic *Bellum Poeni-
cum* by Cn. Naevius – in the latter half of the third century BC.[70]

By the late third century, the Remus legend probably
existed in written form. Naevius wrote a play on 'the upbringing of Remus and Romulus'; and a line survives from a play
called *The Wolf*, probably by Naevius (and perhaps the same
one), in which Amulius of Alba is greeted by someone apparently called Vibe of Veii.[71] That is enough to show that there
were variants or episodes known in the third century which do
not occur in our later literary sources.

On the other hand, one or two items that *do* occur there only
make sense if they come from an earlier context. For example,
Amulius has a daughter, who loves her cousin Ilia like a sister
and successfully pleads for Ilia's life when her pregnancy is
discovered.[72] Plutarch gives her name as Antho, 'flower'. That
must be how it appeared in Fabius Pictor's Greek narrative,
but we may suspect that the name was originally Latin. In
either 241 or 238 BC, the aediles L. Publicius and M. Publicius
built the temple of Flora by the Circus Maximus, next to the
temple of Ceres, Liber and Libera, and instituted the *ludi
Florales*.[73]

Another mysterious minor character with a Greek name is
Faustulus' brother Pleistinos, who appears only to be killed
(with Faustulus) in a pitched battle after the death of Remus.[74]
Plutarch reports that he had helped Faustulus to bring up the
twins. His name can only derive from the Greek πλεῖστοι,
'most numerous', and that in turn suggests a partisan contri-
bution to the perennial debate of Roman republican ideology:
who should have power, the many or the few?[75] It would make
a powerful allegorical point to have two brothers whose names
meant 'Good Fortune' and 'The Many' perish in the aftermath
of Remus' death.

By the end of the third century BC the Remus story had been
'entrusted to letters', as the Romans put it, in the histories of
Fabius Pictor and Cincius Alimentus.[76] From now on the form
of transmission is different. Texts that are meant to be read can

live on beyond their moment of communication; they may be consulted decades or centuries after the circumstances of their composition have been forgotten. Not that the cultural change is total: historiography, both Greek and Roman, had much in common with drama, and historians were well aware of it.[77] But the headlong pace of mythopoeic creativity which we have imagined for the late fourth and early third centuries was hardly possible in a literate culture. The annual games were still important, and new dramatic festivals continued to be instituted; but the most authoritative medium for communicating the significant past had become written history, a genre in which new interpretations appeared at a more leisurely rhythm, measured now in decades.

Even if less ruthlessly topical, however, the historians' retelling of the legend could still be political. Conspicuously in Dionysius, less prominently in Plutarch, the theme of discord, rivalry and selfish ambition presents the twins as an *aition* for the origins of political strife in Rome.[78] Does that come from the struggles of the fourth and early third centuries, or from the time of the Gracchi, or Sulla's civil war? It is impossible to say; just as the historians took up the themes of the dramatists,[79] so too the *populares* of the late Republic renewed the ideology of the early plebeians.[80] It was a real continuity. The Republic always consisted of *plebs* and *patres*,[81] with the permanent possibility of conflict between them.

The clearest example of the politically committed historian is C. Licinius Macer, who before he wrote his history had been one of the tribunes campaigning for the repeal of Sulla's reactionary legislation.[82] His version of the death of Remus dispensed wholly with the leap over the trench (or wall). For Macer, Romulus' cheating in the augury contest led straight into a confrontation, and Remus, with Faustulus, was struck down in the fighting.[83] That version is followed by Livy and Dionysius, both of whom comment on the episode as an example of tragic discord resulting from the pursuit of power.[84] It is very likely that Macer spelt out that lesson too.

Cicero did not like Macer or his history, and was unsympathetic to its political message; he may also have had an uneasy conscience about Macer's suicide in 66.[85] That, I think, is why we hear so little about this very influential work (a basic source for Livy and Dionysius, and still known six centuries later to John Malalas in Antioch), at the time when its impact must have been felt most immediately. I suspect, but of course cannot prove, that Cicero's historical excursus in book II of *De republica* was designed to refute and replace the picture of early Rome that had been presented by Macer twenty years earlier.[86]

Certainly the fratricide story, like that of the death of Romulus the tyrant,[87] was a myth with a meaning for the Rome of the civil wars. 'What hounds the Romans is bitter fate and the crime of a brother's murder, ever since the blood of innocent Remus flowed into the earth, a curse to his descendants.'[88]

REMUS AND AUGUSTUS

In the summer of 43 BC, seventeen months after the Ides of March, the young Caesar, whom we call Octavian, marched with eight legions down the Via Flaminia to Rome. He was nineteen years old. On 19 August the Roman people elected him to the consulship. As Dio reports,[89]

Caesar was extremely proud of the fact that he was to be consul at an earlier age than had ever been the lot of anyone else, and furthermore that on the first day of the election, when he entered the Campus Martius, he saw six vultures, and later, when haranguing the soldiers, twelve others. For, comparing it with Romulus and the omen that had befallen him, he expected to gain that king's sovereignty also.

That was clever. Octavian arrogated to himself both Remus' augury, for the citizen body, and Romulus', for the army. Fifteen years later, when he was reinventing himself as no longer a warlord but a godlike statesman, Octavian chose not to take the name 'Romulus'.[90]

Instead, he became Caesar Augustus. As *princeps*, he took good care to control the exploitation of his name by obsequious poets and playwrights.[91] Virgil, on the other hand, as a personal friend,[92] must have known what would be acceptable. The first great prophetic passage in the *Aeneid*, Jupiter's promise to Venus of the destiny of Aeneas' descendants, culminates in this famous vision of the *pax Augusta* (1 291–6):

> aspera tum positis mitescunt saecula bellis:
> cana Fides et Vesta, Remo cum fratre Quirinus
> iura dabunt; dirae ferro et compagibus artis
> claudentur Belli portae; Furor impius intus
> saeva sedens super arma et centum vinctus aenis
> post tergum nodis fremet horridus ore cruento.

Then shall the harsh centuries grow gentle and set wars aside. White-haired Faith and Vesta, and Quirinus together with his brother Remus, shall be lawgivers. Terrible in their iron bonds, the gates of War shall be shut; within, godless Frenzy shall sit on savage weapons, and roar, hideous with bloody mouth, bound with a hundred brazen knots behind his back.

Quirinus is the deified Romulus – a safe identification for Augustus,[93] since the story of the apotheosis is necessarily incompatible with that of Romulus the tyrant. What is astonishing is the presence of Remus, not only alive but a mortal among gods. In the optimism of the twenties BC, the myth could serve yet another purpose, in the interests of peace, harmony and reconciliation.

But there may have been a more specific reference. M. Agrippa was Augustus' closest friend, his colleague as consul in 28 and 27 BC, and his exact contemporary.[94] He was also a man of modest birth, whom the Roman people cherished as one of their own.[95] In the twenties BC, when they were both in their prime, Agrippa might well have seemed like Remus to Augustus' Quirinus, and according to Servius that was how the prophecy in the *Aeneid* was understood.[96]

Remus and Romulus grew up together in Faustulus' cottage; Agrippa lived in Augustus' house after 25 BC, when his own (which had been Antony's) was destroyed in a fire.[97] According to Varro, Faustulus' cottage was at the top of the Scalae Caci; that was where Augustus lived, between the temple of Victory and the temple of Apollo (fig. 14, p. 123 above).[98] The house of Augustus was one of the exhibits in the vision of primitive and modern Rome with which Propertius introduced his book of Callimachean aetiology in about 16 BC:

> qua gradibus domus ista, Remi se sustulit olim;
> unus erat fratrum maxima regna focus.

> Where yonder house rears up above the Steps, so once did that of Remus; the brothers' great realm was a single hearth.

A contemporary reader would not miss the allusion to Agrippa.[99]

By then, Agrippa was Augustus' deputy, with proconsular *imperium* and tribunician *potestas*; he was married to Augustus' daughter, and his two sons by her were Augustus' adopted sons and heirs; and he had just presided, with Augustus, over the great symbolic festival that marked the New Age of Rome.[100] The poets of this period use Remus, like Romulus, as a symbol of Rome itself: young Tiberius returns to 'the city of Remus', the Parthians must give back 'Remus' standards'.[101] The murder is not only forgotten, it is evidently denied. A line of Propertius makes it clear that the version in which Remus ruled together with Romulus (like Agrippa and Augustus) was common knowledge in the twenties BC.[102] Fratricidal strife was a thing of the past. As Virgil's Jupiter prophesied, the law-givers of Augustan Rome would be Quirinus and his brother Remus together.

The temple of Quirinus had been struck by lightning and burned down at the time of Caesar's war with Pompey. Augustus had to reverse that bad omen. He rebuilt the temple, and dedicated the splendid new building in 16 BC, the first year of the New Age.[103] By great good fortune, we happen to know what it looked like. The pedimental sculpture is reproduced on one of the fragments of the decoration of a Domitianic monument which were found near the Baths of Diocletian in 1901 (fig. 16).[104]

The iconographical scheme is an unusual one. In a pedimental composition, the most important place is naturally in the centre, where there is most room for the god of the temple to be

Fig. 16. Fragment of marble relief, showing the façade of the temple of Quirinus: first century AD. Rome, Museo nazionale: photo by courtesy of the Deutsches Archaeologisches Institut, Rome (inst. neg. 6434).

prominently portrayed. Here, however, the central position is occupied by what looks like a door or gate, with three birds above it flying from right to left. Smaller versions of the door or gate appear symmetrically at each side of the composition, separating the figures into groups of two and three. They are clearly not city-gates; the lattice-work of which they seem to be constructed suggests something much less permanent. The best suggestion yet offered is that each gate represents the single entrance into an *auguraculum* or *templum minus*, the rectangular space, marked off by ropes or railings, in which the rite of augury was carried out.[105] The birds suggest a scene of augury; and since there was a permanent *auguraculum* on the Quirinal,[106] its representation (as the central door) would be an intelligible symbol for the god Quirinus.

The smaller doors to each side must be associated with the seated figures at the far left and far right; two acts of augury are simultaneously taking place.[107] Once this is recognised, the scene becomes intelligible. As was clear from the first discovery of the relief, the seated figures must be Remus and Romulus.[108] Romulus, who will one day be Quirinus, is at the left: the birds are flying towards him, and all but one of the figures in the composition are looking in his direction. A goddess stands beside him and presents him with a cornucopia; next come Jupiter with his eagle and sceptre, helmeted Mars (in the background), and winged Victory conspicuous in high relief.[109]

On Remus' side we have Mercury with his *caduceus*, Hercules (perhaps) with his club, and between them a female figure who could be the Good Goddess.[110] All of them have turned towards Romulus; the one figure who turns to Remus is a goddess whom iconography and topography identify as Murcia.[111] That suggests that Romulus' goddess with the cornucopia may be Pales, eponym of the Palatine, since by the time of Augustus it was accepted that that was where Romulus had watched for his sign.[112]

The Quirinus pediment of 16 BC is a brilliant statement of the meaning of the Remus myth in Agrippa's lifetime. The twins are equal in size, and therefore in status, though one is visibly more favoured by the gods. The dynastic duality implied by the compositional framework was advertised also in the younger generation with the stepsons of Augustus, Tiberius and Drusus, aged respectively 25 and 22 at the time of the dedication of the temple, and jointly responsible for the gladiatorial shows associated with it;[113] it was equally clear in the generation after that, with Agrippa's sons (and Augustus' heirs) Gaius and Lucius, respectively a four-year-old and a babe in arms.

But with Agrippa's death in 12 BC it all began to unravel. Three years later Drusus died, and though the legend could handle that (only one of Mars' twin progeny was destined to be immortal),[114] the deaths of Lucius and Gaius in AD 2 and AD 4 were beyond its resources. After that calamity, everything changed. The next two heirs were Tiberius and Agrippa Postumus,[115] an ill-matched pair whom not even the most ingenious flattery could think of as brothers. Worse, the disinheritance and exile of Agrippa Postumus in AD 6–7 brought about an intensity of dynastic strife that threatened to develop into civil war.[116]

One of the minor episodes in that strife was the banishment of Ovid in AD 8, and the consequent abandonment (at the half-way point) of a masterpiece of Roman mythography, Ovid's calendar poem, the *Fasti*.[117] Various dates in February and March had enabled Ovid to spread himself on the conception, birth and miraculous suckling of Remus and Romulus, and on the stories of the Sabine women and of Romulus' deification.[118] But April brought him to the Parilia, the day of the foundation of Rome, where he told at length the story of the death of Remus; and for the Lemuria in May, the days of the angry ghosts, he summoned up Remus' bloodstained and resentful shade, bitterly complaining to Faustulus and Acca Larentia.[119]

Romulus' grief is tactfully emphasised (Celer gets the blame), but even so, it is a sign of how the message of the myth had changed again. For the disillusioned Rome of Augustus' last years, it signified not harmony but murderous violence. And when, on Augustus' death, it was thought necessary to kill

Agrippa Postumus as Tiberius came to power,[120] no doubt sensible people took care not to mention Remus at all.

MEDIEVAL EPILOGUE

What Augustus left to his successors was an army of twenty-five legions and an empire that stretched from the Atlantic to the Euphrates, from the North Sea to the Nile. Three hundred years before, Remus and Romulus had been founder-heroes for a city-state. Something different, more cosmopolitan, was needed for a world empire; the *Aeneid* and the imperial cult provided it.[121] Three hundred years later, Constantine saw a light in the sky, and the Roman empire adopted the God of the Christians. Three hundred years later still, when power had long since moved to Byzantium, Rome was essentially a city-state again. But now her twin protectors were St Peter and St Paul.[122]

A good myth, however, is inexhaustible, and Remus lived on in some unexpected places. Some time in the tenth century Flodoard of Reims attributed the foundation of his native city to 'the soldiers of Remus' in exile from Romulus' Rome.[123] Reims had once been Durocortorum, chief town of the Remi, whom Caesar describes as constantly loyal to Rome during the Gallic wars.[124] The other Gallic people Caesar trusted were the Aedui, who claimed kinship with Rome via a shared descent from Troy.[125] Did the Remi make a similar claim? Since Durocortorum was where Roman governors were entertained,[126] it is easy to imagine the imperial legate of Gallia Belgica listening to loyal orators asserting the fraternal devotion of the city of Remus to the city of Romulus. Flodoard's legend may well date back to the Roman empire.

Remus' other city is Siena. The tale of Aschio and Seno the sons of Remus is purely medieval, but it mattered enough to the *comune* for a gilded bronze statue of the wolf and twins to be commissioned in 1428, a generation or so before the twins were added to the Capitoline wolf in Rome.[127] It stands now in the Palazzo Pubblico at Siena, a worthy setting for the one surviving monument to Remus.

CHAPTER 10

The other Rome

IMPERIAL PRECONCEPTIONS

The twentieth century has its own myth of Rome, and its own medium (the cinema) for expressing it. At the half-way point of the century, in the heyday of Hollywood when ninety million Americans went to the movies every week,[1] the epic *Quo Vadis* was created at the Cinecittà studios in Rome. The opening scene was the Via Appia – tombs, an aqueduct, umbrella pines against the sky – with marching legions and driven slaves. A 'voice-over' spelt out the message: the power and corruption of imperial Rome, where murder replaces justice and there is no escape from the whip and the sword. Against this pyramid of human misery and slavery is pitted the Gospel of love and redemption. 'This is the story of that immortal conflict . . .'[2]

The novel *Quo Vadis*, by the Polish author and patriot Henryk Sienkiewicz (1846–1916), was published in 1896. It was immediately translated into all major languages (and a good many minor ones, including Gaelic), and its huge success all over the world brought Sienkiewicz the Nobel Prize for Literature in 1905. Similar vast sales had been achieved a little earlier by General Lew Wallace (1827–1905) with *Ben-Hur: a Tale of the Christ*, written while he was Governor of New Mexico and published in 1880. It too became a classic Hollywood epic.[3]

Between the novels and the epic movies there was a third form, equally popular, that of the 'toga-play'. *Quo Vadis* was not a success on the stage, but a play with a very similar plot (arrogant Roman officer redeemed by love of Christian girl) was Wilson Barrett's *The Sign of the Cross*, first published in 1894. *Ben-Hur* was dramatised in 1899, complete with galloping chariots on the stage.[4] Both plays were highly successful. The London production of *The Sign of the Cross* played to audiences of 70,000 per week, some of whom came as if to a religious service. '"Ahs" and "hear, hears" were distinctly audible', noted one critic, 'and I should not have been surprised at an "amen" or a "hallelujah".' 'It suits the taste', said another, 'of a very large section of the public.'[5]

This whole genre of early-Christian melodrama can be traced back to Bulwer Lytton's *The Last Days of Pompeii* (1834), and it was still thriving more than a century later, when Lloyd C. Douglas' novel *The Robe* (1943) sold over three million copies and was translated to the epic screen with Jean Simmons and Richard Burton.[6] Much of the genre's appeal lay in the combination of exciting spectacle with non-sectarian piety, and its popularity reflected the importance of church or chapel in most people's lives.[7] As the influence of organised religion waned in western culture, the genre lost its *raison d'être*. Later Hollywood epics like *Cleopatra* (1963) and *The Fall of the Roman Empire* (1964) depended on spectacle alone; the message had gone, the epic form was empty.[8]

The exception that proved this rule was *Spartacus*.[9] No Christians there, but a powerful message for a different sort of organised religion.

As early as the middle of the eighteenth century [Spartacus] had been elevated in Western European literature into an idealized champion of the cause of the oppressed and enslaved. So it was no mere chance that a small number of extreme German Social Democrats, headed by Karl Liebknecht and Rosa Luxemburg, signed their pacifist appeal during the first World War with the name of Spartacus, and in 1918, when the framework of their organization took shape, they called it the 'Spartacus League'.

Thereafter, Spartacus became an emblematic figure for orthodox Marxism. Stalin himself declared, with a fine contempt for historical evidence, that 'the great slave-uprisings of the declining Roman republic annihilated the slave-owner class and the slave-owner society'.[10]

When Howard Fast wrote his novel *Spartacus* in 1951, he had served a three-month jail sentence for refusing to co-operate with Senator McCarthy's Un-American Activities Committee. No American firm would take the book, so he published it privately; the first commercial edition was with a London publisher in 1952. In December 1953 Fast was awarded the Stalin Peace Prize, but he left the Communist Party after the invasion of Hungary in 1956. The film of *Spartacus* (which won four Oscars) was written by Fast in collaboration with Dalton Trumbo, one of the 'Hollywood Ten' blacklisted by McCarthy's committee. It ends, as *Quo Vadis* began, on the Via Appia with the power and cruelty of Rome; as Appian attests, six thousand rebel slaves were crucified along the Roman road.[11]

The resonances of Roman power for the mid-twentieth century are clear enough.[12] The magistrate's *fasces* became the sign of Fascism; quasi-legionary standards were paraded at Nazi rallies; triumphal arches symbolised totalitarian authority. It was not always so. For the seventeenth and eighteenth centuries, Rome had not been monolithic. She could represent republican virtue, and inspire the founding fathers of the American Revolution.[13] From Shakespeare's *Julius Caesar* to Addison's *Cato*, in England, France and Italy alike, playwrights had used Rome for the great political themes of liberty and autocracy, treason and civil war.[14]

The moment when Rome as a polity gave way to Rome as an imperial power in the conceptual world of western culture was probably 1787, when Johann Gottfried von Herder published Part III of his *Ideas for the Philosophy of the History of Mankind*. For Herder, Rome represented the destructive principle in human history:[15]

Rome destroyed Carthage, Corinth, Jerusalem, and many other flourishing cities of Greece and Asia; as it brought to a melancholy end everything civilised in the south of Europe that lay within reach of its sword . . . We are compelled to think, that Rome was founded by some demon inimical to mankind, to exhibit to all human beings traces of his supernatural demoniacal sovereignty.

Forget Brutus, Cato and the people's tribunes; for Herder there
was only ever one Rome, the enslaving empire.[16]

AN UNFAMILIAR CITY

There *was* another Rome, but the empire and its modern
analogues have effectively buried the memory of it. That is not
surprising. As Polybius declared at the start of it all, the
Roman empire was a phenomenon unique in history.[17] No
wonder it dominates our historical imagination.

Already in Polybius' time the Romans were defining themselves as something ruthlessly *different*. Describing the sack of
New Carthage by Scipio's troops in 209 ('their orders were to
exterminate every form of life they encountered, sparing
none'), the historian adds a comment which is clearly based on
personal experience:[18]

This practice is adopted to inspire terror, and so when cities are taken
by the Romans you may often see not only the corpses of human
beings but dogs cut in half and the dismembered limbs of other
animals . . .

An even more revealing episode was the brutal eradication of
the cult of Bacchus throughout Italy in 186 BC. Rome had
always been hospitable to foreign cults – the Dioscuri and
Apollo in the fifth century, Pan evidently in the fourth, Asclepius, Venus of Eryx and the Phrygian Great Mother in the
third – and Bacchus, as Liber Pater, had been installed in the
Ceres temple at Rome for over three hundred years. But now it
pleased the consuls and the Senate to treat his orgiastic mysteries as a dangerous conspiracy, a plague from outside infecting
virtuous Rome, and they stamped out the cult without
mercy.[19]

In the fourth century BC Rome had been a city-state, 'just
one actor, albeit an important one, on a stage where the
leading parts were played by the Greeks, the Etruscans, and
the Italic peoples who spoke the Osco-Umbrian tongue'.[20]
Between these Italian communities the give-and-take of
mutual influence, even mutual participation, was evidently not

perceived as a threat. Our first evidence for the she-wolf story is on a mirror from Praeneste, showing two Greek gods and a third who was thought of as Sabine.[21] Our first evidence for the twin founders is the monument set up by the Ogulnii, whose name proclaims them non-Roman in origin; Q. Ogulnius' later embassies to Epidaurus (to bring Asclepius) and to Alexandria indicate wide horizons, and no doubt a mastery of Greek.[22] Things were very different by the second century BC. With the defeat of Carthage and the conquest of Greece came a determination to construct a Roman identity which excluded 'foreign' influences as dangerously corrupting.[23] The Rome of the elder Cato would have understood Senator McCarthy's committee very well.

The challenge for the historian is to think away the mind-set of imperial Rome, and the accumulated preconceptions generated by our culture's 'reception' of the Empire, and to imagine, from source material which almost all post-dates the change, a Rome which still thought as a city-state and not as a world power. Usable evidence can be found, if we can only recognise it. A few examples will show how unfamiliar 'the other Rome' turns out to be.

The Roman Republic was the Senate and people, *senatus populusque Romanus*. The late-republican Senate was composed of ex-magistrates who were members for life, with all that that entailed for authority, experience and political weight; but in the early Republic, as we happen to know from a learned antiquarian (one would never have guessed it from the historiographical tradition), senators were the friends and supporters chosen by particular consuls or consular tribunes each year, and presumably served only so long as their man was in office.[24] As for the sovereign people, who in the late Republic voted by secret ballot at electoral and legislative assemblies, the etymology of the word *suffragium* suggests that originally their opinion had been expressed, as at Sparta, by a shout in favour or against, or even by the clashing of weapons; the centuriate assembly did after all consist of the Roman people in arms.[25]

At the games in the Circus Maximus, the chariots in the late

Republic were driven by professionals organised in the four *factiones* of Reds, Whites, Blues and Greens. To call a senator a charioteer was like calling him a bandit or a gladiator.[26] But in the fifth century BC, as we know from a law of the Twelve Tables quoted by Pliny, Roman aristocrats competed in chariot-races just like their Athenian contemporaries; the wreath that crowned the victor was an honour that followed him even to the grave.[27]

The archaic Roman community was divided into three groups, called Titienses, Ramnes and Luceres. What did the names mean? Our sources have no idea, and neither have we.[28] The Roman year was marked on the calendar with 45 festival days in large letters; most of these were named after the divinities honoured on each day, but for the Agonalia, Lupercalia, Feralia, Quinquatrus and Lucaria (seven festivals in all, for there were three Agonalia during the year), the competing explanations offered by our sources show that by the first century BC the meanings of these names had been forgotten.[29]

An even more striking index of the 'otherness' of pre-imperial Rome, even as late as the third century BC, is the design of its coinage. Roman coinage began with two separate sequences: silver (with token bronze fractions), and cast bronze. The first issue in silver appeared at the end of the fourth century BC; then, after a gap of about thirty years, the two sequences were produced in parallel.[30] This was the period of the conquest of Italy and the war with Pyrrhus. How did Rome present herself on her coinage? What were the public symbols of her national identity?

The first three issues of silver didrachms carried the following types, all with the legend ROMANO (fig. 17):[31]

1 Helmeted head of bearded Mars, with oak-spray behind: horse's head on base, with corn-ear behind (*c.* 310–300 BC).
2 Laureate head of Apollo: horse galloping, with star above (*c.* 275–270 BC).
3 Head of Hercules, hair bound with ribbon, club and lionskin over shoulder: she-wolf suckling twins (*c.* 269–266 BC).

Mars is self-explanatory, Apollo and Hercules perhaps somewhat less so. As for the reverse types, why should the horse be a

Fig. 17. Roman silver didrachms, third century BC; photos by courtesy of the British Museum (*BMCRR* Romano-Campanian 1, 22, 28).

Fig. 18. Roman bronze *as*, third century BC; photo by courtesy of the British Museum (*BMC* Italy 48.1).

symbol as significant as the foundation legend itself? Now let us
look at the cast bronze sequence in the same period; the first
four issues appeared probably between 280 and 266 BC.[32] If we
ignore the types of the small denominations,[33] the obverse and
reverse of the *as* and *semis* types of these four issues give us
sixteen images, as follows: Apollo, three times; Roma (in a
Phrygian helmet), three times; Minerva (in a Corinthian
helmet), three times; Pegasus, the winged horse, twice; an
unidentified goddess, twice; Mercury, once; Castor or Pollux,
once; and an unidentified youthful Janus-head, once. Why
Pegasus? Who is the nameless goddess? Whose are the faces on
the Janus-head?

    The last type is particularly puzzling (fig. 18). It appears on
the main denomination of the very first issue of bronze, and
again on an *as* issue of about 241–235, both times with Mercury
on the reverse. Then, with a slight adjustment (a laurel wreath
in the hair instead of a band), it was used for all the gold and
silver issues of 225–214 BC, the so-called *quadrigati*.[34] It must
have been a significant image, but what did it represent, and
why? The conventional identification as the Dioscuri is based
on quite inadequate evidence.[35] It is better to admit our
ignorance.

    These mysterious glimpses of the other Rome should serve to
moderate our certainty about what was or was not possible in
the early Republic. The arguments in this book have conver-
ged on a single conclusion, that the myth of Remus was begun,
developed and essentially completed within a quite short and
specific period of time – twenty years or so, at the end of the
fourth and the beginning of the third centuries BC. It is a fair
question, to ask how that could come about. The medium that
has been suggested is drama, topical and partisan performances at the public *ludi*. Again, it is fair to object that there is no
direct evidence for such a thing at that time. So my final
concern has been to suggest that the argument from silence is
not valid.

    Do we really know enough about early Rome to be able to
say, with confidence, 'That cannot have happened'? It may be
tempting to believe that we do; but the date and nature of our

literary evidence, combined with the twentieth-century predisposition to apply the ethos and ideology of imperial Rome to all stages of the city's history, mean that the temptation must be resisted. Rome as a city-state is a historical phenomenon which is very imperfectly understood, and any attempt to make sense of it must avoid unexamined assumptions based on later conditions.

It is true that the evidence for the period we are concerned with is desperately inadequate; but all that means is that hypotheses have to be carefully argued, and conclusions must be recognised as being necessarily provisional. It is always possible that a better explanation will be offered. What matters for the Remus myth is to recognise that explanation is needed.

Appendix: Versions of the foundation of Rome

Lycophron *Alexandra* 1226–80. Third century BC (possibly a second-century interpolation: West 1984.143–6). Cassandra prophesies:

'As for the fame of my ancestors' race, one day hereafter their descendants will exalt it to the highest, raising with their spears the crown of the first spoils of war and seizing the sceptre and monarchy of land and sea. O wretched fatherland, you will not hide your glory in oblivion, faded in the dark. Such a pair of lion cubs, a race
I outstanding in strength [*rhōmē*], will a certain kinsman of mine leave, the son of Castnia who is also Cheirias, the best in counsel and in battle not to be despised.

In Rhaecelus first will he come to dwell, by the steep headland of Cissus and the horn-bearing Laphystian women. And from Almopia as he wanders back Tyrsenia will receive him, and Lingeus heaving out its stream of hot waters, and Pisa and the lamb-rich glens of Agylla. And with him will a man who is an enemy join together a friendly army, having overcome him with oaths and prayers of supplication, a dwarf who searched out in his wanderings every corner of sea and land, and with him the double offspring of the king of the Mysians (whose spear one day the stay-at-home god of wine will bend, tying his limbs together with willow-branches), Tarchon and Tyrsenus, tawny wolves sprung from Heraclean blood. There he will find a table full of things to eat, a table afterwards devoured by his followers, and understand the memory of ancient prophecies.

And he will found in the places of the Borigoni a populated land beyond the Latins and the Daunians, thirty towers, when he has counted up the offspring of a black sow which he will carry in his ship from the crests of Ida and the Dardanian places, to bear and rear that number of wild boar. Her image, and that of her milk-fed young, he will put up in a single city, modelling them in bronze. And having built a precinct for Myndian Pallenis, he will place in it his ancestral images of the gods. It is these, together with his aged father (having

160

put aside both wife and children and all other rich possessions of wealth), that he will hold in honour, wrapping them in robes at the time when the spear-wielding dogs, having devoured together all the property of his fatherland by casting lots, will offer to him alone the choice to take and carry away from his house whatever gift he wants.

Being judged for this most pious even by his enemies, he will create the country that is most sung in battles, blessed in its late descendants, a bastion around the tall glens of Circaeon and the Argo's famous anchorage, great Aeetes, and the waters of the Marsionid lake of Phorce, and the Titonian stream of the hollow that sinks to unseen depths beneath the earth, and the slope of Zosterius, site of the gloomy dwelling-place of the virgin Sibyl, roofed over by a cavernous pit of shelter.'

Supplementum epigraphicum Graecum XVI 486. Inscription from Chios, late third or (more probably) early second century BC. A benefactor sets up public games and festivals in honour of the Romans in return for their help in war. I translate the text of lines 22–9 as restored in Derow and Forrest 1982.80.

. . . and wishing by all means to make clear the goodwill and gratitude of the people, and to present the citizens maintaining and together increasing what appertains to glory and honour, he produced at his own expense an offering to Rome worth one thousand Alexandrian drachmas, comprising the story of the birth of Romulus the founder of Rome and his brother Remus. According to that story **2** it came about that they were begotten by Ares himself, which one might well consider to be a true story because of the bravery of the Romans.

Sallust *Bellum Catilinae* 6.1. First century BC.

The city of Rome, as I understand it, was originally founded and **3** occupied by Trojans (who were wandering as refugees with no fixed abode under the leadership of Aeneas), together with the Aborigines, a wild race without law or authority, free and uncontrolled.

Diodorus Siculus VII 5.1. First century BC.

Some of the historians have gone astray by supposing that Romulus the son of Aeneas' daughter founded Rome. But that is not the truth: **4** there were many kings in the time between Aeneas and Romulus, and the city was founded in the second year of the seventh Olympiad, 433 years after the Trojan war.

Dionysius of Halicarnassus *Roman Antiquities* 1 72–3. Late first century BC.

Since there is much disagreement both about the date of the foundation and about the founders of the city, I thought I should not discuss these matters in a cursory fashion, as if they were agreed by
5 all. For Cephalon of Gergis, a very early historian, says that the city was founded in the second generation after the Trojan war by those who were saved from Troy with Aeneas, and he declares that the founder of it was Rhomos, the leader of the colony, and that he was one of Aeneas' sons. (He says that Aeneas had four sons, Ascanius, Euryleon, Rhomulos, Rhomos.) This is also the account given by
6 Demagoras, Agathyllus and many others, both about the date and about the leader of the colony.

But the author of the history of the priestesses at Argos, and the events that happened in the time of each of them, says that Aeneas
7 came from the land of the Molossians into Italy, and along with Odysseus [*or* after Odysseus] became the founder of the city. He says that Aeneas named the city after Rhome, one of the Trojan women; weary of wandering, she urged on the other women and together with
8 them set fire to the ships. Damastes of Sigeum and certain others agree with him.

9 But the philosopher Aristotle narrates that some of the Achaeans returning from Troy were seized by a violent storm while rounding Cape Malea. For a time, driven by the winds, they wandered all over the sea, but at last they came to the place in the Opician land which is called Latinion and lies on the Tyrrhenian sea. Delighted at seeing land, they hauled up their ships there and spent the winter making ready to sail at the beginning of spring. But when their ships were set on fire in the night, and they had no means of achieving their departure, by necessity, and not by their wish, they settled their lives in the place where they had come to land. This disaster befell them because of the captive women they happened to be bringing back from Troy; the women burned the ships from fear that the Achaeans' return home would take them into slavery.

10 According to Callias, the historian of the deeds of Agathocles, Rhome was one of the Trojan women who came into Italy with the rest of the Trojans; she married Latinus, the king of the Aborigines, and gave birth to three sons, Rhomos, Rhomulos and Telegonus [. . .] and they founded the city and named it after their mother.

11 The historian Xenagoras says that Odysseus and Circe had three sons, Rhomos, Anteias and Ardeias, who set up three cities and
12 named their foundations after themselves. Dionysius of Chalcis makes Rhomos the founder of the city, but says that according to some he

was the son of Ascanius, according to others the son of Emathion. **13**
And there are others again who say that Rome was founded by **14**
Rhomos the son of Italus and Leukaria, daughter of Latinus.

I could offer many other Greek historians who assign different
founders to the city, but in order not to seem long-winded I shall pass
on to the Roman historians. There is not a single one of the Roman
historians or chroniclers who is ancient; however, each one of them
has taken and recorded something from ancient accounts that have
been preserved in sacred documents.

Of these authors, some say that Rhomulos and Rhomos, the **15**
founders of Rome, were sons of Aeneas. Others say they were the sons **16**
of Aeneas' daughter, without specifying the father, and that they
were given as hostages by Aeneas to Latinus the king of the Aborigines when the treaty was made between the native inhabitants and
the new arrivals; Latinus welcomed them, and not only looked after
them well but even left them as heirs to half his kingdom when he
died with no male descendants.

Others again say that after the death of Aeneas Ascanius inherited **17**
total authority over the Latins, but divided the land and power into
three with his brothers Rhomulos and Rhomos. He himself founded
Alba and some other towns; Rhomos founded Capua, Anchisa,
Aineia (later called Janiculum), and Rome, named respectively after
his great-grandfather Capys, his grandfather Anchises, his father,
and himself. Rome was deserted for some time, but when another
colony arrived, sent out by the Albans under the leadership of
Rhomulos and Rhomos, it received its ancient name. So (it is said)
there were two foundations of Rome, one shortly after the Trojan
war, the other fifteen generations after the first.

If anyone wants to look even further back, a third Rome too will be **18**
found, older than these, that came into being before Aeneas and the
Trojans arrived in Italy. The author of this account is no ordinary or
recent historian, but Antiochus of Syracuse, to whom I have referred
before. He says that when Morges was king in Italy (and at that time
Italy was the coast from Tarentum to Posidonia), there came to him a
man exiled from Rome. This is what Antiochus says: 'When Italus
was growing old, Morges was king; in his time there came a man
exiled from Rome; his name was Sikelos.' So according to the Syracu-
san historian an ancient Rome is found even earlier than the Trojan
war; but whether it was in the same place as the present city,
or whether a different place happened to have the same name,
Antiochus left it unclear and I cannot come to any conclusion either.
I think the above will suffice as an account of the ancient foundations.

Plutarch *Romulus* 1–2. Early second century AD.

The name of Rome is great, and famous throughout mankind; but from whom, and for what reason, the city was so called is disputed among historians.

19   Some say that Pelasgians settled there, after wandering over most of the inhabited world and conquering most of mankind, and that they called the city after their strength [*rhōmē*] in arms.

20   Others say that when Troy was taken some of the Trojans escaped and found ships; driven by the winds, they happened to reach Tyrrhenia and came to anchor at the river Tiber. By now their womenfolk were in despair and unable to endure the sea. One of them, Rhome by name, who had the reputation of pre-eminence in birth and wisdom, suggested to the women that they should set fire to the ships. When it was done, the men at first were angry. But afterwards, having settled by necessity around Pallantion, in a short while they prospered more than they had expected, finding that it was good land and the neighbouring people welcomed them; and so they honoured Rhome, in particular by calling the city after her, since she had been the cause of it. (Ever since then, so it is said, the custom has endured for women to greet their relatives and husbands with a kiss. For that was how the women who burned the ships greeted and embraced the men on that occasion, begging and entreating them not to be angry.)

21   Others say that the Rhome who gave her name to the city was a
22   daughter of Italus and Leukaria; or a daughter of Telephus the son of
23   Heracles, married to Aeneas; or a daughter of Aeneas' son Ascanius.

24   Others again say that the founder of the city was Rhomanos, son of
25   Odysseus and Circe; or Rhomos the son of Emathion, sent from Troy
26   by Diomedes; or Rhomis the tyrant of the Latins, having driven out the Tyrrhenians (who had come to Italy from Lydia, and to Lydia from Thessaly).

27   What is more, even those authors who make Rhomulos the eponym of Rome, in the most authoritative of the versions, do not agree about
28   his descent. Some say he was a son of Aeneas and Dexithea the daughter of Phorbas, and that he was brought to Italy as a baby along with his brother Rhomos; all the other ships were wrecked in the overflowing river, but the one with the children in was tipped gently on to a soft bank; they were unexpectedly saved, and the place was called Rome.

29   Others say that the mother of Rhomulos was Rhome, daughter of the Trojan woman mentioned above and wife of Latinus the son of
30   Telemachus; or Aimulia the daughter of Aeneas and Lavinia, having had intercourse with Ares.

Others again tell a wholly mythical story about his birth. Tarche- **31**
tios was king of the Albans, a most lawless and cruel man. In his
house there occurred a supernatural manifestation: a phallus arose
out of the hearth and remained there for many days. There was in
Tyrrhenia an oracle of Tethys, from which Tarchetios received the
response that a virgin must have intercourse with the apparition, for
she would bear a child of great fame, pre-eminent in courage, good
fortune and strength [*rhōmē*]. And so Tarchetios told one of his
daughters the prophecy, and ordered her to have intercourse with the
phallus; but she thought it unworthy of her, and sent in a slave-girl to
do it. When he found out, Tarchetios was furious. He seized both the
girls to put them to death, but Hestia appeared to him in his sleep and
forbade him to kill them. So he chained them and gave them a
particular task of weaving to do, on the understanding that when
they had finished it they would be given in marriage. They wove by
day, but at night other girls unravelled the weaving on Tarchetios'
orders. When the slave-girl gave birth to twins by the phallus,
Tarchetios gave them to a certain Teratios to destroy them. He took
them and put them down close to the river. Then there came a
she-wolf which suckled the babies, and birds of all kinds brought
morsels of food and fed them, until a herdsman, seeing this with
amazement, ventured to approach and pick the children up. So they
were rescued, and when they grew up they attacked Tarchetios and
overcame him. That at any rate is what a certain Promathion has
related, who put together a history of Italy.

Festus *De verborum significatu* 326–9L, s.v. 'Roma'. Late second century AD.

Cephalon of Gergis, who seems to have written about Aeneas' arrival **32**
in Italy, says that Rome was named after a certain companion of
Aeneas; for having occupied the hill now called Palatine, he founded
a city and called it Rhome. Apollodorus in his *Euxenis* says that the **33**
sons of Aeneas and Lavinia were Maylles, ⟨Ro⟩mulus and Rhomus,
and that the city took its name from Romus [*sic*]. Alcimus says that **34**
Romulus was the son of Aeneas' wife Tyrrhenia, and from Romulus
was born Aeneas' granddaughter Alba, whose son, called Rhodius
[Rhomus?], founded Rome. Antigonus, the writer of an Italian **35**
history, says that a certain Rhomus, born of Jupiter, founded a city
on the Palatine and gave it the name Rome.

According to the compiler of the history of Cumae, some people set **36**
out from Athens to Sicyon and Thespiae; then from those cities,
because of the shortage of dwellings, many of them set out for foreign
parts and arrived in Italy. They were called Aborigines from their

extensive wandering. Those of their number who were subject to the authority of the man [. . .] and his unparalleled strength called the Palatine hill, on which they had settled in large numbers, Valentia, after the strength of their ruler. On the arrival in Italy of Evander and Aeneas with a large number of Greek-speakers, the name was translated and began to be called Rhome.

37   Agathocles, the author of the history of Cyzicus, says that Aeneas, urged on by the prophecy of Helenus, made for Italy carrying with him his granddaughter Rhome, daughter of Ascanius; and that when the Phrygians had taken possession of Italy, and in particular those regions which now are close to the city, she was the first of all to consecrate a temple on the Palatine, to Fides. Afterwards, when a city was being founded on that hill, she who had previously dedicated the place to Fides seemed to be a proper reason to call it Rome. Aga-

38   thocles, indeed, says that there are several authors who claim that Aeneas is buried in the city of Berecynthia close to the river Nolon, and that it was one of his descendants called Rhomus who came to Italy and founded the city named Rome.

39   Caltinus [i.e. Callias?], the historian of the deeds of Agathocles the Sicilian, thinks that among the band of Trojans who fled when Troy was captured was one called Latinus, and that he had a wife Rhome after whom, when Italy had been occupied, he called the city he founded 'Rome'.

40   Lembos, who is called Heraclides, considers that when the Achaeans were returning from Troy they were driven off course by a storm to the regions of Italy, and by following the Tiber upstream arrived where Rome now is. There the captive women, wearied with the sea journey, urged on by the authority of a certain maiden of marriageable age called Rhome, burned the fleet. The city was founded by the Achaeans as a result of their enforced stay, and it was called specifically after the name of the woman whose plan had caused them to fix on that place as their settlement.

41   Galitas [Callias?] writes that since the rule of Italy after Aeneas' death had passed to Latinus, son of Telemachus and Circe, and he had recognised Rhomus and Romulus as his sons by Rhome, the reason for calling the city founded on the Palatine 'Rome' in particular [. . .]

Julius Solinus *Collectanea rerum memorabilium* 1 1–3. Third or fourth century AD.

42   There are some who would like it to appear that Rome was first given her name by Evander, when he found there the town which the young men of Latium had previously built and called Valentia; he kept the meaning of the original name, and Rome was called 'Valentia' in

Greek. Since the Arcadians had occupied it on the summit of the hill, the derivation followed that the most secure parts of cities should be called *arces* ['citadels'].

Heraclides' view is that when Troy was captured certain of the **43** Achaeans came via the Tiber to the area where Rome is now, and that at the urging of Rhome, the noblest of the captive women, who was their companion, the ships were burned, they settled and built defences, and called their town Rhome after her. Agathocles writes **44** that Rhome was not a captive, as was said above, but that as the daughter of Ascanius and the granddaughter of Aeneas she was the reason for that name.

Servius on Virgil *Aeneid* VII 678. Late fourth century AD.

One finds disagreement about the founders of cities, so much so that even the origin of Rome cannot be precisely ascertained. For Sallust **45** says 'The city of Rome, as I understand it, was originally founded and occupied by Trojans, together with the Aborigines'; others say it **46** was founded by Evander, and Virgil follows them when he writes 'The king Evander, founder of the Roman citadel . . .'; others say it **47** was founded by Romulus, as in 'See, my son, under this man's auspices that famous Rome . . .'

Servius 'auctus' on Virgil *Aeneid* I 273. Fourth century AD?

About the origin and founder of the city, different authors give different accounts. Clinias reports that Telemachus' daughter, called **48** Rhome, was married to Aeneas, and Rome was called by her name. [. . .] says that Latinus, son of Ulysses and Circe, called the city **49** Rhome after the name of his dead sister. Ateius asserts that before the **50** arrival of Evander Rome was called Valentia for a long time, but afterwards it was called by the Greek name Rhome. Some say it was **51** called after the daughter of Evander; others, after the prophetess who **52** had foretold to Evander that it was in these regions that he ought to settle. Heraclides says that Rhome, a captive Trojan noblewoman, **53** had sailed there and urged settlement out of weariness of the sea, and that the city was called after her name. Eratosthenes reports that **54** Romulus, [son] of Aeneas' son Ascanius, was the originator of the city. Naevius and Ennius tell us that Romulus the founder of the city **55** was Aeneas' grandson by his daughter. The Sibyl says 'Romans, sons of Rhomos . . .'

Junius Filargyrius on Virgil *Eclogues* 1.19 (text as in Courtney 1993.405). Fifth century AD?

There was a Roma even before Romulus, and Marianus, the **56** poet of the Luperci, shows that Rome acquired its name from

her: 'But the fair golden-haired goddess Roma, the daughter of
Aesculapius, made a new name for Latium, which now all call Rome,
under the very name of her who founded it.'

Procopius *Wars* IV 22.7. Sixth century AD.

57 Among the monuments of the race that have still survived is the ship
of Aeneas, the founder of the city.

John Lydus *De mensibus* IV 4. Sixth century AD.

58 They say that Latinus was Telegonus' brother, Circe's son, and
Aeneas' father-in-law, and that in the course of founding the citadel
of Rome, before the arrival of Aeneas, he discovered a laurel tree by
chance on the site, and so he allowed it to remain there. That is the
reason why they call the Palatine 'Daphne'.

Anthologia Palatina III 19 preface. Ninth or tenth century AD; the epigram itself was inscribed in a second-century BC temple at Cyzicus, but the lemma (possibly by Gregory Magister, Cameron 1993.148–9, 334) dates from the creation of the anthology.

59 On the nineteenth panel are Rhēmos [*sic*] and Rhomulos rescuing
their mother, Servilia by name, from Amulius' punishment. For Ares
seduced her and begot them on her, and when they were exposed a
she-wolf reared them. When they grew up they freed their mother
from her chains, founded Rome, and restored the kingship to
Numitor.

Etymologicum Magnum s.v. 'Rhome'. Twelfth century AD.

60 From Rhomos and Rhomulos the sons of Aeneas.

John Tzetzes on Lycophron *Alexandra* 1226. Twelfth century AD.

61 Rhomos and Rhomulos were born to Priam's daughter Creousa; with
Hector's children Astyanax and Sapernios they founded the city of
Rome.

Notes

1 Polybius IX 1.4; see Bickerman 1952.

2 *SEG* XXVI 1123 ('Lanoios' was the eponym of the Latin city of Lanuvium). On Fabius and his work, see Manganaro 1976.87–93.

3 Dion. Hal. I 71, *OGR* 17–18 etc.; Fabius Pictor fr. 4P. The dynasty was invented to cover the chronological gap between the fall of Troy ('1183 BC', according to Eratosthenes) and the founding of Rome ('747 BC', according to Fabius); cf. Dion. Hal. I 74.1–2. Velleius Paterculus (I 8.4) put the foundation of Rome 437 years after the capture of Troy.

4 Variants on her name at Dion. Hal. I 76.3 (Ilia or Rhea Silvia) and Plut. *Rom.* 3.3 (Ilia or Rhea or Silvia). She is Ilia ('Trojan') in Naevius and Ennius, who do not have the Silvian dynasty (n. 3 above); 'Rhea' is attested in the first century BC (Castor of Rhodes *FGrH* 250 F 5, Varro *LL* V 144).

5 Fabius in *Origo gentis Romanae* (*OGR*) 20.1; Dion. Hal. I 77.2, II 56.6.

6 Alternative version at Dion. Hal. I 79.1–2: Ilia is put to death. According to Ennius, she was drowned and became the bride of the river-god (Tiber or Anio): Enn. *Ann.* I 45 Sk, Porphyrion on Hor. *Odes* I 2.18.

7 Only one man in Plutarch (*Rom.* 3.4), who also gives an alternative version naming Faustulus as Amulius' servant rather than the herdsman who rescued the twins.

8 Fabius *ap. OGR* 20.3; Dion. Hal. I 79.5; Plutarch (*Rom.* 3.5) specifies the Cermalus.

9 Mentioned in *OGR* 20.3, named (as Ficus Ruminalis) in Plut. *Rom.* 4.1; not in Dion. Hal. See also Ovid *Fasti* II 411–12; for the Ficus Ruminalis, see Briquel 1980.301–7.

10 One of a group of herdsmen in Dion. Hal. (I 79.6–9). 'Descendit': *OGR* 20.3.

11 Only in Dion. Hal. (1 79.8), who has already mentioned the Lupercal as having been founded by Evander centuries before (1 32.3–5).

12 Rationalising alternative versions in Plut. *Rom.* 4.3 and 6.1 (cf. Dion. Hal. 1 84.1–4): no she-wolf, Numitor knows and supports. See Gigon 1954.164.

13 Only in Plutarch (*Rom.* 6.2, cf. 4.1 on the Ficus Ruminalis), who may at this point be using an author other than Fabius. *OGR* 21.4, quoting Valerius (Antias?), derives Romulus from ῥώμη, the Greek for 'strength', and Remus from *remor*, allegedly archaic Latin for 'slowcoach': see n. 36 below.

14 Only Plutarch (*Rom.* 6.2, followed by Zonaras VII 2) distinguishes Romulus as the more thoughtful, and a born ruler; according to Dionysius (1 79.12), both twins 'are still celebrated in traditional songs' as demigods.

15 Plut. *Rom.* 6.3, trans. Bernadotte Perrin.

16 Dion. Hal. 1 80.3, σπουδὴν μανικωτέραν.

17 Inspiration specified at Plut. *Rom.* 7.4, Dion. Hal. 1 81.4 (cf. 79.7 and 9 for divine assistance).

18 So Dion. Hal. 1 82.2, 83.3. Plutarch (*Rom.* 8.5–6) has Romulus enter Alba only during the attack itself, as in the (non-Fabian) account at Livy 1 5.7.

19 In Plutarch's version (n. 18 above), it is a combined operation, with Remus in command inside the city and Romulus outside.

20 Plut. *Rom.* 8.7, δραματικὸν καὶ πλασματῶδες (cf. Wiseman 1994.5–16).

21 There is one eccentric variant, Conon *FGrH* 26 F 1.48: Numitor killed by Amulius, the twins ruling in Alba before founding Rome. Servius (on *Aen.* VI 777) has the twins ruling jointly with Numitor in Alba for a year.

22 Plut. *Rom.* 9.1, Dion. Hal. 1 85.2. *Ubi educati erant*: Livy 1 6.3, Val. Max. II 2.9 (*sub monte Palatino*), Florus 1 1.5. Faustulus' hut: Conon *FGrH* 26 F 1.48, Zonaras VII 3 (from Dio?), Solinus 1.18, Tzetzes on Lycophron 1232 *ad fin.*

23 Diodorus XXXVII 11.1 ('oath of Drusus'); Justin XLIII 3.1; Conon *FGrH* 26 F 1.48; Strabo V 3.2 (229), who *also* reports the killing of Remus κατὰ τὴν κτίσιν; Servius on *Aen.* VI 777; Lydus *De mens.* p. 115 (*CSHB*), whose use of the formula 'Remus and Romulus' (p. 203 n. 48) suggests an early source; Lydus *De mag.* 1 3; Malalas VII p. 171 (*CSHB*). Also Maxentius' inscription in the *comitium* (*CIL* VI 33856): 'Marti invicto patri et aeternae urbis suae conditoribus'.

24 Lydus *De mag.* 1 5, Malalas VII pp. 171–2, *Chronicon Paschale* pp. 204–5 (*CSHB*); Cedrenus p. 258 (*CSHB*) has Remus rebel against Romulus.

25 Egnatius in *OGR* 23.6, a very eccentric variant.

26 Val. Max. II 2.9 (see pp. 126–7); Tzetzes on Lycophron 1232 *ad fin.*, followed by Cedrenus p. 189 (*CSHB*); *Vir. ill.* 1.4.

27 Hemina fr. 11P (Diomedes I 384 Keil). For the *Lares Grundiles*, cf. Nonius 164L: Palmer (1970.9–10) translates 'the Grunting Heroes'.

28 E.g. Dion. Hal. I 56 (thirty years from the foundation of Lavinium to that of Alba), Lycophron 1253–8 (thirty Italian cities to be founded by Aeneas).

29 Diod. Sic. VIII 4: οἱ πλεῖστοι (cf. p. 142) voluntarily obey the twins, and come together wherever they order.

30 *OGR* 23.1.

31 Plut. *Rom.* 9.4 (already in the Fabian narrative at 7.1?), Dion. Hal. I 85.4–5; also Livy I 6.4, which suggests a non-Fabian source. Cf. Plut. *Rom.* 8.7, Dion. Hal. I 83.3: signing off from Fabius?

32 Enn. *Ann.* I 72–91 Sk, from Cicero *De div.* I 107–8. Rival texts at Jocelyn 1971.44, Skutsch 1985.76–7; discussion in Skutsch 1961 = 1968.62–85, Jocelyn 1971.60–74, Skutsch 1985.222–38. (Otto Skutsch was a fine scholar, but the way he dealt with Jocelyn's important article in his commentary was unworthy of him.)

33 I would read 'In Murco Remus auspicio se devovet atque . . .', for the following reasons. (i) *se devovet*, the reading of MS *B*, must not be emended away (Jocelyn 1971.62–3, rightly). (ii) *in Murco* is the brilliant suggestion of Skutsch (1961.253–9 = 1968.63–71). (iii) *secundam* seems redundant, since *ex hypothesi* both twins were looking for favourable birds (Dion. Hal. I 86.1); so deleting it is the best way to make the line metrical (Jordan 1885.8, rightly). (iv) The imbalance of *avem*, with no epithet, and *genus altivolantum* (cf. Jocelyn 1971.61) corresponds to that of *Remus* and *Romulus pulcer*, *in Murco* and *in alto Aventino*: only the winner enjoys the decorative descriptions.

34 I tentatively suggest (see previous note): 'On Mount Murcus Remus by his auspicy vows himself to the gods below, and . . .'

35 Who? Jocelyn (1971.67–8) infers from the change of tense a missing line referring to a 'proto-Senate'. Very uncertain. Possibly the twins' respective followers?

36 Valerius (Antias) in *OGR* 21.4: 'alterum vero Remum dictum, videlicet a tarditate, quippe talis naturae homines ab antiquis *remores* dici'. Festus 344L (277M): 'Remeligines et remorae a *remorando* [MS memorando] dictae sunt in Plauto in Casina' (Mueller's emendation is certain, since Plautus *Casina* 804 has *remorantur remeligines*).

37 Dion. Hal. I 85.6, 86.2, Plut. *Rom.* 9.4, *OGR* 23.1 (conflating a 'distant Remuria' version with Remus' auspicy on the Aventine at 23.2); cf. Festus (Paulus) 345L.

38 Romulus on the Aventine is confirmed by the story of his spear-cast to the Palatine (Serv. *Aen.* III 46; Arnobius IV 3, from Varro). Murcus: Skutsch 1961. 253–9 = 1968.63–71; see pp. 113, 115.

39 N. 32 above. Jordan 1885.4–7, Skutsch 1961.262–7 = 1968.75–81, Jocelyn 1971.64–74, Skutsch 1985.231–8: none of these seem to me to be wholly satisfactory.

40 I follow Jordan on *sol albus* (a riddling periphrasis?), and take the single bird as Remus' omen (cf. *avem* at line 75 Sk): the idea that it is a collective singular and not to be distinguished from the later twelve (Skutsch) seems to me arbitrary.

41 I tentatively accept *priora* (Jocelyn) rather than *propritim* (Skutsch) for the MSS *propriam*; but the reading is so uncertain that nothing can depend on it.

42 Ovid *Fasti* IV 815–18 (*pacto statur*); Florus I 1.6–7, *Vir. ill.* 1.4 (*victor*); Val. Max. I 4 pref. (*potior*).

43 See nn. 66–7 below.

44 Dion. Hal I 86.3–4, Plut. *Rom.* 9.5 ('some say'). There are other stories in which cheating works to the benefit of Rome, with divine approval: see for instance Livy I 45.3–7 on the sacrifice of the Sabine ox.

45 Dion. Hal. I 86.3: ὑπὸ σπουδῆς τὲ καὶ τοῦ πρὸς τὸν ἀδελφὸν φθόνου.

46 *OGR* 23.2–4.

47 E.g. C. Flaminius, C. Minucius Rufus, C. Terentius Varro: Livy XXII 3–7, 27–30, 38–49.

48 Enn. *Ann.* XII 363 Sk, Virg. *Aen.* VI 845; Cic. *Att.* II 19.2, *De off.* I 84, *De sen.* 10, Livy XXX 26.9, Suet. *Tib.* 21.5, Ovid *Fasti* II 241–2, Seneca *De beneficiis* IV 27.2.

49 See nn. 16, 36, 45 above.

50 Diod. Sic. VIII 6 (from the *Excerpta Constantiniana*): πολλάκις ἐπαριστέροις βουλεύμασιν ἐπιδέξιος ἀκολουθήσει τύχη. Cf. Dion. Hal. II 5.2 for left and right in the Roman augural system, 'learned from the Etruscans'.

51 Festus 224L, Val. Max. I 6.5. The Festus item shows that there were various explanations for this term, including at least one from Greek ('ex Graeco tractum putant').

52 Festus (Paulus) 345L; cf. n. 36 above.

53 Diod. Sic. VIII 6.1, κατὰ σπουδήν.

54 Diod. Sic. VIII 6.1–3.

55 Plut. *Rom.* 10.2, Tzetzes *Chiliades* 893–901.

56 As in Ovid *Fasti* v 467–72 (cf. IV 837–53).
57 Serv. *Aen.* XI 603, Festus (Paulus) 48L. *Celeres*: Dion. Hal. II
  13.2–3; Plut. *Rom.* 26.2 (associated with Romulus' tyranny),
  Numa 7.4 (disbanded by Numa); Livy I 15.8; Pliny *NH* XXXIII 35
  (forerunners of the *equites*); Lydus *De mag.* I 9. *Tribunus celerum*:
  Pomponius *Digest* I 2.2.15 and 19 (king's second-in-command,
  equivalent of dictator's *magister equitum*), Dion. Hal. IV 71.6,
  75.1.
58 Ovid *Fasti* IV 837 (cf. v 467 *manus temeraria*); Festus (Paulus) 48L,
  Valerius Antias in Dion. Hal. II 13.2, Serv. *Aen.* XI 603.
59 Dion. Hal. I 87.4; contrast Diod. Sic. VIII 6.3 'at the king's
  command'.
60 Diod. Sic. VIII 6.3, Dion. Hal. I 87.4, *Vir. ill.* 1.4, Ovid *Fasti* IV 843
  (cf. *Ibis* 638 *rustica tela*). See White 1967.28–31, 52–6.
61 Jer. *Chron.* p. 146 (ed. Fotheringham): their mother was not
  imprisoned but buried alive, 'iuxta legem in terram defossa est'.
62 *Ibid.* p. 152 (under the third year of the sixth Olympiad): 'Remus
  rutro pastorali a Fabio Romuli duce occisus.' Festus (Paulus) 77L
  on 'Fovi qui nunc Favi [i.e. Fabii] appellantur', Plut. *Fab. Max.*
  1.2. Cf. Krämer 1965.384 n. 33, and (for Fabii as *celeres*) Montanari 1976.114–15.
63 Florus I 1.8, 'dubium an iussu fratris occisus est [Remus]'.
64 Yes: Enn. *Ann.* I 94–5 Sk, Diod. Sic. VIII 6.2, *Vir. ill.* 1.4. No: Ovid
  Fasti IV 841.
65 In *Vir. ill.* 1.4, Celer is a centurion.
66 Ovid *Fasti* v 452, Remus *male velox*; cf. IV 843 *nec mora*.
67 E.g. Ovid *Fasti* IV 833–6, Jupiter's sign of approval for the ditch
  and walls; *Vir. ill.* 1.4, 'ut [urbem] prius legibus muniret quam
  moenibus, edixit . . .'; Zonaras VII 3, *aition* for the death sentence
  on anyone crossing the *vallum* of a Roman camp.
68 Livy I 7.2, *volgatior fama*; cf. Plut. *Rom.* 10.1, Tzetzes *Chiliades* 899
  ('some say he was killed by Romulus himself'). Ovid (*Fasti* IV
  845–8) adapts the punch-line to the Celer story.
69 Livy I 7.2, *OGR* 23.5 (Licinius Macer), Serv. *Aen.* I 273, VI 779,
  Zonaras VII 3.
70 Dion. Hal. I 87.1–3 (cf. Plut. *Rom.* 10.1, adding the death of
  Faustulus' brother Pleistinos, who is mentioned nowhere else). As
  Pais notes (1913.299 n. 1), θανάτου τοῦ ταχίστου τυχεῖν alludes
  to the Celer story even while replacing it.
71 *OGR* 19.5 for his version of the begetting of the twins – by Amulius
  in a dawn mist; Malalas VII pp. 178–80 (*CSHB*) for his version of
  the she-wolf – the nickname of a human foster-mother.
72 Cf. Serv. *Aen.* VI 779 (Remus killed by Romulus' men in the

conflict): 'fabulosum enim est quod a fratre propter muros dicitur interemptus.'

73 Cic. *De rep.* II 4: 'dicitur . . . perhibetur . . . ut iam a fabulis ad facta veniamus.' Cf. Velleius Paterculus I 8.4: 'Romulus, son of Mars, having avenged the wrongs of his grandfather, founded the city of Rome . . .'

74 Cic. *De rep.* II 5–12. He even rationalises the 'hasty Romulus' motif: 'atque haec quidem perceleriter confecit' (12).

75 Cic. *De off.* III 40–1, *peccavit igitur*.

76 N. 24 above: Lydus, Malalas, etc. Compare the joint rule of Romulus and T. Tatius (also short-lived): Livy I 13.4–14.3, etc.

77 Cf. Wiseman 1979.39 = 1987.232 on Lydus *De mens.* IV 114 and Cicero *pro Caecina* 88, *Philippic* III 20 (the Gauls attack the Capitol by means of tunnels); also n. 71 above for Licinius Macer in Malalas.

78 πόλεμοι ἐμφύλιοι in Malalas (p. 172), followed by the *Chronicon Paschale* (pp. 204–5) and George Cedrenus (p. 258); *pestilentia* in Servius on *Aen.* I 276, 292.

79 Serv. *Aen.* I 276, 292, VI 779.

80 Ovid *Fasti* IV 849–56, on which see Bömer 1958.279–80, Drossart 1972. For 'invito frater adempte, vale' (852), cf. Catullus 68.20, 92; 101.6, 10.

81 Scholiasts on Horace *Epistles* II 2.209. Cf. Ovid *Fasti* II 599–600 on Lala/Lara. Kretschmer 1909.294 compares *peregrinus/pelegrinus*, and points out that the old spelling was *lemores* (from *remores?*); visible ghosts, especially of murder victims, might be thought of as 'delaying' (*remorantes*) in this world because not yet received into the next (Plautus *Mostellaria* 498–503).

82 Ovid *Fasti* V 445–9. The Lemuria honoured the *taciti manes* (V 422); Tacita (II 572) and Mania (Varro *LL* IX 61, Festus 114L etc.) were two of the names of the nymph whose story Ovid tells at *Fasti* II 583–616: she was raped by Hermes as he took her to the underworld, and became the mother of the twin Lares (see pp. 70–1). For the associations of Tacita, Mania and Acca Larentia, see Tabeling 1932.14–81; for their application to the Ovid narrative, Drossart 1972.196–8.

83 Dion. Hal. I 87.3, Plut. *Rom.* 11.1; cf. n. 37 above.

84 Justin XII 2.5–11 (Diomedes' Aetolians), cited to explain Alexander of Epirus' failure to capture Brundisium *c.* 335 BC; Zonaras VIII 3 (rebellious Praenestines, 281 BC) – from Dio? See respectively Briquel 1976b and 1986. A similar equivocation in the Pythian oracle given to Ap. Claudius in 48 BC: Val. Max. I 8.10 *Euboeae coela obtinebis* (cf. Lucan I 194–236, which shows he hoped for a *regnum*).

85 Prophecy of Cumaean Sibyl, presumably to Aeneas, about Remus' death: Propertius IV 1.49–50. Warning oracle to Amulius: Tzetzes on Lycophron 1232 (cf. Krampf 1913.41 for parallels). Supposed appearance of Vesta to Amulius: *OGR* 19.4. 'Oracle of Tethys' and appearance of Vesta: Plut. *Rom.* 2.4–5 (see pp. 58, 61). Appearance of Aeneas to Ilia: Enn. *Ann.* 1 38–50 Sk (cf. 60 Sk, Venus to Ilia).

86 See above, nn. 33–4.

87 See above, nn. 12, 71. For the technique, see Feeney 1991.31–2, Fox 1993.44–5.

88 Cf. above nn. 22, 26–30, 42.

89 Justin XXVIII 2.8–10 (Aetolians, *c.* 293 BC); cf. Lucan 1 95, 'fraterno primi maduerunt sanguine muri'.

90 Augustine *City of God* III 6, cf. XV 5. For a full list of Christian authors on the fratricide, from Minucius Felix to Leo the Great, see Wagenvoort 1956.172.

91 Hor. *Epodes* 7; cf. 16.1, 'altera iam teritur bellis civilibus aetas'.

92 For 'fratricide as the founding myth of Rome', see Pontone 1986.

93 Cain and Abel (not twins, anyway) do not offer an adequate parallel; see Strasburger 1968.35 (= 1982.1047), Bremmer 1987a.37.

94 Cf. West 1988.160 on the possible significance of the twinship of Neleus and Pelias (*Odyssey* XI 235–57). The story of their conception, with a speech by the divine rapist, is close to Fabius Pictor's account of Remus and Romulus (Trieber 1888.570 and passim).

95 Herodotus VI 52, citing Spartan tradition. Cf. How and Wells 1912.2.82–3: 'the most probable origin of this anomaly [the dual kingship] is the fusion of two distinct communities whose chiefs shared the throne'.

96 Scholia on Euripides *Orestes* (ed. Dindorf 2.240): Acrisios ruled in Argos, Proitos in Tiryns.

97 That must always have been horrific. Krämer (1965.356–7) tries to justify it as 'native severity', not fratricide 'in the strong sense' – which I think is special pleading.

2 MULTIFORM AND MANIFOLD

1 Puhvel 1987.290.

2 Ibid. 4, 37.

3 Ibid. 4, 19, 20.

4 Ibid. 191 (triangulation), 39, 162.

5 Ibid. 165 ('it is conceivable . . .'); presented without hesitation at 177, 181, 197, 285.

6 Ibid. 284–9.

7 Tac. *Germ.* 2.3; an alternative reading gives Mannus as the *origo* and his three sons as the *conditores*.

8 Müllenhoff 1900.112–14; Much 1967.51.

9 Puhvel 1987.286.

10 Ibid. 107–10, 286.

11 Lincoln 1975–6, Puhvel 1975–6 ('Remus et frater'). 'Deserves serious consideration' (Versnel 1976.400), but the Dumézilian Briquel (1980.345 n. 48) is sceptical.

12 Lincoln 1975–6.135 n. 36; Puhvel 1975–6.153 n. 56; Puhvel 1970.170 n. 29.

13 Lommel 1950.253; Puhvel 1970.170 (my italics).

14 Puhvel 1975–6.153; cf. Lincoln 1975–6.135.

15 Lincoln 1975–6.129–32; Puhvel 1975–6.154; Puhvel 1987.107–10.

16 Güntert 1923.324, 337; Pokorny 1959.230, 505; cf. Lincoln 1975–6.129, 137.

17 Lincoln 1975–6.129 (my italics).

18 Lommel 1950.255 n. 3.

19 Puhvel 1987.64: 'whose twin, and why, will be speculated upon in chap. 17'.

20 Lincoln 1975–6.125 n. 24.

21 Puhvel 1975–6.154, phrased a little more cautiously in 1987.286.

22 Puhvel 1987.286–7.

23 Eliade 1954.18, cited by Puhvel 1975–6.154 n. 58, Lincoln 1975–6.138 n. 71, and Burkert 1962.367 (whom Puhvel also cites). Eliade himself refers the reader to his 'commentaries on the legend of Master Manole' – a book published in Romanian in 1943 which I have never seen cited elsewhere.

24 Lincoln 1975–6.138, Puhvel 1975–6.154, Eliade 1982.108, 449.

25 Puhvel 1975–6.153, cf. 1987.288.

26 Kretschmer 1909.294, 303, whence Puhvel 1975–6.151–2, cf. 1987.288. See below, p. 203 n.48.

27 Florus I 1.8 (cf. p. 124); Kretschmer 1909.301–2 (independently of Florus), whence Puhvel 1975–6.149, 155 n. 59, 1987.287.

28 Puhvel 1975–6.156, 1987.289; Lincoln 1975–6.138, 'the conclusion is inescapable'. *Contra* Bremmer 1987a.37, 'etymological juggling'.

29 Puhvel 1987.289.

30 Ibid. 288–9, cf. 1975–6.155.

31 'The badly misapplied mythical theme of senatorial quartering of the body of the "tyrant" Romulus was hardly what Rome needed' (Puhvel 1987.289 = 1975–6.157); 'Rome got stuck with a subsequently inconvenient set of twin founders and had to rid

itself of one of them by the clumsy and guilt-laden expedient of legendary fratricide' (Puhvel 1987.287 = 1975–6.150).

32 Puhvel 1987.287–8 = 1975–6.150.

33 Puhvel 1975–6.148–9, 152–3. On Dumézil's 'tri-functional theory' – a wonderful intellectual construct, but based on totally inadequate evidence – see Momigliano 1984a (= 1987.135–59), and Belier 1991. Poucet (1985.171–9, cf. 302, 311) does his best to incorporate Dumézil's vision into a historical argument.

34 Dumézil 1974.260–2 = 1970.249–51.

35 Dumézil 1974.263 = 1970.252. I quote from Philip Krapp's translation.

36 Ibid. Cf. Bremmer 1987a.36: '*pace* Dumézil, the Roman twins do not perform anything remotely comparable'.

37 Dumézil 1974.264–6 = 1970.254–5; cf. Briquel 1976a.75–6.

38 See above, pp. 2–4.

39 Dumézil 1973.147 (trans. Derek Coltman), cf. 1968.88; Schilling 1960.192 n. 2 = 1979.353 n. 2; Briquel 1977 passim (pointing out that the 'wrong' twin predominates).

40 Ovid *Fasti* II 425–52. See pp. 84, 127.

41 See pp. 57–61: in any case, the story may not be about the conception of the *twins*.

42 Puhvel 1987.59–60, 228–9.

43 Ward 1968, ch. 2.

44 Ward 1968.27.

45 E.g. Ward 1968.6–7, on the mother, names, and hostility of the twins.

46 Krappe 1930.254: 'il s'agit d'une ancienne légende dioscurique'. See his ch. 4 for Dioscurism in general.

47 Krappe 1930.90, Ward 1968.5.

48 Krappe 1930.91; not in Ward.

49 Krappe 1930.53 and in Wood 1933.136.

50 Adolf Diessmann (Engl. trans. L. R. M. Strachan) in Wood 1933.xiii; cf. also p. v (editor's preface): 'it is not given to many of us "to wear the weight of learning like a flower" or to impart fascination to the results of research by selective simplicity, literary grace, and the charm of romance'.

51 H. G. Wood in the *Dictionary of National Biography*, quoting F. J. A. Hart (Clare College, Cambridge). As Wood observes, 'he had become interested in twin-lore and pushed his speculations to daring lengths'.

52 Krappe 1933.147.

53 Harris 1906.135.

54 Harris 1913.321.

55 Puhvel 1987.7–20, cf. 210 for 'dioskourism'. Harris and Krappe are briefly referred to by Briquel (1976a.73 n. 1, 97 n. 69; 1977.253 n. 3, 255 n. 11), and by Dulière (1979.16–17).

56 For a revealing detail, cf. Ward 1968.6: '[the Divine Twins'] names may be differentiated by Ablaut, for example, "Romus" and "Remus" (Romulus is a secondary form)'. No reference given, but the idea comes from Harris 1906.59 (cf. 1927.8).

57 Harris 1927.2–3, 16–17; Krappe 1933.152; Puhvel 1975–6.148 (on Kretschmer).

58 Briquel 1977.258: 'le cas des jumeaux romains constitue un anomalie'. Bremmer 1987a.38: 'the murder of Remus remains very much an enigma'.

59 Cf. Briquel 1980.269: 'Il vaut donc mieux ne pas chercher à interpreter la légende romaine en fonction d'un schéma mythique préexistant, établi sur des parallèles ethnographiques ou une comparaison indo-européenne, et se contenter de partir des documents qui sont à notre disposition.' But Briquel nevertheless goes on to a Dumézilian analysis.

3 WHEN AND WHERE

1 Niebuhr 1811.155–6 = 1828.189 (I quote from Hare and Thirlwall's translation), justifying the interpretation of Romulus' twelve vultures as twelve Etruscan *saecula* (Vettius *augur*, quoted by Varro in Censorinus *De die natali* 17.15).

2 Totila was the Ostrogothic king who captured Rome in 546 and 549. The Lombard invasions followed (568–72), and Gregory's treaty with the Lombard king Agilulf in 605 effectively brought about the division of Italy that lasted till the nineteenth century.

3 Sentinum: Livy x 27–30, Zonaras VIII 1 (pp. 117–120). Actium: Virgil *Aeneid* VIII 671–713, Propertius IV 6.11–68, etc. Pons Milvius: Lactantius *De mortibus persecutorum* 44, Eusebius *De vita Constantini* 27–38.

4 The Theseus legend was familiar about two generations earlier at neighbouring Caere: see Menichetti 1988.112 (the Tragliatella *oinochoe*) and 123 (the Regia plaque).

5 See Ampolo 1988, esp. 155–9; also Momigliano 1989.75–6, Torelli 1989.39–48.

6 For these interrelated phenomena, see Hölscher 1978, Harris 1979.10–34, Raaflaub 1986, Wiseman 1986.89–90 (= 1994.38–9), Hölkeskamp 1987.114–203, and the challenging reassessment of Millar 1989.

7 The bibliography is endless; but see in particular three excellent recent books: Brunt 1988 (with North 1989a); Zanker 1988; Raaflaub and Toher 1990.

8 'Conversion of Europe': Jones 1948. Analyses of the period from contrasting viewpoints in Brown 1978, Barnes 1981.

9 See Weinstock 1971, Price 1984.

10 If the Velienses and Querquetulani in Pliny's list of the *populi* 'who used to receive meat at Mt Alba' (Pliny *NH* III 69) represent two of the previously independent communities. On the 'pre-urban' centres, see Mazzarino 1966.1.193–4, Ampolo 1988.165–9.

11 For the Tiber as a frontier, as late as the third century BC, see Gellius *NA* xx 1.46–7 (quoting the Twelve Tables), Livy VIII 14.5, 20.9, XXVI 34.7; Dion. Hal. I 28.1, Juvenal VIII 264–5. The right bank was always the *ripa Veientana*: *CIL* VI 31547–8, 31555, cf. Hor. *Odes* I 2.14 (*litus Etruscum*).

12 For the *via salaria* (and the *via campana* from Rome to the coast), see Coarelli 1988.131–6.

13 I quote (respectively) Gruen 1990.11, Cornell 1975.23; cf. also Bremmer 1987a.25. For the opposite view, cf. Mazzarino 1966.1.190, 197; Strasburger 1968.14.

14 West 1988.159–71.

15 Ibid. 172. For the 'orientalising period', see Strøm 1971, Burkert 1992; for archaic Greek commerce and its effects, see Mele 1979. It is not clear to me why West, who emphasises Phoenician–Euboean contacts as early as the ninth century, puts the 'orientalising' of Argive and Theban myth only in the sixth (West 1985.149–54).

16 *Iliad*: 'Nestor's cup' at Ischia (*SEG* XXVI 1144). *Odyssey*: the Aristonothos crater at Caere (Menichetti 1988.111). Respectively late eighth and mid-seventh century BC, both pots may predate the epics in the form we have them.

17 Strøm 1971, esp. 140–71, 201–6.

18 Solin 1983, on *SEG* XXXI 875.

19 See above, nn. 4 and 5.

20 *SEG* XXVII 671, XXXII 940–1017; see pp. 59–60.

21 Timaeus *FGrH* 566 F 71 (Massalia founded 599?), Herodotus I 165–7 (*c.* 540–535).

22 Strabo IV 1.4 (179), 1.5 (180). The first-century BC historian Pompeius Trogus (epitomised in Justin XLIII 3–4) reported a Romano-Phocaean alliance 'in the time of king Tarquin'.

23 See Sommella Mura 1981, Menichetti 1988.122. The identification is certain: the same group, with the goddess just behind the

24 hero's shoulder, is on a fifth-century bronze candelabrum in the
Metropolitan Museum, New York (Rogers Fund 1961: 61.11.3).

24 Livy I 7.4–14; Virgil *Aeneid* VIII 184–305; Propertius IV 9; Ovid
Fasti I 465–586.

25 Hellanicus *FGrH* 4 F 111 (Dion. Hal. I 35.2–3).

26 Not *on* the hill, as Michels (1953.42) points out: see Dion. Hal. I
31.3, 32.3, 84.3, II 1.3; Virg. *Aen.* VIII 363 (the *regia*).

27 From the Arcadian *Pallantion* and *Lykaion*: see pp. 77–9.

28 Eratosthenes quoted by the scholiast on Plato *Phaedrus* 244b (p. 61
Ruhnk); Evander in this version is the son of the 'Italian Sibyl'.

29 Small 1982.3–12: (*a*) a fourth-century mirror in the British
Museum, (*b*) Cassius Hemina in *OGR* 6.7 ('Evandri servus nequi-
tiae versutus et praeter cetera furacissimus'). A favourable view of
'Kakios' in Diodorus IV 21.2 (source unknown).

30 Plut. *Moralia* 278b–c, Dion. Hal. I 31.1, Strabo V 3.3 (230),
Solinus 1.10. For 'Themis' as the name of a prophetess, see the
Codrus Painter's scene of Aegeus before the Pythia, named as
Themis (illustrated in Fontenrose 1978.205).

31 Acilius fr. 1P (Strabo V 3.3, 230), sometimes attributed to Coelius
Antipater. A century earlier (n. 28 above), Eratosthenes identified her as the Italian Sibyl.

32 Livy V 47.2, Gellius *NA* XVIII 7.2, Solinus 1.13 etc. The Carmentes
(plural) were birth-goddesses: Varro in Gellius *NA* XVI 16.4,
Tertullian *Ad nat.* II 11, Augustine *City of God* IV 11.

33 Festus (Paulus) 77L, cf. 78L: *fovea* = Fovi = Favi (*a fovendo*) = Fa-
bii; cf. p. 173 n. 62 above for a more primitive version of the same
etymology. Evander's daughter: Silius Italicus VI 627–36, cf. Plut.
Fab. Max. 1.1 ('a nymph or a local lady'), Juv. VII 14. For
Polybius (cited in Dion. Hal. I 32.1), Evander's daughter was
Lavinia, and her son by Hercules was Pallas, eponym of the
Palatine.

34 Servius *auctus* on *Aeneid* VIII 336; Cato fr. 56P (Solinus 2.7); *CIL*
XIV 3555. For the great temple complex of Hercules Victor at
Tibur, see Coarelli 1987.85–103.

35 That is, only one or two generations after his divinity (as opposed
to hero status) was first recognised, in Attica early in the sixth
century: see West 1966.417, 1985.169.

36 See Page 1973 (for the papyrus fragments) and Brize 1980 (for the
poem's impact on archaic art).

37 Pausanias VIII 3.2; according to the *Suda*, Stesichorus was born at
Pallantion and went to Sicily as an exile.

38 Dion. Hal. XIX 2.1; Serv. *Aen.* I 532, Dion. Hal. I 13.1 (citing
Pherecydes, mid-fifth century BC).

39 As argued by Bayet 1920, esp. 99–103, 119–20. The new evidence strengthens Bayet's view of 'les origines de l'arcadisme romain'.
40 Dion. Hal. 1 31–3.

4 WHAT THE GREEKS SAID

1 Momigliano 1984b.438.
2 On the 'first treaty' with Carthage (Polybius III 22), see Scardigli 1991.47-87; also Walbank 1957.337-445 (with previous bibliography), Alföldi 1965.350-5 (sceptical), Ampolo 1987.84-5. I think Walbank is right to accept the genuineness of the treaty itself, but not of the consular date evidently attached to it (Polybius III 22.1, Walbank 1957.339).
3 Polybius I 1.5-6; Walbank 1957.40.
4 The resentment is clear from Dionysius' need to refute it in the age of Augustus: Dion. Hal. 1 3.6-5.3; cf. Gabba 1991.191-2, 195-6 (with earlier bibliography).
5 See West 1984, who makes a powerful case for the Italian elements in Lycophron's *Alexandra* (including the Rome passage) having been later additions for second-century BC audiences in southern Italy.
6 That is why I do not share Tim Cornell's radical agnosticism about the date and significance of the Greek versions (Cornell 1975.16-27). 'Scrittori tardi possono rispecchiare tradizioni antichissime' (Pasquali 1949.906).
7 *Anth. Pal.* III 19 (no. **59**); cf. Polybius XXII 20, Plutarch *Moralia* 480d.
8 Hellanicus *FGrH* 4 F 84 (no. **7 = 20**).
9 See in particular Schwegler 1853.400-10; Preller 1883.305-40; Niese 1888, esp. 483-97; Pais 1913.303-9; Rosenberg 1914b.1077-9, 1083-9; Schur 1921; Pasquali 1949.906-8; Phillips 1953; Mazzarino 1966.1.203-7, 2.53-9; Strasburger 1968.11-13; Schröder 1971.62-89; Cornell 1975.3-8, 16-27; Momigliano 1984b.437-62; Ampolo and Manfredini 1988.262-76.
10 Niese 1888.482.
11 Cornell 1975.22 n. 1 (on no. **26**). Cf. ibid. 21: 'Some Greek scholars discussed the origins of peoples for purely antiquarian reasons and without any ulterior motive.' I find that hard to believe for the *creation* of stories.
12 Homer *Odyssey* x 133 – XI 10; real geography is left behind at IX 82. See Strabo 1 2.12-14 (22-3) for Eratosthenes on Homer's fantasy world; and Juvenal xv 13-26, Lucian *True History* 1 3 and Dio Chrysostom 11.34 for Odysseus' narrative as the 'lying story' *par excellence*.

13 *Odyssey* XII 3–4, trans. Walter Shewring.

14 See West 1966.398–9, 432–7 (cf. 417, 430); 1985.125–37; for the 'Hesiodic tradition', Lamberton 1988.22–4, 137–9. West dates the Circe passage to the second half of the sixth century (1966.436, 1985.130); Phillips (1953.56) and Mele (1987.173) put it earlier.

15 Hesiod *Theogony* 1008–20; I omit line 1014, interpolated to harmonise with the *Telegony* tradition (West 1966.434–5).

16 Hecataeus *FGrH* 1 F 62 (from Stephanus Byzantinus). The evidence for Stesichorus bringing Aeneas 'to the west' is not strong (Horsfall 1979), but not necessarily false either (Momigliano 1984b.444 and n. 2). Thucydides (VI 2.3) knew a tradition of refugee Trojans settling in Sicily, and there is good evidence for late sixth-century Etruscan knowledge of the story of Aeneas bringing Anchises and the Penates (Momigliano 1984b.445).

17 West 1966.436: relevant to Corcyra ('Phaeacia')? A later tradition made the Ausones of central Italy the descendants of Odysseus and Calypso: ps.-Scymnus 229 (fourth century BC), Festus (Paulus) 16L. Otherwise, of Circe: see n. 30 below.

18 Eratosthenes in Strabo 1 2.14 (23), scholiast on Apollonius Rhodius IV 311. For the islands, cf. Phillips 1953.55, 62–4.

19 Tirelli 1981.48 and tav. xva (a late sixth-century mirror in Paris); Weinstock 1946.111–12, on Martianus Capella 1 49.

20 Aeschylus in Theophrastus *Hist. plant.* IX 15.1; Pliny *NH* VII 15, XXV 11.

21 Hesiod *Theogony* 859–68. Note γαῖα πελώρη at 858 – interpreted as Peloris, like 'Aitna' at 860 (cf. West 1966.393)?

22 Hesiod fr. 149 Merkelbach/West (Diodorus IV 85.5).

23 For very early traditions being transplanted northwards, compare Herakles and Pallantion (p. 42) and the burning of the ships by the Trojan women (p. 51).

24 Theophrastus *Hist. plant.* v 8.1 and 3; Meiggs 1982.243–6, Mazzarino 1966.1.193–4.

25 Nonnos *Dion.* XXXVII 12–13, with Κίρκη and λόχμη at the end of adjacent lines, as in XIII 330–1.

26 Peek 1968–75.578 gives the full list (it includes also the Maurusii of the north African desert). For the 'wilderness', cf. Eratosthenes (scholiast on Plato *Phaedrus* 244b) on the Italian Sibyl: ἡ ἐν ἐρημίᾳ τῆς Ἰταλίας τὴν διατριβὴν λαχοῦσα.

27 Peek 1968–75.11.

28 Hesiod *Theogony* 1013–16 (p. 46 above). The emphasis on the *rock* may be significant: cf. XIII 332 for Circe's 'rocky' palace; Theophrastus (n. 24 above) stresses the rocky nature of her 'island' at Monte Circeo; 'rock-loving' (φιλοσκόπελος) is used by

Nonnos otherwise only of wild beasts, gods of the wild, and herdsmen or hunters (Peek 1968–75.1697).

29 So Preller 1883.308, rightly; also Phillips 1953.55. On the nature of Faunus, see Brelich 1976.66–83; he was identified with Pan (Serv. *Aen.* VI 775 etc.), the god of Nonnos' native city Panopolis. (Cf. Alföldi 1965.238–9: 'Agrios can be none other than the mythical personality, Silvius, the founder of Alba.' But his arguments seem to me inadequate.)

30 Servius *auctus* on *Aeneid* VIII 328, Lydus *De mens.* I 12; Steph. Byz. s.v. *Prainestos*, Solinus 2.9 (from Zenodotus).

31 Appendix nos. **24, 49** (both anonymous), **11** (Xenagoras *FGrH* 240 F 29). Cf. also no. **58** (Lydus), combining the Hesiodic and Virgilian genealogies.

32 Early: Pasquali 1949.906; Strasburger 1968.11–12; Mele 1987.175. Late: Classen 1963.451–2, 1971.480; Cornell 1975.20–1.

33 Above, n. 3; Momigliano 1989.85–6, Ampolo 1987.84.

34 West 1985.27–8; ibid. 1–11 passim for the genealogical literature of the seventh, sixth and fifth centuries BC.

35 *Epicorum Graecorum fragmenta* (ed. Davies) 71–3, cf. Severyns 1963.96–7.

36 Serv. *Aen.* VI 107; Theophrastus *Hist. plant.* V 8.3, Pliny *NH* XV 119; Homer *Odyssey* XI 74–8, XII 10–15. Hero-cult of Odysseus: Phillips 1953.55, 61.

37 Hyginus *Fabulae* 127, probably from the *Telegony*.

38 Festus 116L; Dion. Hal. IV 45.1, Livy I 49.9; Horace *Odes* III 29.8, Ovid *Fasti* III 92, etc. Mele (1987.174) notes the contrast with Diodorus VII 5.9 and *OGR* 17.6 (Tusculum founded from Alba).

39 No. **14** = **21** (anonymous).

40 *Leuke*: Dion. Hal. I 66.1. See Rosenberg 1914b.1086, Classen 1963.448 n. 9, Schröder 1971.84. The old idea that Leukaria represents Luceria, the colony founded by Rome in 315 (Niese 1888.490–1, Pais 1913.306), would reverse the relationship of Leukaria and Rhomos.

41 So Niese 1888.492, rightly.

42 No. **48** (Cleinias *FGrH* 819 F 1).

43 An insoluble textual crux: either reading is possible. 'After' would make sense if this tradition gave Aeneas the daughter of Telemachus as his wife (see previous note); 'with' is implied by Lycophron 1242–5 (no. **1**).

44 No. **7** = **24** (Hellanicus *FGrH* 4 F 84). Hellanicus' contemporary and neighbour Damestes of Sigeum told the same story (no. **8**, Damastes *FGrH* 5 F 3); Mazzarino (1966.1.203–6) gives Damastes the priority.

45 See in particular Rosenberg 1914b.1077–8, Schur 1921.146–8. Prinz (1979.153–7) calls Hellanicus the first Greek author to take an interest in the west – an astonishing judgement.

46 No. **9** (Aristotle fr. 609 Rose); followed by Heraclides Lembos, no. **40** = **50** = **53** (fr. 1, Müller *FGH* III 168).

47 Lycophron 921, 1075 and scholia; Strabo VI 1.12 (262); scholiast on Theocritus 4.24.

48 As in Hesiod (Rosenberg 1914b.1077). For stories moved north from Magna Graecia to Latium, cf. n. 23 above.

49 West 1985.1–7.

50 So Schur 1921.147–8.

51 Lycophron *Alexandra* 1226–49 (no. **1**); good analysis in Schur 1921.138–41. For the date of this passage of 'Lycophron', see n. 6 above.

52 No. **22** (anonymous), on which see Briquel 1991.185; cf. Dion. Hal. I 29.2. Also 'Tyrrhenia the wife of Aeneas' in Alcimus (no. **34**, p. 165).

53 Dion. Hal. I 28.3 (Hellanicus *FGrH* 4 F 4); Phillips 1953.58. For the traditions on Odysseus in Etruria alluded to by Lycophron, see Phillips 1953.60–1, 65–6.

54 Herodotus I 94 on the Lydian emigration under Tyrrhenus.

55 No. **26** (anonymous); Pais 1913.308, Briquel 1984.514–18, Ampolo 1987.85.

56 Justin XLIII 1.9, scholiast on Lycophron 1232; Dion. Hal. I 43.1 (alleged to be Faunus' own son). For the background, see Wiseman 1987.301; for Herakles at Rome, pp. 39–42 above.

57 Virg. *Aen.* VIII 313; nos. **42**, **51**, **52** (all anonymous). See above, p. 41.

58 No. **34** (Alcimus *FGrH* 560 F 4); see Rosenberg 1914b.1083, Classen 1963.448; Pasquali (1949.907) suggests that 'Tyrrhenia' alludes to the Hesiodic tradition.

59 Alba: see n. 40 above (an elaboration of the *Telegony*?). The Latin League's authority over Rome in the fifth and early fourth centuries BC is implied by L. Cincius in Festus 276L (*iussu nominis Latini*).

60 No. **10** (Callias *FGrH* 564 F 5) = **39** ('Caltinus', garbled). Latinus' parentage in no. **41** ('Galitas'), attributed to Callias by Mommsen (1881.4–5); *contra* Jacoby 1955.2.310 n. 31. No. **29** (anonymous) has the same, but with Rhome as the *daughter* of the Trojan lady.

61 Dion. Hal. I 72.5 (text completed from Syncellus); see Pais 1913.308, Classen 1963.449.

62 There is no need to suppose that 'Rhomos' is here already the Greek for Remus. Cf. Soltau 1909.113 n. 1: 'Nie Zwillinge!'

63 No. **17** (anonymous); see Niese 1888.490, Pais 1913.308, Classen 1963.450. Campanian chronicle: Schur 1921.143–6, Gabba 1967.145.

64 See above, p. 169 n. 3.

65 See above, n. 16, with Dion. Hal. 1 73.3 (named after the Trojan Capys); see Martin 1971 for a speculative reconstruction.

66 No. **25** = **13** (anonymous); Justin VII 1.1; Perret 1942.467.

67 On the simultaneous impact of Alexander and Rome, see Mazzarino 1966.2.55–6. Arrian VII 15.5 (Aristus of Salamis *FGrH* 143 F 2) reports the story that Alexander predicted Rome's power and enquired about her constitution (cf. Polybius, n. 3 above); according to Clitarchus (*FGrH* 137 F 31, Pliny *NH* III 57), the Romans sent an embassy to Alexander.

68 *Iliad* XX 302–8; *Homeric Hymns* 5.195–7; see Gabba 1974.630–1, 1976.84–8, Momigliano 1984b.451–2 on Demetrius of Skepsis (Strabo XIII 1.53, 608).

69 No. **38** (reported by Agathocles *FGrH* 472 F 5).

70 See above, nn. 16, 42, 43.

71 For Lavinium, see Alföldi 1965.246–68, Torelli 1984.189–236.

72 E.g. the Geganii and Nautii? Wiseman 1974.153–4 = 1987.207–8.

73 See above all Gabba 1976, Momigliano 1984b.437–62, Gruen 1990.11–15: Trojan origin was a usefully adaptable diplomatic concept *vis-à-vis* the Greek world.

74 No. **3** = **45**, **57**. Sallust's source evidently combined it with the story of the Aborigines, who named their city Valentia, later Hellenised as *Rhome*: no. **36** = **42** = **50**, cf. no. **19** (Pelasgians); for the story of the Pelasgians at Rome, already current in the third century BC (Baton of Sinope *FGrH* 268 F 5), see Briquel 1984.495–522.

75 Nos. **1** ('Lycophron', n. 6 above), **15** (anonymous Roman), **17** (n. 63 above), **60**, **61**. Rhomylos only: no. **54** (Eratosthenes *FGrH* 241 F 45). Rhomos only: no. **38** (n. 69 above).

76 No. **12** (Dionysius of Chalcis *FGrH* 840 F 10).

77 Nos. **23** (anonymous), **37** = **44** (Agathocles *FGrH* 472 F 5)

78 Festus 328L (no. **37**).

79 Roman *Pistis*: *LIMC* IV 2.70 (early third-century coins of Locri), Diod. Sic. XXVI 4.1, Polybius II 11.5, Plutarch *Flamininus* 16.4; Niese 1888.494–5, Gabba 1974.632. Ritual: Livy I 21.4, Serv. *Aen.* I 292, VIII 636; Pasquali 1949.906–7. Temple: Cicero *De nat. deorum* II 61: A. Calatinus (*cos.* 258) triumphed in 257; no doubt the temple was built *ex manubiis*.

80 No. **5** (Hegesianax *FGrH* 45 F 9, early second century).

81 No. **33** (Apollodorus *FGrH* 840 F 40b): *Mayllem* [*Ro*]*mulum Rhomumque*.

82 No. **28** (anonymous).

83 Steph. Byz. s.v. *Dexamenai*; Dion. Hal. I 50.4.

84 Strabo VII 7.6 (325), Polybius XXI 26–30, Livy XXXVIII 3–9. It was from there that Fulvius Nobilior brought the statues of the Muses to decorate his triumphal monument, the temple of Hercules Musarum (Pliny *NH* XXXV 66).

85 Plut. *Rom.* 2.2; cf. Ovid *Fasti* IV 291–328. See Bremmer 1987c, Gruen 1990.5–33, for mythographic and political analysis (respectively); both list extensive previous bibliography.

86 No. **56** (Marianus, second century AD?). Asklepios/Aesculapius: Livy X 47.7, *epit.* 11; Ovid *Metamorphoses* XV 622–745; Plut. *Mor.* 286c–d, etc.

87 Niese 1888.482: p. 45 above.

88 No. **34**, p. 52 above.

89 No. **10**, pp. 52–3 above. Three brothers also in nos. **17** (first part) and **33**: not homogeneous enough to count as an archaic 'triad' (n. 34 above).

90 No. **5**, p. 54 above. The issue is complicated by the fact that later Greek authors narrating the twins story frequently call Remus 'Rhomos'.

91 I.e. nos. **15**, **16**, **17** (second part), **28**, **41**, **60**, **61**.

92 Nos. **28**, **17** (p. 53 above).

93 Dion. Hal. I 73.2 (no. **16**), cf. Diod. Sic. VII 5.1 (no. **4**).

94 See above, p. 169 n. 3. This was the version used by Naevius and Ennius (no. **55**).

95 No. **35** (Antigonus *FGrH* 816 F 1); date inferred from Dion. Hal. I 6.1 (between Timaeus and Polybius?). Schröder (1971.81–2) suggests that Antigonus' Rhomos was the son of Aeneas' daughter and Zeus.

96 As Schröder (1971.79) points out, 'Ilia' was pointless as the name of the twins' mother after the invention of the Alban dynasty. Rhea and the Magna Mater: Schwegler 1853.428, Pais 1913.286–7; denied (surely wrongly) by Niebuhr 1828.176, De Sanctis 1907.217 = 1956.212, Gigon 1954.158–9.

97 No. **30** (anonymous); see Wiseman 1993.183–4 for the Aemilii and their myths. Niese (1888.496) puts Aemilia in the context of Aemilius Paullus' victory at Pydna in 168 BC.

98 Cornell 1975.25–7 (though his conclusions are too sweeping).

99 No. **2**: text in Derow and Forrest 1982.80 (whose supplements I translate) and Moretti 1980.37; commentary in Derow and Forrest 1982.85–6, Moretti 1980.48–53. On epigraphic criteria the date should be mid to late third century BC, but the most plausible historical context is 189–188 (Derow and Forrest 1982.86–91).

100 No. **59**: n. 7 above.

101 Cic. *Academica* II 56, 84–5 (mid-third century BC) for the original Servilii *gemini*. It is fortuitous that the two Roman names imported into the story are Aem-ilia and Serv-ilia? Cf. n. 96 above for the obsolescence of Ilia, 'the Trojan'.

102 No. **31** (Promathion *FGrH* 817 F 1); Plut. *Rom.* 2.3–6 (μυθώδη πανάπασι), 3.1–8.7 (τοῦ δὲ πίστιν ἔχοντος λόγου μάλιστα καὶ πλείστους μάρτυρας); Gigon 1954.154 rightly emphasises the deliberate contrast.

103 Dion. Hal. VII 5–6 (Porsenna and the Aricians), from the 'Cumaean chronicle': see Alföldi 1965.56–72, Cornell 1989.257–64.

104 Vulcan: Ovid *Fasti* VI 626–36, Dion. Hal. IV 2.2–3, Plut. *Mor.* 323C. *Lar familiaris*: Pliny *NH* XXXVI 204, Dion. Hal. and Plut. as above. *Di conserentes*: Arnobius V 18.

105 Late: Mommsen 1881.6 n. 2, Gabba 1967.147–9, Cornell 1975.26, Bremmer 1987b.50. Early: Perret 1942.462, Accame 1959.155, Mazzarino 1960.93–4 and 1966.1.196–9, Alföldi 1973.327–8 and 1974.182. Strasburger (1968.15–16 = 1982.1027–8) takes an intermediate position.

106 'Teti' in Ampolo and Manfredini 1988.273 is Thetis, and therefore not relevant. Heurgon (1961.314), assuming a confusion with Thetis, identifies the oracle as the sixth-century temple of Leucothoe (also a Nereid) at Pyrgi, the port of Caere.

107 Homer *Iliad* XIV 201, 302, Nonnos *Dion.* VIII 160; e.g. Catullus 88.5 (*ultima Tethys*), Archias *Anth. Pal.* VII 214.6 (Τηθύος εἰς πέρατα), Diod. Sic. XVII 104 (Alexander's altar).

108 Herodotus VII 140.2 (attributed to the Pythia), cf. Tzetzes *Chiliades* IX 812 (Bakis), with Fontenrose 1978.171: the opening phrase is 'characteristic of Bakid and Sibylline oracles'.

109 Herodotus I 164–7 (Phocaeans), 170 (Bias of Priene), V 124.2 (Aristagoras of Miletus). Cf. Virg. *Aen.* VIII 333 on Evander coming to Italy: *pelagique extrema sequentem*.

110 Heraclides Ponticus fr. 102 Wehrli (Plut. *Camillus* 22.2); Gottschalk 1980.15–22, 112–27 (on Heraclides' interest in Empedocles and Pythagoras).

111 Iamblichus *Vita Pyth.* 241 (from Aristoxenus: see Diogenes Laertius VIII 14); Gabba 1967.156–9. Cf. Epicharmus fr. 295 Kaibel – no doubt a fourth-century pseudo-Epicharman text, but quite possibly based on a reference to Pythagoras and Rome in the genuine works of the early-fifth-century Sicilian dramatist.

112 Pallottino 1981.44 (my translation), cf. 1991.77–8; Ridgway 1988.668–70. See above, p. 179 nn. 20–2.

113 Iamblichus *Vita Pyth.* 5; Plut. *Rom.* 2.4.

114 So Strasburger 1968.22 (= 1982.1034), rightly. Indirect citation by Plutarch: Mazzarino 1960.389, 1966.1.197 and 2.66–7, Ampolo and Manfredini 1988.275.

115 Mazzarino 1960.390 and 1966.1.195–7, on Aristotle fr. 248 Rose (*Liber Aristotelis de inundacione Nili*).

116 Gisinger 1957.1286 ('somewhere in north-west Africa'). Nonnos (*Dion.* xxxi 103–5) associates the Chremetes with Mt Atlas.

117 E.g. *de ameo* for Ἐξαμίου, *nakithemius* for Ἀπολλοθέμιδος, *Arthaxerxes*, *Athinagoras*, etc. Mazzarino assumes (surely wrongly) that 'Promathos' is right and Plutarch's 'Promathion' an error.

118 So Strasburger 1968.22 = 1982.1034. Classen's idea (1963.452) that all 'Rhomos' versions are late is too schematic, and requires special pleading on no. **11** (Xenagoras).

119 See above, n. 104; Thomsen 1980.58–64; Coarelli (1983.198–9) suggests that the Promathion story could have been created at the time of Servius' seizure of power.

120 Festus (Paulus) 84L, Varro in Augustine *City of God* vii 13, Censorinus 3.1; sometimes identified with the Lar, who was the phantom phallus in some versions of the Ser. Tullius story (Censorinus 3.28, n. 104 above).

121 Festus 492L (*Tages Geni filius*); Cic. *De divinatione* ii 50–1, Ovid *Metamorphoses* xv 553–9, Lydus *De ostentis* 2–3; Tages identified as Tarchon in Strabo v 2.2 (219). For the relevance of Tarchetios (and of Pythagoras) cf. Schultz 1916.

122 Varro in Augustine *City of God* vii 13 for his association with Genius; Macrobius *Sat.* 1 8.5 on the unbinding of his statue as the birth of the gestated seed.

123 Varro *LL* vi 23–4 (with Fay 1914.246) and Plut. *Mor.* 272e on the connection of Larentalia and Saturnalia; Accius in Macrobius *Sat.* 1 7.36–7 (masters serving).

124 Lydus *De mens.* fr. 6 (with Weinstock 1950.46); Pliny *NH* xxviii 39.

125 See n. 99 above on the date of the Chios inscription. Diocles may be earlier in the third century.

126 'Nie Zwillinge!' (n. 62 above).

127 See nn. 58–9 above.

128 Tethys' oracle: nn. 111–12 above.

129 See nn. 70–82 above.

130 Etruscan solar cult, Monte Circeo hero cult? See nn. 19 and 36 above.

5 ITALIAN EVIDENCE

1 Mommsen 1845.301 = 1908.15 (my translation).
2 Detailed discussion and bibliography in Dulière 1979.28–43; see also M. E. Micheli in Cristofani 1985.54–63.
3 Details and bibliography in Dulière 1979.23–7.
4 Dulière 1979.40–2, figs. 12, 14, 15.
5 Crawford 1974.403–4 (no. 388), assuming that the type represents the Capitoline wolf herself; though the attitude is not the same, the distinctive treatment of the hair on the neck and spine certainly suggests that.
6 Livy XXII 1.12 ('signum Martis Appia via ac simulacra luporum sudasse'), x 27.8–9 ('hinc victor Martius lupus . . . gentis nos Martiae et conditoris nostri admonuit'). Note that she-wolves are not specified in either context.
7 Dulière 1979.18 and fig. 1; Momigliano 1984b.387 = 1989.59 and fig. 16 (assuming it to be a wolf).
8 Jurgeit 1980.272–5; his suggested identification (Caeculus), followed without argument by Pairault Massa 1992b.164, is certainly possible, but the Bologna parallel means that it does not have to be a local story.
9 See Binder 1964.123–250: over 120 examples of *die Aussetzung des Königskindes*. Telephus, Paris: Apollodorus III 9.1, 12.5. Cyrus: Herodotus I 107–22.
10 See Adam and Briquel 1982.34–6 for the details.
11 G. Koerte in *Etruskische Spiegel* v (Berlin 1897) 172; Dulière 1979.72–3.
12 Adam and Briquel 1982.36–48, esp. 47: 'Même en supposant une extrême habileté à un graveur moderne, la cohérence de tous les details de la représentation avec un groupe précis de miroirs n'était pas réalisable à l'époque de la découverte.'
13 Klügmann 1879; Jordan in Preller 1883.2.347 n. 3; Peter 1886.1465–6; Rosenberg 1914b.1082–3; Adam and Briquel 1982.51–3; Wiseman 1991.116–17; Pairault Massa 1992a.141–4, 1992b.178–9; Weigel 1992.293; Wiseman 1993.
14 Adam and Briquel 1982.54; cf. 57 on 'la forte proportion des éléments non canoniques par rapport aux éléments canoniques'.
15 Pairault Massa 1992a.141, 1992b.178; *contra* Adam and Briquel 1982.53, rightly. She also assumes that the two birds are the *picus* (woodpecker) and *parra* (nightjar?) mentioned by Servius on *Aen.* I 275 as present at the suckling of Remus and Romulus; the *picus* was Mars' bird, the *parra* Vesta's (Hyginus in Nonius 835L), which makes them appropriate helpers of the sons of Mars and a

Vestal Virgin. But although the identification as a nightjar is not certain (André 1967.118–19, Capponi 1977.449–51 n. 31), 'it is very improbable that the *parra* was an owl' (Poultney 1953.471). The presence of the owl is evidence for the scene *not* being of Remus and Romulus.

16 Adam and Briquel 1982.51.

17 Pairault Massa 1992a.143, 1992b.179, 'concepito sotto forma di un antico re agreste' – i.e. in a form *not* appropriate to her explanation.

18 Wiseman 1993.4–5. For the iconography of Pan in the fourth century, see Brommer 1956.968–82, Borgeaud 1988.53, Hübinger 1992.206; for Quirinus defined by his spear, see Ovid *Fasti* II 477–8, Festus (Paulus) 43L, Plut. *Rom.* 29.1, Servius on *Aen.* I 292, Isidore *Orig.* IX 2.84.

19 Ovid *Fasti* II 583–616 (611–16 quoted); cf. V 129–46 on the Lares Praestites.

20 Cf. Adam and Briquel 1982.41 on the 'double symmetry' of the composition, both horizontal and vertical, concentrating attention on the central scene.

21 Varro *LL* VI 13, 'ab inferis et ferendo, quod ferunt tum epulas ad sepulcrum' (so too Ovid *Fasti* II 569); Festus (Paulus) 75L, 'a ferendis epulis vel a feriendis pecudibus'.

22 Ovid *Fasti* V 79–106, etc.: full references in Maltby 1991.360.

23 Ovid *Fasti* V 129–30, 663–70; for Mercury see also Livy II 21.7, Festus (Paulus) 135L, Martial XII 67.1, etc.

24 Bona Dea Subsaxana, 1 May: Ovid *Fasti* V 148–50, Macrobius *Sat.* I 12.21, Lydus *De mens.* IV 80. Bona Dea identified as Maia and Earth and associated with Mercury: Cornelius Labeo in Macrobius *Sat.* I 12.20–1. Grove of Bona Dea: Propertius IV 9.21–70 (forbidden to men, 51–60); the rape may have been an *aition* for the prohibition, as Faunus' rape of Bona Dea herself was for other elements in her cult (Macrobius *Sat.* I 12.24–5, cf. Butas in Arnobius *Adv. nat.* V 18). Bona Dea as a goddess of the underworld: Macrobius *Sat.* I 12.23 (Proserpina, Hecate).

25 Nonius 197L, Porphyrio and ps.-Acro on Hor. *Epist.* II 2.209, etc.

26 Ovid *Fasti* II 547–56: the *parentatio* offerings were designed to prevent it. For Februus as Dis Pater or Pluto, see Servius on *Georgics* I 43, Lydus *De mens.* IV 25, Isidore *Orig.* V 33.4.

27 Ovid *Fasti* II 610, *infernae nympha paludis*.

28 Ovid *Fasti* II 633–4. Grateful: Caristia (22 Feb.) as Χαριστία implied at Josephus *Ant. Jud.* XIX 272.

29 Hermes talks to Pan because Pan is his son (*Homeric Hymn* 19,

Herodotus II 145.4, Pindar in Servius on *Georgics* I 16, Plato *Cratylus* 408b).

30 Schwegler 1853.432–5, even before the mirror was known; rejected without argument by Mommsen 1881.1 n. 1, surely wrongly.

31 Livy X 23.11–12; cf. XXII 1.12 (n. 6 above) for the temple of Mars outside the Porta Capena.

32 E.g. Soltau 1909.121–2, Dulière 1979.58–62; *contra* Carcopino 1925.23–4.

33 Virg. *Aen.* VIII 631–4, Livy I 4.6; cf. Dion. Hal. I 79.6, Ovid *Fasti* II 418, *OGR* 20.3 (licking).

34 Crawford 1974.137; 1985.30–2.

35 His colleague was Q. Fabius Pictor, whose family claimed descent from Hercules (Plut. *Fab. Max.* 1.1, Festus (Paulus) 77L, Sil. It. *Pun.* VI 627–36); see Altheim 1938.144–50 for the possible significance of the coin-types (*pace* Crawford 1974.714).

36 Terror of Gauls: Livy X 10.12, 21.2–3, 26.13; cf. 28.8–9 for the battle itself. Threatening prodigies: Livy X 23.1–2, Zonaras VIII 1 (pp. 118–20).

37 Dion. Hal. IV 61.2, Plut. *Cam.* 31.4; cf. Livy I 55.6, V 54.7 (*caput rerum*).

38 For good reason: Vitruvius *Arch.* I 7.1.

39 Livy X 27.8–9 (n. 6 above).

40 Cic. *Brutus* 55 (on Ti. Coruncanius), cf. *De domo* 136 (on 154 BC). Also *antiqui commentarii* on theatrical festivals, third and second centuries BC: Cic. *Brutus* 60 (death of Naevius), 72 (Livius Andronicus in 240).

41 Livy IV 3.9 (secret), X 6.3–9.2 (*lex Ogulnia*).

42 Livy X 23.12 (*infantium conditorum urbis*), contrast 27.9 (*conditoris nostri*). See above, pp. 5–6.

43 As suggested by Rosenberg 1914b.1080.

44 *CIL* VI 33856: 'Marti invicto patri et aeternae urbis suae conditoribus dominus noster imp. Maxent[iu]s p. f. invictus Aug.' And on the side: 'Dedicata die XI Kal. Maias per Furium Octavianum v. c. cur. aed. sacr.'

45 Dion. Hal. I 79.10; Diodorus XXXVII 11.1 (Italian oath to Livius Drusus, 91 BC).

46 Martianus Capella II 160; contrast 155 on the Lares, between Sun and moon.

47 Varro *LL* V 54, Livy I 4.5, Ovid *Fasti* II 411–12, Plut. *Rom.* 4.1, Festus 326L, Pliny *NH* XV 77, Tac. *Ann.* XIII 58, Serv. *Aen.* VIII 90, *OGR* 20.3–4. The earliest evidence for the *ficus* is on the pottery of Cales, *c.* 250–180 BC (Dulière 1979.67–71, figs. 176–80).

48 Pliny *NH* xv 77. Lupercal (or Cermalus): Varro *LL* v 54, Serv. *Aen.* vIII 90. Comitium: Tac. *Ann.* xIII 58; also on the *anaglypha Traiani* (Torelli 1982.98–106, plates IV.1 and 2).

49 Dion. Hal. I 79.8. Festus 168–70L (the Comitium fig-tree as *ficus Navia*) may imply that *ad ficum Ruminalem* was still the Lupercal, despite Pliny and Tacitus.

50 Plut. *Rom.* 19.7, Festus (Paulus) 34L, etc.; cf. C. Titius in Macrobius *Sat.* III 16.15.

6 THE LUPERCALIA

1 Rationalising historians who insisted on a human foster-mother still had to call her a *lupa*: see Livy I 4.7, Plut. *Rom.* 4.3, Dion. Hal. I 84.4, Lactantius *Inst. div.* I 20.2, *OGR* 21.1–2 (from Valerius Antias), etc.; for a different explanation, Licinius Macer fr. 2P.

2 Varro *LL* v 54, Plut. *Rom.* 3.5 (Fabius Pictor *FGrH* 809 F 4a).

3 Varro in Festus 332L (cf. 326L), Plut. *Rom.* 4.1, *QR* 57 (*Mor.* 278c), *Mor.* 320d, Pliny *NH* xv 77. *Rumis/ruma* as *mamma*: Varro *RR* II 11.5 and in Nonius 246L, Augustine *CD* IV 11 (Varro *Ant. div.* fr. 113 Cardauns), on the goddess Rumina.

4 Ovid *Fasti* II 421, Serv. *Aen.* vIII 343; cf. Plut. *Rom.* 21.3 on the Lupercalia. Ficus Ruminalis at Lupercal: Serv. *Aen.* vIII 90, Ovid *Fasti* II 411–22. Ficus Ruminalis at Cermalus: Varro *LL* v 54, Plut. *Rom.* 3.5–4.1, *Mor.* 320c ('near'); implied at *OGR* 20.3–4. Lupercal at Cermalus: implied in Ovid *Fasti* II 381–422, Clem. Alex. *Stromateis* I 108.3.

5 Clem. Alex. *Stromateis* I 108.3; cf. Eratosthenes in the scholiast to Plato *Phaedrus* 244b (Wiseman 1995). Eratosthenes on Sibyls: *FGrH* 241 F 26 (Varro in Lactantius *Div. inst.* I 6.9, Suda s.v. *Sibyllai*).

6 Ovid *Fasti* I 467, Dion. Hal. I 31.1, Plut. *Rom.* 21.2, *QR* 56 (*Mor.* 278c), *OGR* 5.2, Martianus Capella II 159, Isidore *Orig.* I 4.1; cf. Virg. *Aen.* vIII 340 (from *canere*), Solinus 1.10, Serv. *Aen.* vIII 336, Augustine *CD* IV 11.

7 Serv. *Aen.* vIII 90, cf. 63 ('quasi ripas ruminans et exedens').

8 Plut. *Rom.* 4.1, *OGR* 20.4, Festus 332L (distinguished from the Varronian etymology).

9 Plut. *Mor.* 320c; cf. Serv. *Aen.* vIII 90, for the Tiber flowing by the Lupercal.

10 E.g. Theocritus 1.15–18, Longus *Daphnis and Chloe* II 26–7; see Borgeaud 1988.111.

11 Virg. *Aen.* vIII 343–4 and Servius; Dion. Hal. I 32.3; cf. Plut. *Rom.*

21.3, *QR* 68 (*Mor.* 280c) on the Lupercalia, Ovid *Fasti* II 423–4 on the Luperci.

12 Servius on *Aeneid* VIII 343: 'ergo ideo et Evander deo gentis suae sacravit locum et nominavit Lupercal, quod praesidio ipsius numinis lupi a pecudibus arcerentur.'

13 Ibid.: 'sub monte Palatino est quaedam spelunca, in qua de capro luebatur, id est sacrificabatur; unde et Lupercal nonnulli dictum putant.' Cf. Quintilian I 5.66, the same derivation for the Lupercalia.

14 Dion. Hal. I 31–2; cf. Virg. *Aen.* VIII 333–6, Ovid *Fasti* I 465–542, Pausanias VIII 43.2, *OGR* 5.

15 Dion. Hal. I 32.4–5, 79.8.

16 Dion. Hal. I 80.1 (Tubero fr. 3P); cf. Livy I 5.1–3.

17 The best discussions, giving references to earlier bibliography, are Smits 1946.19–32, Ulf 1982 and Pötscher 1984.

18 Wiseman 1995, concentrating on the identity of the deity or deities concerned.

19 Ovid *Fasti* II 267–8.

20 *Sacerdotes*: Varro *LL* v 83 and 85, Serv. *Aen.* VIII 663. *Hieropoioi*: Dion. Hal. I 80.2 (Tubero fr. 3P), Dio XLIV 6.2. See Ulf 1982.44–51, who has to ignore or explain away these passages because he believes the Luperci were not priests of any sort.

21 Varro *LL* v 85, *Fasti Praenestini* 19 March, Ovid *Fasti* III 259–60, etc. For Luperci and Salii mentioned together, cf. Virg. *Aen.* VIII 663 (with Servius); the Salii too were supposedly Arcadian in origin (Plut. *Numa* 13.4 on Salios of Mantinea).

22 Cic. *Cael.* 26 (*sodalitas*); *ILS* 2676, 4948 (*collegium*); *ILLRP* 696, *ILS* 1924, 2676, 9039 (*magistri*). For a possible meeting-house (third or fourth century AD), see Dulière 1979.255–9.

23 L. Herennius Balbus was a member, but also a champion of old-fashioned morality at the Caelius trial (Cic. *Cael.* 25–30); presumably he had not been running about naked with the young men a month and a half earlier.

24 Plut. *Rom.* 21.4–5; Pötscher 1984.233–40.

25 Hide: Plut. *Rom.* 21.5, Dion. Hal. I 80.1 (Tubero fr. 3P), Serv. auct. on *Aen.* VIII 343, *OGR* 22.1, Festus (Paulus) 76L, Ovid *Fasti* II 445–6, Val. Max. II 2.9, Propertius IV 1.25; cf. Plut. *Caes.* 61.2, *Ant.* 12.1 ('shaggy thongs'). Butchery: Bruit Zaidman and Schmitt Pantel 1992.224–7.

26 Ovid *Fasti* II 361–80, esp. 363 and 373 for the spits; Romulus' laugh (377) may be an allusion to the ritual laugh reported by Plutarch. Cf. *OGR* 22.2–3 for games and feats of strength.

27 *ILS* 1923, 4948, *CIL* VI 33421; Festus (Paulus) 78L, *Faviani*

et Quintiliani; Festus 308L; Ovid *Fasti* II 377–8, Fabii and Quintilii.

28 Luperci as performers (*ludii*): Varro in Tertullian *Spect.* 5.3 (*Ant. div.* fr. 80 Cardauns). Planned theatre at Lupercal, implying performance: Velleius I 15.3. *Spectaculo sui*: Val. Max. II 2.9.

29 Ovid *Fasti* II 373–80; for a similar prohibition, applied to the Pinarii at the Ara Maxima sacrifice to Hercules, see Livy I 7.13, Veranius in Macrobius *Sat.* III 6.14, Dion. Hal. I 40.4, etc.

30 Val. Max. II 2.9, 'epularum hilaritate ac vino largiore provecti'.

31 Mommsen 1864.17. For the alternative explanation, '*cut* from the womb', see Pliny *NH* VII 47, Festus (Paulus) 50L, etc.

32 *Discurrere*: Ovid *Fasti* II 285 (of Faunus); Festus (Paulus) 49L, *OGR* 22.1, Tertullian *De spect.* 5 (Varro *Ant. div.* fr. 80 Cardauns), Minucius Felix *Octavius* 22.8, Gelasius *Adv. Andromachum* 17 (*CSEL* 35.1 p. 458). Greek equivalents: Plut. *Rom.* 21.5, *Caes.* 61.2, *Ant.* 12.1, *QR* 68 (*Mor.* 280b–c). Running *round*: Dion. Hal. I 80.1 (Tubero fr. 3P), Plut. *Rom.* 21.4, 21.8.

33 Varro *De gente pop. R.* fr. 21 Fraccaro (Augustine *CD* XVIII 12), *LL* VI 34; cf. Ovid *Fasti* II 32, V 102. For *lustrare* as *circumagere*, see (e.g.) Cato *Agr.* 141.1.

34 Lupercal: Dion. Hal. I 80.1 (Tubero fr. 3P), Plut. *Rom.* 21.4. Comitium: Cic. *Phil.* II 85, Dio XLIV 11.2, XLV 30.1, Appian *BC* II 109, etc. (Rostra, Forum).

35 Varro *LL* VI 34. For the Lupercalia as *dies februatus*, see Varro *LL* VI 13, Festus (Paulus) 75–6L, Censorinus 22.14–15, Plut. *Rom.* 21.3, *QR* 68 (*Mor.* 280b).

36 Festus (Paulus) 42L, 49L, respectively on *crepae* and *crepi*, both implausibly derived from *crepitus*. For the Luperci as goats, see Pötscher 1984.232–45.

37 To Silvanus? See Wiseman 1995 on Pliny *NH* XV 77. Did the dog sacrifice take place at this point (n. 45 below)?

38 Justin XLIII 1.7, on Evander's foundation of the Lupercal: 'ipsum dei simulacrum nudum caprina pelle amictum est, quo habitu nunc Romae Lupercalibus decurritur.'

39 Tubero fr. 3P (Dion. Hal. I 80.1, p. 79 above); Ovid *Fasti* V 101 (*cinctuti*), cf. Val. Max. II 2.9 (*cincti*); Plut. *Rom.* 21.5 (*perizōmata*). Also called *campestre* (Isidore *Orig.* XIX 22.5, 33.1), and identified by Augustine as the fig-leaf covering of Adam and Eve: Genesis 3.7 (*perizōmata* in the Vulgate), Augustine *CD* XIV 17 (*campestria*).

40 Augustus: Suetonius *Aug.* 31.4. Imperial iconography: Veyne 1960, Schumacher 1968–9 (Taf. 10–11), Wiseman 1995.

41 Val. Max. II 2.9 (*obvios*), *OGR* 22.1 (*occursantes quosque*), Plut. *Rom.* 21.5–6, *Caes.* 61.2, *Ant.* 12.1 (*tous empodōn*, etc.).

42 Orosius IV 2.2 (date), Augustine *CD* III 18 (Aesculapius); Livy fr. 14W–M (Gelasius *Adv. Andr.* 12, *CSEL* 35.1 p. 457), from book XIII or XIV; Ovid *Fasti* II 425–52 (aetiology). See Otto 1913.183–5, Holleman 1974.20–1. An Arcadian parallel at Pausanias VIII 23.1: women flogged at the Dionysus festival at Alea, after consultation of Delphi (about infertility?).

43 Festus (Paulus) 49L, 75–6L: 'obvias quasque feminas ferire', 'quo die mulieres februabantur a Lupercis' (n. 35 above for *februare*); Servius auctus on *Aen.* VIII 343, cf. Juvenal II 148.

44 Plut. *Rom.* 21.6; Varro *LL* VI 34, Ovid *Fasti* II 32, V 102. Cf. also Dion. Hal. I 80.1 (Tubero fr. 3P), quoted at p. 79 above.

45 Plut. *Rom.* 21.5 (mentioned separately from the goat sacrifice at the Lupercal), *QR* 68 = *Mor.* 280b–c. Note that Silvanus (n. 37 above) is regularly portrayed with a dog: e.g. Dorcey 1992, illustrations 1, 2, 7, 10.

46 Varro in Censorinus 22.15: 'salem calidum ferunt quod februum appellant' (n. 35 above); cf. Ovid *Fasti* II 23–4 on *februa* as toasted spelt with salt.

47 Servius auctus on *Ecl.* 8.82: *adiecto sale cocto* (see previous note). On 15 September the *praetor maximus* of the archaic city drove a nail into the Capitoline temple wall to mark the year (Livy VII 3.5–8 cites the inscription).

48 Vesta's fire: Livy V 52.7, Val. Max. IV 4.11, Plut. *Numa* 9.5, etc. Capitol as *caput rerum*: Livy I 55.6, V 54.7, *Vir.ill.* 8.4, Florus I 7.9; cf. Dion. Hal. IV 61.2, Plut. *Cam.* 31.4 ('head of Italy').

49 Cic. *Cael.* 26, trans. Austin 1952.81.

50 Varro in Augustine *CD* XVIII 17; see Burkert 1983.84–93 on the *Lykaia*.

51 See for instance Ulf 1982.95–144 (explaining the ritual), Bremmer 1987a (explaining the myth).

52 Pp. 46–8 above, on Hesiod *Theog.* 1011–16, Nonnos *Dion.* XIII 328–32, XXXVII 56–60. Faunus as king: Dion. Hal. I 31.2, 43.1, Suetonius *Vitellius* 1.2, Justin XLIII 1.6–9, etc.

53 C. Acilius *FGrH* 813 F 2 (Plut. *Rom.* 21.7), Ovid *Fasti* II 267–8, 361, 423–4, etc.

54 See above, n. 36.

55 Eratosthenes: n. 5 above. Mirror: p. 68 above.

56 Dates, probably more or less reliable (and confirmed by archaeological evidence for the Castor temple): Livy II 42.5, IV 29.7, *epit.* XI.

57 Tibullus II 5.25–30, trans. White 1993.182. Tibullus' contemporary Propertius, in a similar context, imagined a skin-clad ploughman (*arator*) as a proto-Lupercus (Prop. IV 1.25–6).

58 See Cairns 1979.79–81 for the multiple allusions. Pales was an eponym of the Palatine (Solinus 1.15).
59 See above, nn. 47–8 (archaic); Gelasius *Adv. Andr.* 13–15 (late fifth century AD).
60 See above, nn. 5–13.
61 See above, nn. 4 and 11–13.
62 Servius auctus on *Aen.* 1 273. For Vestals getting water from the Tiber, cf. Val. Max. VIII 1.abs.5 (Tuccia).
63 Pan and caves (e.g. Euripides *Helen* 186–90): Borgeaud 1988.49–51. Cave of Mars: Virg. *Aen.* VIII 630, Fabius Pictor *Ann. Lat.* fr. 4P (*spelunca Martis*).
64 See above, nn. 50–1 (wolves), 11 (Lykaion).
65 Varro in Arnobius *Adv. Nat.* IV 3. In Varro's account (n. 50 above), the Luperci were *lupi*, and so, no doubt, the *lupa* was Luperca.
66 C. Acilius *FGrH* 813 F 2 (Plut. *Rom.* 21.7), Ovid *Fasti* II 359–80, Servius auctus on *Aen.* VIII 343.
67 Tubero fr. 3P (Dion. Hal. 1 80.1–2), Livy 1 5.3; cf. *OGR* 22.1–3 (from the *libri pontificales*), where Remus' capture arises from the 'games' element in the Lupercalia (n. 26 above).
68 Butas in Plut. *Rom.* 21.6; Val. Max. II 2.9.
69 Ovid *Fasti* II 425–52: infertility among the Sabine women.
70 Explicit at Dion. Hal. 1 79.11. The apologetic tone of Livy 1 4.9 and Plut. *Rom.* 6.2–3 implies a hostile version that called them brigands and robbers: see Strasburger 1968.32 = 1982.1044.
71 E.g. Dion. Hal. 1 79.8, 80.1 (p. 79 above); Livy 1 5.1–2, Val. Max. II 2.9, Ovid *Fasti* II 421–4.

7 THE ARGUMENTS

1 Momigliano 1982.8 = 1985.106.
2 Niebuhr 1828.174. Not in the 1811 edition: no doubt Niebuhr got the idea during his years as ambassador in Rome (1816–23).
3 Dion. Hal. 1 85.6, 87.3; Plut. *Rom.* 9.4, 11.1; *OGR* 23.1; cf. Ennius *Ann.* 1 77 Sk (pp. 6–7 above), Festus (Paulus) 345L.
4 Niebuhr 1828.187 n. 568, 1849.39 (where 'three miles' is evidently a Freudian slip). S. Paolo is about 3.2 km from the Palatine (five Roman miles would be 7.4 km), and about 2.4 km from the line of the Servian wall (thirty *stadia* would be 5.76 km). See pp. 114–16.
5 Niebuhr 1849.40.
6 Niebuhr 1828.248–51 (quotation from p. 250), 1849.46–50.
7 Festus (Paulus) 345L, Dion. Hal. 1 86.2, Plut. *Rom.* 9.4; Niebuhr 1849.39–40.

8 Niebuhr 1828.251; cf. 1811.177–80, 1849.10–14 on the 'lays of ancient Rome'.

9 Ovid *Fasti* II 615, V 143 (p. 70 above); Schwegler 1853.434–5, cf. 417, 435–6 on Niebuhr.

10 Schwegler 1853.436–8.

11 Festus (Paulus) 345L; Gellius *NA* XIII 14.5–6, Seneca *De brev. vit.* 13.8; Schwegler 1853.438–40.

12 Neither Schwegler nor Niebuhr mentioned the explanation of the name Remus *a tarditate* (*OGR* 21.5), though the *remores* in that passage have the same etymology as the *aves remores* in Festus.

13 Mommsen 1881.2 n. 1: 'der politische Begriff des Königs und der sacrale des Lar weit aus einander liegen'.

14 Cassius Hemina fr. 11P (p. 5 above); Mommsen 1881.10–12, cf. 19–21.

15 Mommsen 1881.9. Cf. 16 n. 2, dismissing as irrelevant both Remuria and the *aves remores*; as for *OGR* 21.5 (n. 12 above), the derivation from *remorari* 'has no basis in the legend itself'.

16 Mommsen 1881.21: 'mit der übrigen Remusfabel steht sie . . . in einer gewissen Disharmonie'.

17 Benedict Niese, in an important article in 1888, followed Mommsen but was more chronologically precise: the story of the twins as sons of the war-god should belong no earlier than the end of the fourth century (Niese 1888.495–6).

18 Schulze 1904.219, 368, 579–81.

19 *Inscr. Ital.* XIII 1.24–5, 362–3, Livy III 33.3 (*Romulius* in the MSS); cf. Tac. *Ann.* VI 11 on Romulius Denter, 'city prefect under Romulus'. *Tribus*: Festus (Paulus) 331L, 'Romulia' tribe on land taken from Veii by Romulus; *CIL* VI 10211, Varro *LL* V 56 (fifth tribe, after the four *urbanae*).

20 Festus (Paulus) 38L.

21 A sixth-century *rumelnas* is now known from Orvieto (i.e. Volsinii): De Simone 1975.135.

22 I.e. *ruma* (Schulze 1904.581)? Note *Roma* spelt *Ruma* on a second-century BC milestone from Vulci (*ILLRP*² 1288).

23 Kretschmer 1909.288–94.

24 Kretschmer 1909.295–302 (quotation from p. 302).

25 Propertius III 9.50; Kretschmer 1909.301–2. Cf. also Florus I 1.8 on Remus as the *prima victima* – wrongly (I think) dismissed by Kretschmer as a mere 'rhetorical expression'.

26 Festus (Paulus) 6–7L, offering various implausible explanations; Kretschmer 1909.302–3 (also for the order of names *Remus et Romulus*). However, Kretschmer does not mention Lydus *De mag.* I 5 on Remus as the elder.

27 He offered only *CIL* XI 1554 (Faesulae). Remmii occur at Rome, but the only known senatorial Remmius, in the nineties BC (*Vir. ill.* 66.2, cf. Cic. *Rosc. Am.* 55), is much too late to be of any significance.

28 Mesk 1914.12–14, explicitly after Schulze.

29 Mesk 1914.14–15; Pais 1913.299.

30 Rosenberg 1914a.597–8, 1914b.1079 (cf. n. 27 above); 1914b.1074–7 (Romulus and *ruma*), 1077–9 (Greek etymologies), 1079–83 (fifth-century twins).

31 Rosenberg 1914b.1090.

32 Last 1928.365–8. Contrast the scepticism of Gaetano De Sanctis and Karl von Holzinger, both of whom rejected Schulze's theory: De Sanctis 1907.207 = 1956.203, Holzinger 1912.197.

33 Carcopino 1925.73: 'the Luperci created Romulus and Remus'.

34 Carcopino 1925.67–75; dismissed by Last (1928.367–8).

35 Carcopino 1925.60–1. A similar idea had been suggested by Soltau (1909.125), and rejected by Holzinger (1912.195–7).

36 Carcopino 1925.76.

37 'Die Sage . . . *politischen* Impulsen entstammt' (Strasburger 1968.20 = 1982.1031).

38 Classen 1963.454–7; cf. 1965.402 (the twins symbolised 'eine ursprungliche Zweiheit' – not explained).

39 Strasburger 1968.23 = 1982.1044. Detailed argument at 24–6 = 1036–8 (1); 28–31 = 1040–3 (2); 32 = 1044 (3); 33–5 = 1045–7 (4); 35–7 = 1047–9 (6); 5 and 7 not discussed. See 27–8 = 1039–40 (also Jocelyn 1971.52–3) on 'suckled by a wolf, therefore wolfish by nature'.

40 Jocelyn 1971.54–5, 56–7 (cf. Plut. *Rom.* 9.6–7).

41 Strasburger 1968.7–8, 38–43 = 1982.1019–20, 1050–5.

42 E.g. Classen 1971.482–3, Schröder 1971.163, Alföldi 1974.107, Cornell 1975.6–11, Momigliano 1984b.439–40.

43 Momigliano 1984b.440; cf. Cornell 1975.11 ('most myths contain elements that are embarrassing to moralists').

44 Item 1, for example, is merely the corollary of the honorific 'son of Mars' motif.

45 See above, p. 45: Niese's article is referred to with approval by Strasburger (1968.19 = 1982.1031).

46 Grant 1971.102 ('Reminii' may be a misprint); Schröder 1971.155; Cornell 1975.28–9. The ancient explanation of the name is dismissed by Grant in a footnote as 'fanciful' (*OGR* 21.5, Grant 1971.245 n. 34).

47 Grant 1971.102; Schröder 1971.65. Similarly, the fratricide 'is an extremely common theme in the mythologies of the world' (Grant

1971.110), but no parallels are offered for its presence in a foundation-legend.

48 Cornell 1975.29–31, giving proper credit to Schwegler on the Lares (n. 9 above).

49 Cornell 1975.29. Presumably the argument falls if the name *can* be explained? Cornell does not mention the derivation *a tarditate* (*OGR* 21.5).

50 Cornell 1975.29–30, referring to Weinstock 1971.332 on earlier versions of the Alföldi thesis ('no evidence, no discussion, and no proof was produced, and yet the assertion was often repeated . . .').

51 Alföldi 1974.69 (my translation). See Binder 1964 for the 'exposure of the royal child' motif, 1964.74–5 on the twins as double kings in the 'original myth' of Rome.

52 Alföldi 1974.69–71 (Turks), 72 (special pleading on duality).

53 Alföldi 1974.74, referring to 1965.239 n. 1 (also to 1965.277–8 on Lavinium – i.e. Dion. Hal. 1 59.4–5 – but suckling is not involved there either). The reference at 1965.239 to 'the authentic atmosphere of the genuine legend of Roman origins' is a clear *petitio principii*.

54 Alföldi 1974.76 (my translation); cf. pp. 63–5 above.

55 Alföldi 1974.91, 117, 171–2.

56 Cf. Alföldi 1974.119, citing διχῇ at Dion. Hal. 1 85.4 and ignoring τριχῇ at 1 80.2; neither version, of course, tells us anything about Eurasia in the second millennium BC.

57 Alföldi 1974.105–6 (my translation), evidently accepted by Cornell (1975.31).

58 Cf. Alföldi 1974.116–17 on the 'very ancient' names of Remus and Romulus (following Schulze and Rosenberg).

59 Alföldi 1974.157 (my translation); cf.165–6 on Romulus' 'elimination' of Remus.

60 Momigliano 1977b.162 = 1980.685: 'Dopo la lettura del suo libro, rimaniamo per Roma arcaica al punto di prima.'

61 Versnel 1976.392, 399.

62 Binder 1964.29–38, Alföldi 1974.107–50; Versnel 1976.398.

63 Briquel 1980.267–300, esp. 294–5, 299–300.

64 Bremmer 1987a.36–7 on twins (the Romans 'used this atypical position to accentuate the special status of their founders'), 37–8 on the fratricide (an excellent critical analysis, but no solution).

65 Momigliano 1989.58–9 (= 1984b.386–7).

66 Niese 1888.482 (p. 45 above).

67 See above, nn. 2–5.

68 See above, nn. 25–6.

69 *OGR* 21.5; cf. nn. 12, 15, 46 and 49 above.

8 THE LIFE AND DEATH OF REMUS

1 Tac. *Ann.* I 1: 'urbem Romam a principio reges habuere; libertatem et consulatum L. Brutus instituit.'

2 Sall. *Cat.* 6.7 (*binos imperatores*), Livy II 18.8 (*pari potestate*), Dion. Hal. IV 73.4 (like Spartan kings), Plut. *Publ.* 1.4, etc. Explicit statement at Eutropius I 9.1: 'hinc consules coepere, pro uno rege duo, hac causa creati, ut si unus malus esse voluisset, alter eum habens potestatem similem coerceret.'

3 Livy II 7.5–6, Dion. Hal. V 12.3, 19.1, Plut. *Publ.* 10.1, 11.1.

4 Mommsen 1887.77: 'das heisst Genossen, Collegen'. The Romans derived the word from *consulere* (Cic. *De or.* II 165, etc.) or *consilia* (Dion. Hal. IV 76.2).

5 Livy III 55.12, VII 3.5 (from L. Cincius' collection of documents); cf. Festus 276L (quoting Cincius), 518L (quoting the *Twelve Tables*).

6 Livy IV 13.7 (L. Minucius), where the anachronistic position of *praefectus annonae* is due either to Livy himself or to his source – no doubt Licinius Macer, who discovered the *libri lintei* in the temple of Moneta on the Capitol (Livy IV 20.8).

7 Cic. *Rep.* II 56 (*novum genus imperii*), Livy II 18.8, Dion. Hal. V 70.1, 73.1–2, etc.; Festus 216L (*magister populi*).

8 Cic. *Rep.* II 61.3, Livy III 33.1 (*iterum mutata forma civitatis*).

9 Livy IV 7.1 (*pro consulibus*), Dion. Hal. XI 62.1.

10 Tac. *Ann.* I 1: 'dictaturae ad tempus sumebantur, neque decemviralis potestas ultra biennium neque tribunorum militum consulare ius diu valuit' (sixty years?). Cf. Claudius in *ILS* 212.1.28–36.

11 Ogilvie 1965.230–1; Drummond 1989.186–8; Momigliano 1975.308–16 (quotations from pp. 313 and 316).

12 Drummond 1989.173–6 (quotation from p. 176); cf. 176–7 for the historical inference about the origin of the Republic.

13 Wiseman 1979.12–16 on the second century BC (cf. 45–6 on the sort of research that was involved).

14 Pinsent 1975.64 (on 385–342 BC); cf. 19 on the supposed chronicle of the *pontifex maximus*: 'There should be little doubt that such meagre records of that kind as were made or as survived were subjected over the years to a great deal of amplification, misinterpretation and even plain invention in support of different political and constitutional theories.'

15 For the sceptical argument, see Wiseman 1987.293–6 (with addenda at 384); *contra*, Cornell 1986 and 1989.248–50.

16 Momigliano 1975.309. Cf. Ogilvie 1965.231: 'the collegiate principle of equal *imperium* was a feature of the Roman constitution which . . . the Romans themselves regarded as primeval'.

17 But the Brutus legend implies that *he*, not a pair of consuls, will be the ruler of Rome (Livy I 56.10, Dion. Hal. IV 69.3, *Vir. ill.* 10.3, Dio II 12); Virgil's phraseology (*Aen.* VI 817–18) implies as much.

18 Momigliano 1975.298.

19 Namely 423, 421, 413–409, 393–392. (The consular *fasti* are conveniently reproduced in *CAH²* VII 2.628–44.)

20 Mommsen 1881.11–12, 20–1; cf. 22, dating the legend 'between the expulsion of the kings and the Samnite wars'.

21 Livy VI 35.5, 37.10 (quotation, from a speech of '369 BC'), 40.15–41.3 (Ap. Claudius' opposition), VII 1.1.

22 Dion. Hal. XIV 22 ('ten years of *stasis*'), Florus I 26 (*seditio*), Ovid *Fasti* I 643–4 (secession of *plebs*), Diodorus XV 75.1, Plut. *Cam.* 39.1 (*anarchia*); Livy VI 35.10 (no magistrates for five years), 42.9 (*ingentia certamina*, 'nearly' a secession).

23 Livy VII 17.10–18.10, 19.5–6, etc. (backlash); VII 42.1–2: 'invenio apud quosdam L. Genucium tribunum plebis tulisse ad plebem . . . utique liceret consules ambos plebeios creari' (cf. Zonaras VII 25.9).

24 Thus Cornell 1989.334–9; see Billows 1989 for detailed discussion, with a convincing explanation for the false tradition.

25 Mommsen 1881.1: 'Ein Doppelgründer für ein als Einheit empfundene Institution ist ein innerer Widerspruch.'

26 Dulière 1979.53 ('on est tenté, en effet, d'attribuer à ce geste une portée politique'), followed by Coarelli 1985.90. 'Power-sharing': Cornell 1989.338, 342.

27 See n. 22 above. Appius' speech: Wiseman 1979.77–92, esp. 84–5. Camillus: Livy VI 42.4–8, Plut. *Cam.* 40–2.

28 Livy VI 42.9–10 (Everyman translation, 1914), cf. Kraus 1994.330.

29 Livy VII 9.5 ('quaesita ea propriae familiae laus'), cf. VII 37.8, 39.3 for likely Licinian items.

30 *Vir. ill.* 20.2. Livy (VII 2.1) puts Stolo's consulship in 364, the Capitoline *fasti* put it in 361; both sources call L. Sextius Lateranus (*cos.* 366) the *primus e plebe*.

31 Ovid *Fasti* I 637–44 (following a secession of the *plebs*), Plut. *Cam.* 42.3–4.

32 Plut. *C. Gracchus* 17.6, Appian *BC* I 26.120, Augustine *CD* III 25; see Levick 1978, esp. 218–20. For Camillus and the late-republican *popularis* tradition, cf. Livy V 32.8 and *Vir. ill.* 23.4: a tribune called L. Appuleius Saturninus has him exiled in 391.

33 Macer on Sulla: Sall. *Hist.* III 48M. Macer on dictators: Dion. Hal. v 74.4 (fr. 10P), cf. 77.4–5 (on Sulla), with Gabba 1960.218, 1991.142. See also Gabba 1960.207–16 on the *patrum auctoritas*, reintroduced by Sulla to control the tribunes (cf. Macer in Sall. *Hist.* III 48.15M).

34 Cf. Livy v 18.3: *concordia* in the story of P. Licinius Calvus and his son (evidently from Macer). Also IX 46.3–6: Macer's favourable treatment of Cn. Flavius, and the latter's shrine to Concordia (cf. Pliny *NH* XXXIII 19); see Levick 1978.220–1.

35 Livy VI 42.11–12: 'sedatae discordiae sunt . . . tandem in concordiam redactis ordinibus.'

36 See above, nn. 23–4. Pinsent (1975.13–14, 65, 69) even entertains the possibility that Genucius was really the first plebeian consul.

37 Livy VII 6.8–9; Ovid *Met.* xv 565–621 ('ut victor domito veniebat ab hoste'), Val. Max. v 6.3 ('praetori paludato portam egredienti'). The gate was the Porta Raudusculana, on the road to Ostia; Pliny (*NH* XI 123) attributes the Cipus story to *Latia historia*, and in Ovid Cipus is promised rule over *Latiae arces* as well as Rome.

38 Varro *De vita pop. R.* fr. 94 Riposati (P. Aelius Paetus), Pliny *NH* X 41 (Aelius Tubero), Frontinus *Strat.* IV 5.14 (C. Aelius, or Caelius or Laelius?); Val. Max. v 6.4, 'before the battle of Cannae', but the Aelii flourished in the following generation (consuls in 201 and 198, censors in 199 and 194).

39 Explicit in Ovid on Cipus: *Met.* xv 577, *Tyrrhenae gentis haruspex*.

40 The Aelian homestead was *in agro Veienti* (Val. Max. IV 4.8), and the inscription of an early *C. Genucio Cleusino prai[tor]* has recently been found at Caere (*Studi Etruschi* 52 (1984) 404, *Archaeological Reports* 32 (1985–6) 107); the *Genucii Clepsinae* named on the consular *fasti* for 276, 271 and 270 evidently owe their *cognomen* to a false transcription of *clevsina*, a fourth-century aristocratic family at Tarquinii.

41 Livy X 9.2 (C. Genucius and P. Aelius Paetus); Zonaras VIII 1 (p. 120) for the successful prophecy of 'Manius the Etruscan' in 296.

42 Curtius ('362 BC'): Livy VII 6.1–6, Varro *LL* v 148, Val. Max. v 6.2, Pliny *NH* xv 78, Zonaras VII 25. Decii (340 and 295 BC): Livy VIII 9, X 28, etc. The Curtius story also involves the *haruspices*: Varro *LL* v 148; cf. Livy VII 6.3 (*vates*), Dion. Hal. XIV 11.1 (Sibylline Books).

43 Marcius: Mommsen (1879.113–52) analyses the traditions; see especially *Vir. ill.* 19.2 for a consulship ('491 BC') unknown to the *fasti*. Brutus: see n. 17 above; Livy II 5.5–8, 6.6–9; Dion. Hal. v 8,

15.1–2; Plut. *Publ.* 6, 9.1–2. For the disputed question whether – and if so, how – M. Brutus the tyrannicide was descended from L. Brutus, see Posidonius *FGrH* 87 F 40 (Plut. *Brutus* 1.6–7), Dio XLIV 12.1.

44 *OGR* 21.5; cf. Ennius *Ann.* fr. 77 Sk (pp. 6–7 above) for *Remora*.

45 *OGR* 23.4, cf. Diodorus VIII 6; p. 8 above.

46 Alcimus *FGrH* 560 F 4 (Festus 326L): son of Aeneas and Tyrrhenia, father of Alba, whose son Rhomos founded Rome; see p. 52 above.

47 Promathion *FGrH* 817 F 1 (Plut. *Rom.* 2.4); see p. 59 above.

48 Lydus *De mag.* 1 5: Remus elder, Romulus thoughtless (πράττων ἀλόγως τὰ προσπίπτοντα). Romulus as *Altellus* at Festus (Paulus) 6L may imply subordinate status: 'fit diminutive . . . ab alterno altellus'. The canonical order of the names 'Remus et Romulus' implies Remus' seniority: see Naevius in Donatus on Terence *Ad.* 537 (*Alimonium Remi et Romuli*), Cassius Hemina fr. 11P, Varro in Festus 332L, Cic. *De leg.* 1 8, Diodorus VIII 3, 5, Verrius Flaccus *Fasti Praen.* 23 December (*Inscr. Ital.* XIII 2.138–9), Tac. *Ann.* XIII 58, Festus (Paulus) 106L, Polyaenus VIII 2, Serv. *Aen.* VI 777, Justin XLIII 2.7, Lydus *De mens.* p. 115 Bekker; cf. also Steph. Byz. s.v. *Tabioi* (οἱ περὶ 'Ρέμον); Kretschmer 1909.303.

49 Strength: *OGR* 21.5, Festus 326L. Vigour: Ovid *Fasti* II 396.

50 Dion. Hal. I 80.3, 86.3; Diodorus VIII 5.1, 6.1; Cic. *Rep.* II 12; Ovid *Fasti* V 452, 467; cf. also Lydus *De mag.* 1 5 (n. 48 above).

51 Festus 345L, 287L; Ennius *Ann.* 86–9 Sk, Diodorus VIII 5 (pp. 7, 9 above).

52 The Genucii Augurini in the consular *fasti* for 451, 445 and 399 are automatically suspect, as retrojections of the plebeian augur: Mommsen 1864.65–8 (cf. Pinsent 1975.14: the Genucii after 300 were 'in a position to affect the early Fasti').

53 Dion. Hal. I 86.2, cf. 85.6 for Remoria.

54 Festus (Paulus) 345L: 'Remuria ager dictus, quia possessus est a Remo, et habitatio Remi Remona [perhaps 'Remu < ria >' in the full Festus text, 344L]. sed et locus in summo Aventino Remoria dicitur, ubi Remus de urbe condenda fuerat auspicatus.' Plut. *Rom.* 9.4 (*Remonion, Rignarion*), *OGR* 23.1; cf. also *ILLRP* 252, *Remureine* (i.e. a goddess Remurina?), one of a group of archaising inscriptions from the Palatine.

55 Seneca *De brev. vit.* 13.8 on its exclusion from the *pomerium*, 'aut quod plebs eo secessisset, aut quod Remo auspicante illo loco aves non addixissent'. Cf. Propertius IV 1.50 for *Remus Aventinus*.

56 Festus (Paulus) 135L, Serv. *Aen.* VIII 636, *Vir. ill.* 5.2; Skutsch

1961.253–8 = 1968.64–9. *Saxum* and Bona Dea: Ovid *Fasti* v 147–58, Cic. *De domo* 136; Brouwer 1989.302–3, 400–2.

57 Varro *Ant. div.* fr. 131 Cardauns (Augustine *CD* IV 16, cf. Arnobius *Adv. gent.* IV 9); Humphrey 1986.60–1, 95–7 (shrine and statue illustrated at 96, fig. 38).

58 Cic. *Att.* IV 1.5, Juvenal III 10–20. Potters' quarter: Varro *LL* v 154. Commercial area outside Porta Capena: E. Rodriguez Almeida in Steinby 1993.118–20 on the *areae Carruces, Pannaria* and *Radicaria*. Mercury temple: Apuleius *Met.* VI 8.2 (*retro metas Murtias*); Livy II 27.5–6, Val. Max. IX 3.6 (founded by *populus*). Shops and workshops in Circus Maximus: Dion. Hal. III 68.4, Tac. *Ann.* XV 38.

59 Livy I 33, Dion. Hal. III 43.2 (*ad Murciae* and Aventine respectively): *nova multitudo*, ἑτέρα πόλις. Rowdy: Livy I 33.8. Marcius as a *popularis* king: Virg. *Aen.* VI 815–16; the plebeian Marcii Reges claimed descent from him (Suet. *Iul.* 6.1).

60 Pliny *NH* XV 120–1; cf. Varro *LL* v 154 (myrtle grove), Plut. *QR* 20 = *Mor.* 268e for Murcia as Venus Myrtea.

61 E.g. Sall. *Hist.* I 11M, *Cat.* 33.4 (letter of Manlius), *Jug.* 31.6 and 17 (speech of Memmius), *Hist.* III 48.1M (speech of Macer).

62 Livy *epit.* XI: 'plebs propter aes alienum post graves et longas seditiones ad ultimum secessit in Ianiculum'; Pliny *NH* XVI 37, Pomponius *Digest* I 2.2.8 (*multae discordiae*), Augustine *CD* III 17 (act of war).

63 See Raaflaub 1986.207: 'the last phase provided the model for the entire conflict'.

64 Cic. *Brut.* 54, *Corn.* ap. Asconius 76C, Livy II 32.2, Dion. Hal. v 45.2, Festus 422–4L, Ovid *Fasti* III 663–4, Val. Max. VIII 9.1, Pomponius *Digest* I 2.2.20, etc.

65 Aventine: Piso fr. 22P, Sall. *Jug.* 31.17, Cic. *Mur.* 15, Livy III 54.8. Both: Cic. *Rep.* II 58, Sall. *Hist.* I 11M. (Varro *LL* v 81 says they went to Crustumerium.)

66 Sall. *Jug.* 31.17, Diodorus XII 24.5, Dion. Hal. XI 43.6, Pomponius *Digest* I 2.2.24; implied at Florus I 24.3?

67 Cic. *Rep.* II 63, cf. *Corn.* ap. Asconius 77C (where *Romae revertuntur* may imply a previous occupation of the *mons sacer*).

68 Livy III 50.13–15, 51.10–12, 52.1–3, 54.9–11.

69 Plut. *C. Gracchus* 16.4, Appian *BC* I 26.115, Orosius v 12.6 for the Diana temple as Gracchus' base; cf. Dion. Hal. XI 43.6 on the second secession. Ogilvie however (1965.311, 489) takes the Aventine versions as early.

70 *OGR* 23.1, Dion. Hal. I 85.6.

71 Strabo v 3.2 (C230) on 'Phestoi', Dion. Hal. VIII 36.3 (cf. Livy II 39.5, I 23.3) on the camp of Coriolanus.

72 Festus 442–4L, cf. Cic. *Brut.* 54, Livy II 32.2, III 52.3.

73 Livy I 9.8, 10.2, 11.1; Dion. Hal. II 35.2–7, Plut. *Rom.* 17.1.

74 See above, p. 196 n. 4 ('three miles'), followed by Gell 1834.2.191. The monti del Trullo, on the right bank near Magliana, are about the right distance, but not plausible as a city site.

75 Dion. Hal. I 85.6; also *Ined. Vat. FGrH* 839 F 1.5 (probably from Dionysius).

76 Ennius *Ann.* in Porphyrio on Hor. *Odes* I 2.18; Ovid *Amores* III 6.45–82, *Fasti* II 598; Hor. *Odes* I 2.13–20, Statius *Silvae* II 1.99–100. See Nisbet and Hubbard 1970.26, Skutsch 1985.212.

77 Dion. Hal. I 87.3, Plut. *Rom.* 11.1; cf. Festus (Paulus) 345L, *habitatio Remi*.

78 Citizen colonies: Antium 338, Tarracina 329, Minturnae 296, Sinuessa 296. Latin colonies: Cales 334, Fregellae 328, Luceria 314, Saticula 313, Suessa Aurunca 313, Pontian islands 313, Interamna Lirenas 312, Sora 303, Alba Fucens 303, Narnia 299, Carseoli 298. Roads: Via Appia 312, Via Valeria 307? (Livy IX 43.25).

79 Livy X 33.9 (begun *c.* 307 BC, dedicated 294); Wiseman 1981 = 1987.187–204, Pensabene 1988.

80 Livy X 13.2–4, 16.3–8, 18.1–2, 21.11–15.

81 Livy X 10.12, 13.5, 21.2, 26.13.

82 Livy X 23.11–12; p. 72 above.

83 Dion. Hal. I 32.2–33.1; Wiseman 1981.35–7 = 1987.187–9. Palatine from Pallas: Polybius in Dion. Hal. I 32.1. Lupercal as Lykaion: p. 78 above.

84 Zonaras VIII 1, cf. Livy X 23.1–2 (*prodigia multa*).

85 Cic. *De div.* II 70, distinguishing Roman augury of his time from that of other peoples, and other times in Rome. For Cicero's time, see Linderski 1986, North 1989b.584–5, Beard 1990.39–40; for a hypothetical reconstruction of earlier conditions, see Wiseman 1992 = 1994.49–67. For *augur* as 'prophet', see for instance Ovid *Met.* III 348–9, 511–12 (Tiresias), XII 18 (Calchas), *Amores* III 5.31–3 (dream-interpreter).

86 College of 300 BC: Livy X 9.2. Cn. Marcius and his brother, famous prophets and *nobili loco nati*: Cic. *De div.* I 89, 115, II 113; Livy XXV 12.3, Festus 162L, (Paulus) 185L, Isidore *Orig.* VI 8.12. Marsyas: Serv. *Aen.* III 359. For Minucius and 'Publius' (i.e. Publicius?), see Wiseman 1991.118–19.

87 E.g. Appian *BC* I 24, II 18, III 7, V 96, Plut. *Aristides* 15.3.

88 Lucian *Pseudologistes* 12: τὴν μακρὰν καὶ ἀπευκτὴν καὶ ἀπαίσιον καὶ ἄπρακτον . . . ἡμέραν. Scholiast on Oppian *Halieutica* 372 (cf. 399): ἀπαίσιον ἄδικον, μισητὸν καὶ κακὸν, φοβερὸν, ἀπρεπές.

89 For milk and honey (cf. Exodus 3.8), see Nisbet and Hubbard 1978.321–2 on Hor. *Odes* II 19.10–12 etc.

90 Plut. *Pelopidas* 21–2 (371 BC), giving all the classic precedents. Calchas: Aeschylus *Agam.* 198–204. Fourth-century attitudes: Phainias of Eresos fr. 25 Wehrli (reporting human sacrifice before Salamis), Theophrastus fr. 584a (= Porphyry *De abst.* II 27.2, 'up to the present day'). Third century: Phylarchus *FGrH* 81 F 80. Cf. Hughes 1991.191: 'If anything, the extant literature gives an impression of an increase in human sacrifices in Classical and Hellenistic times [as opposed to Homer].'

91 Livy x 26.13 ('Gallici tumultus praecipuus timor civitatem tenuit'), cf. 10.12, 21.2.

92 Plut. *Marcellus* 3.3–4, Zonaras VIII 19 (228 BC), Livy XXII 57.6 (216 BC), Plut. *QR* 83 = *Mor.* 283f–284c (114 BC); see Reid 1912, Briquel 1976b.75–9, Fraschetti 1981 (esp. 78–85 on the third occasion), Cornell 1989.322. The sources clearly imply that those were not the only examples of human sacrifice at Rome: Livy XXII 57.6, Pliny *NH* XXVIII 12, XXX 12, Lactantius *Inst. div.* I 21.

93 Briquel 1976b, on Justin XII 2.5–11 (siege of Brundisium by Alexander the Molossian), Lycophron 1056–7, scholiast on Lycophron 602, 1056.

94 Zonaras VIII 1, cf. Dio VIII fr. 36.28.

95 Livy x 31.8, 47.6, Val. Max. I 8.2 (*trienno continuo*), Orosius III 21.8, 22.4–5; *Vir. ill.* 22.1, Ovid *Met.* XV 622–744, Lactantius *Inst. div.* II 7.13, etc.

96 E.g. Hesiod *WD* 243, Herodotus VII 171.2; Obsequens 13, 22, Dio LIV 1.1–2 (Rome: 165, 142 and 22 BC).

97 Livy x 33.9. Cf. x 29.14, 29.18, 42.7 for Jupiter Victor – evidently a temple to Capitoline Jupiter in the Victory precinct on the Palatine (Dio XLV 17.2, cf. XLVII 40.2).

98 Arnobius *Adv. nat.* VII 47, 'ex libris fatalibus vatumque responsis'.

99 Pensabene 1988.56, 1990.87–90.

100 Vaglieri 1907.187 (two walls, same quarry-marks), 189–91 (grave), 190 (blocks reused for monument); monument and grave-slab illustrated at 192–3, figs. 8–9.

101 Cup illustrated at Vaglieri 1907.193, fig. 10. For the monument, cf. Pensabene 1990.87 (my italics): 'Questi [blocchi di tufo], disposti irregolarmente, sembrano costituire come la fondazione di un *altare* o di una colonna.'

102 Vaglieri 1907.191, 205 (but 'la necropoli . . . continuò ad esistere sino al sec. IV' is inconsistent with Vaglieri's own results: see next note).

103 Vaglieri 1907.191 n. 1: 'È risultato anche dell'esame posteriore del livello dei singoli sepolcri, come questa tomba sia stata fatta quando già il terreno era stato notevolmente abbassato; dei sepolcri più antichi invece non rimane che la parte più profonda.'

104 Vaglieri 1907.187: 'Parve questo un muro di cinta, per la perfezione tecnica, . . . il perfetto combacciamento dei blocchi, la conservazione degli spigoli, il posamento accurato e sistematico sul piano di fondazione dimostrando all'evidenza non trattarsi di rifacimenti, ma di un muro conservato nella sua forma originale e con massi estratti dalle cave espressamente per questa costruzione.'

105 Vaglieri 1907.190 n. 1: 'Non sarebbe troppo inverosimile il supporre, che si sia voluto testimoniare la presenza di un sepolcro importante con questa specie di tumulo immesso nell'*agger* di terra compreso tra i due muri di cinta.' Cf. also Pensabene 1990.87–90, who notes that this area was never disturbed by later rebuilding; he interprets it as a sort of *hērōon*.

106 Festus 310–12L, *Oxyrhynchus Papyri* XVII 2088.14–17; Wiseman 1981.44–5 = 1987.196–7; cf. Vaglieri 1907.187 (n. 104 above). Good photographs in Nash 1968.2.112–13.

107 Homer *Iliad* XII 3–9, cf. VII 449–50; examples of proper procedure at Pausanias I 42.1 (Megara), IV 27.6–7 (Messenia, 369 BC). Cf. *Gromatici veteres* I 141 Lachmann (with Burkert 1983.39) on Roman boundary stones.

108 Sartori 1898.5–19 (quotation translated from p. 5).

109 Malalas VIII 1 and 13 (pp. 192, 200–1 Dindorf); cf. also IX 13, X 10, XI 9 (pp. 221, 235, 275 Dindorf) for alleged similar sacrifices by Augustus, Tiberius and Trajan at Ancyra and Antioch.

110 E.g. Atkinson 1916.7–11 (woman, Lowbury Hill temple); Penn 1960.121–2 (four babies, Springhead temple); Meates 1979.1.104 (baby, Lullingstone villa).

111 Aeschylus *Eumenides* 764–74, Euripides *Heraclidae* 1026–44, Sophocles *OC* 1518–39; see Visser 1982, Kearns 1989.48–55.

112 Festus (Paulus) 18L: 'Argea loca Romae appellantur, quod in his sepulti essent quidam Argivorum inlustres viri.' Cf. Festus 450L, Dion. Hal. I 38.2–3, Ovid *Fasti* V 621–62, Plut. *QR* 32 (*Mor.* 272b): commutation of archaic human sacrifice?

113 Varro *LL* V 54; Pensabene 1990.90, adducing the evidence for a hut, variously attributed to Romulus, Remus and Faustulus, at

the top of the Scalae Caci (Solinus 1.18, Propertius IV 1.9, Plut. *Rom.* 20.4).

114 Livy XXII 57.6; cf. Pliny *NH* XXX 12 for a *senatus consultum* banning it in 97 BC. For the secrecy surrounding 'talismanic' graves, cf. Plut. *Mor.* 578b, with Faraone 1992.115–16.

115 See nn. 104–5 above. For similar concealment of an ill-omened monument, see Coarelli 1985.254–7 on the Caesarian and Augustan *rostra*.

116 Propertius III 9.50, 'caeso moenis firma Remo'; Florus I 1.8, 'prima certe victima fuit munitionemque urbis novae sanguine suo consecravit.'

117 Ovid *Fasti* II 375–8, *OGR* 22.1; see above, p. 193 (n. 27), p. 196 (nn. 66–7), p. 199 (n. 56).

118 Ovid *Fasti* II 374, 'haec certe non nisi victor edet.' See above, p. 81 for the unprivileged status of the Quinctiales; pp. 5–6 and 74 for twin founders; n. 48 above for Remus as the elder.

119 Val. Max. II 2.9, with Wiseman 1995. Cavalry: Polybius VI 25.3 (naked), *Ined. Vat. FGrH* 839 F 1.3 (borrowed from Samnites), Varro *LL* VII 57 (portrayed in Aesculapius temple).

120 Ovid *Fasti* II 425–52; see p. 84 above.

121 Livy I 12.3–6, Dion. Hal. II 50.3, etc.; Livy X 36.11, 37.14–16.

122 Serv. *Aen.* VII 709; contrast Livy I 13.4 ('civitatem unam e duobus faciunt'), Dion. Hal. II 46.2 (*isopsēphoi*), Plut. *Rom.* 19.7, etc.

123 Velleius I 14.6 and 8, referring to the Sabines of Cures (Taylor 1960.59–64), which was where T. Tatius came from (Dion. Hal. II 36.3, 48.1, etc.). Mommsen (1886 = 1906.22–35) pointed out the context of the legend.

124 Plut. *Rom.* 26.2, *Numa* 7.4; Pliny *NH* XXXIII 35, etc.; see above, p. 173 (n. 57), and n. 119 above for the historical context.

125 Cic. *Rep.* II 20, *De leg.* I 3, Dion. Hal. II 63.3–4, *Inscr. Ital.* XIII 3.86 (= *ILS* 64), Ovid *Fasti* II 491–512, Plut. *Rom.* 28.2–3; Livy X 46.7, Pliny *NH* VII 213.

126 See pp. 65–71 above on the Praenestine mirror.

127 Adam and Briquel 1982.40, cf. 48.

128 See above, pp. 54–5.

9 THE USES OF A MYTH

1 See Cornell 1991 for an excellent discussion of the evidence.

2 Thomas 1992, esp. ch. 6. Her view of Roman culture as 'more bookish' refers only to the late Republic and Empire (Thomas 1992.151, 158).

3 Especially in the two collective volumes *Vergangenheit in mündlicher Überlieferung* (e.g. Ungern-Sternberg 1988, Timpe 1988) and *Studien zur vorliterarischen Periode im frühen Rom* (e.g. Rix 1989, Schmidt 1989). See also Zorzetti 1990; and cf. Wiseman 1989.133–6 (= 1994.29–34), 1994.6–16.

4 Niebuhr 1811.177–80, 1849.10–14; Cato fr. 118P (Cic. *Tusc.* 1 2.3, iv 2.3, *Brutus* 75), cf. Varro *De vita pop. R.* fr. 84 Riposati (Nonius 107–8L), Val. Max. ii 1.10, Hor. *Odes* iv 15.25–32.

5 Dismissed: Schwegler 1853.53–73, Lewis 1855.1.202–37, etc. 'Peculiarly fruitless speculation': Horsfall 1987.10. Learned and judicious overview in Momigliano 1957 (= 1960.69–87, 1977a.231–51).

6 Rathje 1983, 1990; doubted (needlessly, I think) by Holloway 1994.191–2.

7 Rösler 1990; cf. Wiseman 1989.134 = 1994.31–2.

8 Zorzetti 1990 (esp. 297: 'What we see is the cultural model of an archaic *polis*'); cf. Wiseman 1994.7–8, 12.

9 Macaulay 1842.7; cf. 6–7 on 'that peculiar character, more easily understood than defined, which distinguishes the creations of the imagination from the realities of the world in which we live'.

10 Plut. *Rom.* 8.7, Dion. Hal. iii 18.1, Livy i 46.3 (*scelus tragicum*), Dion. Hal. ix 22.3, Livy v 21.9. See Wiseman 1994.17–21 for the common ground of drama and historiography; also Walker 1993.364–70 on Dionysius' narrative of the triplets' duel making the reader a spectator.

11 *Populus Romanus* as audience at *ludi scaenici*: Cic. *Sest.* 106, 116, *Pis.* 65, *Att.* ii 19.3, xiv 3.2; *Har. resp.* 22–5 (*ludi Megalenses*), *Sest.* 117–18, *Phil.* i 36 (*ludi Apollinares*); see in general Nicolet 1980.361–73. C. Fannius, consul in 122 BC, defined the privileges of citizenship as political meetings and festival games (*contiones, ludi, dies festi*): Malcovati 1955.144 fr.3.

12 E.g. Beard 1993.48–9, 56–7 (I quote her phrase from p. 56); cf. Finley 1983.126–7 and Wiseman 1994.x–xii.

13 Augustine *CD* vi 5 = Varro *Ant. div.* frr. 7–9 Cardauns. Cf. *CD* iv 27: Varro evidently cited the *pontifex maximus* Q. Scaevola on the *tria genera deorum*.

14 Augustine *CD* vi 5–7 passim. Varro *Ant. div.* fr. 10 Cardauns: 'prima, inquit, theologia maxime adcommodata est ad theatrum.' Cf. also *CD* iv 26: 'cur ergo ludi scaenici, ubi haec dictitantur cantitantur actitantur, deorum honoribus exhibentur, inter res divinas a doctissimis conscribuntur?'; also vii 33 (Varro on *theatrorum fabulae*), xviii 10, 12–13, etc.

15 Augustine *CD* IV 27 (Scaevola, n. 13 above): 'quod multa de dis fingantur indigna'. Varro *Ant. div.* fr. 7 Cardauns: 'multa contra dignitatem et naturam immortalium ficta'.

16 Augustine *CD* IV 26, VI 6–10 passim: 'eant adhuc et theologian civilem a theologia fabulosa, urbes a theatris, templa ab scaenis, sacra pontificum a carminibus poetarum, velut res honestas a turpibus, veraces a fallacibus, graves a levibus, serias a ludicris, adpetendas a respuendis, qua possunt conentur subtilitate discernere!' (VI 9). Cf. VIII 1: 'fabulosa vel civilis, theatrica vel urbana [theologia]'.

17 Cic. *De leg.* I 47. *Praetextae*: Festus 249L, Hor. *AP* 286–8. E.g. Naevius' *Alimonium Remi et Romuli*, Ennius' *Sabinae*, Accius' *Brutus* and *Decius* (or *Aeneadae*), Cassius' *Brutus*, Pomponius Secundus' *Aeneas*. (Also on contemporary subjects, such as Naevius' *Clastidium*, Ennius' *Ambracia*, Pacuvius' *Paullus*, and the pseudo-Senecan *Octavia*.)

18 Ovid *Fasti* IV 326; Wiseman 1979.94–9 for the development of the story. Cf. Seaford 1994.276–7: Attic tragedy regularly provides aetiologies for the origins of cults.

19 Festus (Paulus) 103L. *Ludi* mentioned in Plautus: *Casina* 23–8, *Poenulus* 36–42, 1011–12; cf. *Miles* 991, *Persa* 436, *Poenulus* 1291 on *ludi circenses*.

20 Ovid *Fasti* III 785–6; cf. Cic. *Verr.* v 36, 'mihi ludos sanctissimos . . . Cereri Libero Liberaeque faciundos'. The *ludi Cereales* are first attested in 202 BC (Livy XXX 39.8); the aedile Memmius who first put them on (attested on a coin issue of 56 BC: Crawford 1974.451, no. 427) is undatable and may be legendary.

21 Tertullian *De spect.* 5, 10 (*CSEL* XX 7, 12), Ausonius VII 7.29–30.

22 Dion. Hal. VI 17.2–3, 94.3, Tac. *Ann.* II 49.1; Alföldi 1965.92–100 argues for a foundation date around 400 BC. For the triad of divinities, see Cic. *Verr.* v 36 (n. 20 above), Livy III 55.7, XXXIII 25.3, XLI 28.2, *Fasti Antiates* 19 April (*Inscr. Ital.* XIII 3.9); also Cic. *De nat. deorum* II 62, who insists on the non-identity of Liber and Dionysus.

23 Ps.-Cyprian *De spect.* 4 (*CSEL* III 3.6–7); Dion. Hal. VII 10.1, 17.2.

24 Temple: Pliny *NH* XXXV 154 (from Varro?) on the artists Gorgasus and Damophilus. Cult: Cic. *Verr.* v 187, *Balb.* 55, Val. Max. I 1.1, Festus (Paulus) 86L. Dionysia: Festus (Paulus) 103L, Tertullian *De spect.* 10, Ausonius VII 7.29.

25 Pausanias I 2.5, 20.3, 29.2, 38.8: the cult was brought from Eleutherai, where it had been established by the eponymous Eleuther. For the bilingual calque, see Hyginus *Fab.* 225: 'Eleuther primus simulacrum Liberi patris constituit.'

26 Tragedy and comedy: Taplin 1993, passim. Satyr-play: Wiseman 1988.3–8 = 1994.71–8. Neighbours: Taplin 1993.40–1, 'the Italianization of Greek comedy, well-known to us through Plautus and Terence, has begun around the bay of Naples by soon after 350.' For the international (or at least Panhellenic) attraction of the Great Dionysia in the fourth century, see Aeschines *in Ctes.* 34, 43.

27 Livy III 55.13; cf. X 23.13, XXVII 36.9, XXXIII 25.2–3 for reports of the plebeian aediles' activities at the temple. Raaflaub 1986.207 (p. 114 above).

28 Servius on *Aen.* III 20 ('in liberis civitatibus simulacrum Marsyae erat, qui in tutela Liberi patris est'), II 359 (augury), IV 58 (statue); Hor. *Sat.* I 6.115–17 and scholiasts, Pliny *NH* XXI 8–9 (statue); Torelli 1982.98–106, Coarelli 1985.91–119, Wiseman 1988.4–5 = 1994.73–4. On Dionysus Eleuthereus as appropriate to a free city without distinctions of status, see Seaford 1994.243–7.

29 *Pace* Scullard 1981.196 ('These games, first mentioned in 216 BC, were probably established in 220 when C. Flaminius was censor and built the Circus Flaminius in which they may have been held before probably being transferred to the Circus Maximus'). But the only evidence for the *ludi plebeii* at the Circus Flaminius (Val. Max. I 7.4) is grossly anachronistic and cannot be taken seriously; the Circus Flaminius was not a chariot-racing track and 'was *never* intended to be a regular equivalent to the Circus Maximus' (Humphrey 1986.540–5, quotation from p. 544). The reference to the *ludi plebeii* in 216 (Livy XXIII 30.17) offers no more than a *terminus ante quem*.

30 Plut. *Publ.* 14.3 (Ides of September), Cic. *Att.* IV 1.6 (theatre on 7 September). The early-imperial calendar *fasti* give 5–19 September for the *Romani* and 4–17 November for the *plebeii*, but they were shorter than that in the Republic.

31 Cic. *Rep.* II 36, Livy I 35.9, *Vir. ill.* 6.8, Eutropius I 6.1; cf. ps.-Asconius 217 St (*sub regibus instituti*). Temple: Livy I 38.7, 55.1, Dion. Hal. III 69.1, IV 59.1, Tac. *Hist.* III 72.2, Plut. *Publ.* 14.1.

32 Ps.-Asconius 217 St: 'plebeii ludi, quos exactis regibus pro libertate plebis fecerunt. an pro reconciliatione plebis post secessionem in Aventinum?' For the traditions on the secessions, see p. 204 above (nn. 64–9).

33 Livy VI 42.12–14 (Everyman trans., 1914); see above, pp. 107–8. The *ludi magni* were the *ludi Romani*: Livy I 35.9, Festus (Paulus) 109L, ps.-Asconius 217 St.

34 *Vir. ill.* 20.2; p. 108 above.

35 Livy VII 2.1–3. For the Varronian account of the history of

Roman drama that follows (2.4–13), see Schmidt 1989; there is no reason to consider it historically accurate (Wiseman 1994.12–13).

36 Lydus *De mens.* IV 149. It was one of the three days in the year when the '*mundus* of Ceres' was open, offering a way to the underworld (Festus 126L, 144L, Varro in Macrobius *Sat.* I 16.18).

37 Theophrastus *Hist. plant.* V 8.2; Homer *Odyssey* X 552–60 (Elpenor), Diodorus XIV 102.4 (Roman colony, 393 BC), Cic. *De nat. deorum* III 48 (colonists' cult of Circe).

38 Hesiod *Theogony* 1011–16; pp. 45–8 above.

39 Tertullian *De spect.* 8, Lydus *De mens.* I 12; see Humphrey 1986.91–5 on Sol at the Circus Maximus.

40 Livy I 35.8 (*designatus locus est*), cf. Pliny *NH* XXXVI 102, Suet. *Jul.* 39.2 (Caesar); Humphrey 1986.60–77.

41 Dion. Hal. VI 94.3; Tertullian *De spect.* 8, Apul. *Met.* VI 8.2, *Notizie degli scavi di antichità* 1931.344 line 79 (*metae Murciae*); Varro *LL* V 154 ('intimus Circus ad Murciae vocatur').

42 'vocaverunt . . . deam Stimulam quae ad agendum ultra modum stimularet, deam Murciam quae praeter modum non moverat ac faceret hominem . . . nimis desidiosum et inactuosum' (Augustine *CD* IV 16, cf. 11: Varro *Ant. div.* frr. 130–1 Cardauns). For Murcia, see above, p. 113.

43 Ovid *Fasti* VI 501–18, Livy XXXIX 12.4, 13.12; cf. *CIL* VI 9897 (*lucus Semeles*).

44 See above, pp. 190 (n. 24), 203 (n. 56).

45 Daughter: Varro *Ant. div.* fr. 218 Cardauns (Macrobius *Sat.* I 12.27). Sister and wife: Lactantius *Inst.* I 22.9, cf. Arnobius *Adv. nat.* I 36, V 18. Phaunos, son of Circe and companion of Dionysus: pp. 47–8 above.

46 Mart. Cap. I 50, with Weinstock 1946 on the origin of the material.

47 Pales and Palatine: Solinus 1.15. Faunus from *favor*: Labeo in Macrobius *Sat.* I 12.22 (Fauna), Servius auctus on *Georg.* I 10; implied at Dion. Hal. I 31.2, Justin XLIII 1.6, *OGR* 5.3 (favourable reception of Evander), and Servius on *Aen.* VII 314 (*propitius*).

48 Ennius *Ann.* I 72–7 Sk, pp. 6–7 above; later versions substitute a simpler Palatine/Aventine polarity.

49 See above, pp. 110–11.

50 *Ludi compitalicii* in January, in honour of the Lares: Pliny *NH* XXXVI 204 (founded by Ser. Tullius), Cic. *Pis.* 8 with Asconius 7C (popular), Propertius II 22.3–6 (*theatra*). *Ludi* of Hercules (12 August?): *ILLRP* 701, 703; cf. Crawford 1974.399, no. 385 (*denarii* of M. Volteius, 78 BC), Hercules in the company of Jupiter, Liber, Ceres, Magna Mater and Apollo, all recipients of

public *ludi*. *Ludi Capitolini* on 15 October, in honour of Jupiter Feretrius: Piso fr. 7P (founded by Romulus), Livy v 50.4 (founded in 390), Ennius *Ann.* fr. li Sk (boxing and running). Later, there were the *ludi Florales* (established 241 or 238 BC), *Apollinares* (212 BC), *Megalenses* (191 BC), *Victoriae* (82 BC), etc.

51 Temporary theatres were erected in front of the relevant temples (Cic. *Har. resp.* 24, Augustine *CD* II 4, 26 etc.; Hanson 1959.9–26), so the *ludi scaenici* of the Roman Dionysus must have been held in the Circus Maximus itself. Where the stage plays were performed at the *ludi plebeii* is not known.

52 Plut. *Theseus* 28.2; *Gentleman's Magazine* 44 (1774) 17, quoted in Sutherland 1975.14. Cf. D. W. Griffiths on *Birth of a Nation* (1914), quoted in Sorlin 1980.viii–ix: 'You will see what actually happened. There will be no opinions expressed, you will merely be present at the making of history . . . The film could not be anything but the truth.'

53 Stesichorus fr. 192 *PMG*; see Bowie 1993.23–7. Cf. Egnatius on the survival of Remus (*OGR* 23.6).

54 Overlooking the Circus (Ovid *Fasti* v 669), 'behind the *metae Murciae*' (Apul. *Met.* VI 8.2). Were there *ludi Mercuriales*? The *collegium Mercurialium* is mentioned together with the *collegium Capitolinorum* (*ILS* 2676, Cic. *QF* II 6.2), and the latter was responsible for the *ludi Capitolini* (n. 50 above).

55 See above, p. 190 n. 24. For the archaic context, cf. Seaford 1994.269: 'the enactment of myth . . . precedes the emergence of drama' (ibid. 273 for how the development may have taken place).

56 E.g. Servius auctus on *Aen.* VIII 343 (Pan as Enyalios), Butas in Plut. *Rom.* 21.6 (Luperci *aition* of waving swords), Diomedes *Gramm. Lat.* 1 475–6 Keil (Inuus as the son of Bellona); see Wiseman 1995 for the argument.

57 Joint rule: pp. 5–6 above. Hymns: Dion. Hal. 1 79.10. Oaths: Diodorus XXXVII 11.

58 See above, pp. 8–9.

59 Livy VIII 30–6, Val. Max. II 7.8, III 2.9, etc.

60 Pliny *NH* XXXIV 26, Plut. *Numa* 8.10 (also the wisest: they chose Pythagoras).

61 Val. Max. II 2.9; see above, pp. 126–7.

62 Ovid *Fasti* II 359–82, cf. *OGR* 22.1.

63 For *ludi* at the dedication of temples, cf. Livy XXXVI 36.3–7 (Magna Mater and Iuventas, 191 BC), XL 52.1–3 (Juno Regina and Diana, 179), XLII 10.5 (Fortuna Equestris, 172).

64 See above, pp. 9–10. Sacrifice: pp. 117–25.

65 Livy x 36.11, 37.15 (Jupiter Stator vowed 294), 46.7 (Quirinus dedicated 293).

66 See above, p. 127.

67 Secession: p. 204 n. 62 above. Defeat at Arretium: Orosius III 22.12–14, cf. Polybius II 19.8. Tarentines: Dio IX 39.5–8, Zonaras VIII 2. Praenestines (revolt at the news of Pyrrhus' arrival): Zonaras VIII 3.

68 This may be the context for some at least of the phenomena discussed by Strasburger (pp. 96–7 above). For a crisis (in 276) evidently leading to an elaboration of the story, see p. 84 above on Ovid *Fasti* II 425–52.

69 *ILLRP* 309, with Wachter 1987.301–42 (the first two lines were later deleted); cf. Zevi 1970.66–7 on *apud vos*.

70 For a controversy about the date of Livius Andronicus, see Cic. *Brut.* 71–6, Gellius *NA* XVII 21.42–5: according to Accius and Porcius Licinus (late second century BC), Livius came to Rome in 209; according to Varro and Atticus (mid-first century BC), his first play was produced in 240, and Naevius' in 235. The 'early' chronology was based on documentary evidence (*antiqui commentarii*: Cic. *Brut.* 72, cf. 60), and most modern scholars accept it (e.g. Gratwick 1982.78). But as Mattingly points out (1993.166–8), Accius and Porcius were well placed to know the facts.

71 Donatus on Terence *Ad.* 537, Festus 334L; Powell 1988.146 on Cic. *De sen.* 20, arguing that the reference there is not to the *Lupus*. The date of Fabius Pictor's source Diocles of Peparethos (Plut. *Rom.* 3.1, 8.7) is not known; did he write before or after Naevius?

72 Plut. *Rom.* 3.3, Dion. Hal. I 79.2.

73 Velleius I 14.8 (241), Pliny *NH* XVIII 286 (238), Ovid *Fasti* V 277–330; Tac. *Ann.* II 49.1 (position of temple).

74 Plut. *Rom.* 10.2; at Dion. Hal. I 84.3 Faustulus' brother is called Faustinus.

75 Cic. *Rep.* II 39: 'quod semper in re publica tenendum est, ne plurimum valeant plurimi'. *Pauci* and *multitudo*: Sall. *Jug.* 41.6–7, *Hist.* III 48.6 (Licinius Macer), etc. πλεῖστοι: see above, p. 171 n. 29.

76 *FGrH* 809 F 3–6, 810 F 1–3. *Mandare litteris*: Cic. *De or.* II 52, *Acad.* II 2, etc.

77 Walbank 1960 (= 1985.224–41), Wiseman 1994.1–22.

78 Dion. Hal. I 85.4–6, 86.1, 87.1–2; Plut. *Rom.* 7.1.

79 E.g. Livy I 46.3 (*tragici*), V 21.9, Dion. Hal. III 18.1, IX 22.1–3, Plut. *Rom.* 8.7.

80 E.g. Licinius Macer's speech in Sall. *Hist.* III 48.1, 6, 12, 15 (*maiores*); Sall. *Cat.* 33.4 (C. Manlius), *Jug.* 31.6, 17 (C. Memmius), *Hist.* I 55.23 (M. Lepidus); Cic. *Pro Cornelio* in Asconius 76–8C.

81 Sall. *Hist.* I 11–12, IV 45, Tac. *Ann.* IV 33.2, etc.

82 Tribune in 73: n. 80 above.

83 *OGR* 23.5; cf. also Malalas VII 179–80 (Macer fr. 1P) on Romulus' *hubris*.

84 Livy I 7.1–2 (6.4 *avitum malum, regni cupido*); Dion. Hal. I 87.1–3 (*eris, philoneikia*, etc.).

85 Cic. *De leg.* I 7 (history), *Brut.* 238 (character); *Att.* I 4.2, Val. Max. IX 12.7, Plut. *Cic.* 9.1–2 (trial and suicide in Cicero's praetorship).

86 On *De republica*, Cicero's 'most enduring act of statesmanship and poetry', see Zetzel 1994.23–32.

87 Dion. Hal. II 56.3–5, Plut. *Rom.* 26.1–3; cf. Livy I 16.4, Val. Max. V 3.1; for the contemporary political relevance, see Plut. *Pompey* 25.4 (67 BC). Sulla as Romulus: Sall. *Hist.* I 55.5 (M. Lepidus).

88 Hor. *Epodes* 7.17–20 (pp. 15–16 above); Nisbet 1984.6–8, suggesting the influence of Sallust's *Histories* (Macer is chronologically more likely).

89 Dio XLVI 46.2–3 (Loeb translation); Appian (*BC* III 94) and Suetonius (*Aug.* 95) mention only the twelve vultures.

90 Suet. *Aug.* 7.2, Dio LIII 16.7, Florus II 34.66.

91 Suet. *Aug.* 89.3: 'admonebatque praetores ne paterentur nomen suum commissionibus obsolefieri'. Mention of the praetors confirms the theatrical context (Dio LIV 2.3). Cf. Pliny *Paneg.* 54.1–2 (*ludis et commissionibus*) for Trajan's similar precautions.

92 See White 1993 for the nature of the relationship.

93 As at *Georgics* III 27: *victor Quirinus* in the East, 29 BC.

94 Nic. Dam. *FGrH* 90 F 127.16; cf. Pliny *NH* VII 46 for Agrippa's age.

95 Dio LIII 31.4, LIV 29.3–8.

96 Servius on *Aen.* I 292: 'vera tamen hoc habet ratio, Quirinum Augustum esse, Remum vero pro Agrippa positum.'

97 Dio LIII 27.5; cf. Val. Max. II 2.9 for Faustulus.

98 Varro in Solinus 1.18; cf. Conon *FGrH* 26 F 48.8, with Wiseman 1981.45–6 = 1987.197–8 (Faustulus' hut 'in the temple of Jupiter' probably refers to the Jupiter temple in the precinct of Victory, Dio XLV 17.2). Augustus: Dio LIII 16.5 (where Romulus had lived), cf. Dion. Hal. I 79.11 (Romulus' hut 'on the flank of the Palatine facing the Circus'); Carettoni 1983.7–16, Zanker 1988.51–2, 67–8.

99 Propertius IV 1.9–10, with Beaujeu 1974.68–72.

100 Dio LIV 12.4 (*trib. pot.*, 18 BC), 18.1 (adoption of Gaius and Lucius, 17 BC); Aug. *Res gestae* 22.2, *CIL* VI 32323.53, 103–4, 120, 139, 165 (*ludi saeculares*, 17 BC). For Agrippa at 'the height of power' (*eis pleiston hupsous* probably translates *in summum fastigium*), see Gronewald 1983 on Augustus' funeral speech for him.

101 *Anth. Pal.* IX 219.3 (Diodorus 1.3 Gow–Page); Propertius IV 6.80. So too Statius *Silvae* II 7.60 (cf. IV 6.79); but at Martial X 76.4 and Juvenal X 73 the reference is to the *plebs* in particular.

102 Propertius II 1.23, *regnaque prima Remi*; to suppose, as many commentators do, that *Remi* here is merely a metrical variant for *Romuli* makes nonsense of the legend. Joint rule: pp. 5–6 above.

103 Dio XLI 14.3 (49 BC), LIV 19.4, Aug. *Res gestae* 19.2.

104 Hartwig 1904, Koeppel 1980; Paris 1988 for full bibliography.

105 Berczelly 1978.73–4 and plate XI(a); suggested to me independently by Fausto Zevi. *Templum minus*: Festus 146L, Serv. auct. on *Aen.* IV 200, Varro *LL* VII 13; Linderski 1986.2274–8.

106 Varro *LL* V 51 (from the *sacra Argeorum*). It was on the *collis Latiaris*, which perhaps bore the same conceptual relationship to the temple of Quirinus as the *auguraculum* on the Capitoline *arx* did to the temple of Jupiter Optimus Maximus; cf. Varro *LL* V 158, Martial V 22.4 for the Quirinal *Capitolium vetus*.

107 For the necessity of sitting, see Festus 470–2L, Servius on *Aen.* IX 4, Livy I 18.7, etc.

108 Hartwig 1904.27–9; implausibly doubted by Paris 1988.31–3.

109 Jupiter may be Jupiter Victor in particular (so Palmer 1976.55), whose temple was on the Palatine in the precinct of Victory: n. 98 above.

110 Suggested by Palmer 1976.55. Mercury probably (p. 190 n. 24 above) and Hercules certainly (Propertius IV 9, Macrobius *Sat.* I 12.28) were associated in myth with the grove of Bona Dea 'below the Rock'.

111 Iconography (raised right arm): p. 113 above. Topography: Hartwig 1904.30.

112 Hartwig 1904.30, alluding to Virgil *Georg.* III 1, 294 (others identify her as Vesta). Romulus on Palatine: Dion. Hal. I 86.2, etc.

113 Dio LIV 19.5. For Tiberius and Drusus as quasi-twins (analogous to the Dioscuri), see Ovid *Fasti* I 705–8, Dio LV 27.4 (temple of Castor).

114 *Consolatio ad Liviam* 239–46 (probably Tiberian in date); cf. Hor. *Odes* IV 4.27–8 on 'Augusti paternus in pueros animus Nerones'.

115 Suet. *Aug.* 65.1, *Tib.* 15.2, Velleius I 104.1; for the background, see Levick 1976.47–51.

116 Suet. *Aug.* 19.2, Tac. *Ann.* I 4.2; Levick 1976.57–61.

117 Exile: Levick 1976.60–1, Syme 1978.215–21. Date of *Fasti*: Herbert-Brown 1994.229–33, arguing for AD 4–8 (*contra* Syme 1978.21–36, 'AD 1–4').

118 Ovid *Fasti* II 381–424, 481–512, III 11–86, 179–234.

119 Ovid *Fasti* IV 807–62, V 445–84.
120 The classic account is in Tac. *Ann.* I 6 (cf. II 40.3).
121 Virgil as a 'sacred text': e.g. Hist. Aug. *Hadrian* 2.8 on the *sortes Vergilianae*. Imperial cult, 'constructing the reality of the Roman empire': Price 1984.234–48.
122 Cf. Leo Magnus *Sermones* 82.1 (*In natali apostolorum Petri et Pauli*, AD 441: *Patr. Lat.* LIV 422), addressing Rome: 'isti sunt sancti patres tui verique pastores, qui te . . . multo melius multoque felicius condiderunt quam illi quorum studio prima moenium tuorum fundamenta locata sunt: ex quibus is qui tibi nomen dedit fraterna te caede foedavit.' For Christian use of the fratricide, see above, p. 175 n. 90.
123 Quoted in Jacks 1993.273 n. 32: 'probabilius ergo videtur, quod a militibus Remi patria profugis urbs nostra condita vel Remorum gens instituta putatur.'
124 Caes. *BG* II 3.2, V 54.4, VI 12.7, VII 63.7, VIII 6.2.
125 Caes. *BG* I 33.2 etc., with Braund 1980. Trojan Gauls: Lucan I 427–8 (Arverni), Ammianus XV 9.5.
126 Strabo IV 3.5 (C 194).
127 Jacks 1993.30–1, 86–9; Dulière 1979.25–6 (bibliography at 226 n. 433), and figs. 19 and 20.

10 THE OTHER ROME

1 Wood 1975.12.
2 MGM 1951: director Mervyn Le Roy, screenplay by John Lee Makin and S. N. Behrman, Sonya Levien.
3 Twice, in fact (both produced by MGM): 1925, directed by Fred Niblo, and 1959, directed by William Wyler.
4 Mayer 1994.1–10 (the genre), 104–87 (*The Sign of the Cross*), 188–290 (*Ben-Hur*).
5 Mayer 1994.16 (quoting G. W. Foote and Clement Scott, 1896), 109 (audience numbers).
6 Twentieth-Century-Fox 1953, directed by Henry Koster.
7 Mayer 1994.4–5, 109–10.
8 See Wood 1975.165–88 on the rise and fall of the Hollywood epic.
9 Universal 1960, directed by Stanley Kubrick.
10 See Rubinsohn 1987 passim: quotations from pp. 1 and 6. Cf. Mayer 1994.314 for a Garibaldine Spartacus in an Italian film of 1913: 'he leads a popular revolt and captures Rome . . .'
11 Appian *BC* I 120. Cf. Mazzarino 1960.392, from a lecture given on the Capitol for the anniversary of the foundation of Rome: 'Si esprime, in questa leggenda [the Promathion version, pp. 57–61

above], l'anima democratica della antichissima Roma di Servio Tullio. È una Roma assai diversa da quella Roma imperialistica e schiavistica che soffocò nel sangue la gloriosa rivoluzione di Spartaco; une Roma migliore, ed a noi gran lunga più vicina.'

12 Cf. Eames 1975.245 on the original idea for *Quo Vadis*, vetoed by Louis B. Mayer, that it should be given a political slant, 'equating Nero with modern dictators'.

13 See Reinhold 1979.228–31, MacKendrick 1989.294–315, Vance 1989.1.10–30; cf. Mayer 1994.19 on George Washington and Addison's *Cato*.

14 E.g. Shakespeare, *Julius Caesar* (1599?); Jonson, *Sejanus* (1603); Shakespeare, *Coriolanus* (1608?); Jonson, *Catiline* (1611); Corneille, *Cinna* (1641), *La mort de Pompée* (1642); Monteverdi, *L'incoronazione di Poppea* (1642, libretto by Busenello); Corneille, *Othon* (1664); Racine, *Britannicus* (1669); Addison, *Cato* (1713). Late examples of the influence of this tradition are Robert Graves' crypto-republican Claudius (*I, Claudius* and *Claudius the God*, 1934; BBC television serial, 1976), and Fast's anachronistic left-wing senator 'Gracchus'.

15 Herder 1787.223, 290 = 1909.151, 197; translation by T. Churchill (1803) quoted in Haskell 1993.226, 227–8.

16 Herder 1787.289 = 1909.197 (cf. Haskell 1993.227): 'Da fühlt die Seele, nur Ein Rom sei je in der Welt gewesen . . .'

17 Polybius I 1.5–6 (written about 140 BC): what could be more important than to discover 'by what means and under what system of government the Romans succeeded in less than fifty-three years [220–167 BC] in bringing under their rule almost the whole of the inhabited world, an achievement which is without parallel in human history?' (trans. Ian Scott-Kilvert).

18 Polybius x 15.4–5 (trans. Ian Scott-Kilvert).

19 Livy XXXIX 8–19 (*coniuratio* at 8.1–2, 14.8, 15.10, 16.3; plague, 9.1; offence against ancestral custom, 15.2–3 and passim); *ILS* 18 = *ILLRP* 511 (*coniurare* at line 13). Good discussions, from very different viewpoints, in Seaford 1981.56–8 and Gruen 1990.34–78).

20 Pallottino 1991.20.

21 See above, pp. 68–71. Quirinus as Sabine: Varro *LL* v 73, vi 68; Festus (Paulus) 43L, Lydus *De mag.* I 5, etc.

22 See above, pp. 72–6. Epidaurus: *Vir. ill.* 22.1–2, Val. Max. I 8.2. Alexandria: Dion. Hal. xx 14.1, Val. Max. IV 3.9. Cf. Münzer 1920.83–9, esp. 88–9 (my translation): 'Unquestionably, he should be regarded as one of the respected Italian nobility who were persuaded to move to Rome at that time, and who immedi-

ately laid claim to an appropriate status there as well.' Compare the Praenestine Q. Anicius, curule aedile in 304 (Pliny *NH* xxxiii 17).

23 For 'the pivotal time . . . when the Roman elite felt compelled to articulate national values and to shape a distinctive character for their own corporate persona', see Gruen 1992 (quotation from p. 1; see 52–83 for the elder Cato).

24 Festus 290L: 'ut reges sibi legebant sublegebantque quos in consilio publico haberent, ita post exactos eos consules quoque et tribuni militum consulari potestate coniunctissimos sibi quosque patriciorum et deinde plebeiorum legebant.'

25 *Suffragium*: Vaahtera 1993. Sparta: Thuc. 1 87.2 (cf. Homer *Iliad* 1 22). *Comitia centuriata*: Laelius Felix in Gellius *NA* xv 27.5.

26 Cic. *In toga candida*, quoted by Asconius 88C (on C. Antonius): 'in exercitu Sullano praedonem, in introitu gladiatorem, in victoria quadrigarium'. (However, Claudius Quadrigarius was a respectable historian.)

27 Pliny *NH* xxi 7; Rawson 1981.2–4 = 1991.390–3. Athens: e.g. Aristophanes *Clouds* 14–16, Plut. *Alcibiades* 11. (Messalla as a charioteer in *Ben-Hur* is of course an anachronism.)

28 Varro *LL* v 55, Propertius iv 1.29–32, etc.

29 List of archaic *feriae* in Degrassi 1963.364–5; for the etymologies, see Maltby 1991, under the respective names.

30 For details and argument, see Crawford 1985.25–51, esp. 28–30, 38–42.

31 Crawford 1974, nos. 13, 15, 20. For the date of no. 13, see Crawford 1985.29.

32 Crawford 1974, nos. 14, 18, 19, 21. For the full range of types, see the table at Crawford 1974.717.

33 Crawford 1974.716: 'the types of the lower denominations were doubtless selected entirely at random'.

34 Crawford 1974, nos. 28–34; 1985.52–3.

35 Crawford 1974.715 n. 1: the type was used again on the *denarii* of C. Fonteius about 114 BC, with a ship on the reverse; his relative Mn. Fonteius six years later, also with a ship on the reverse, had laurelled (but separate) heads of the Dioscuri, identified by the twin stars above (Crawford 1974, nos. 290, 307). If the stars were ever found with the Janus-head type, it would be a different story. With no other identification, why should it not be a beardless Janus? But if it were, what would that signify?

Bibliography

Accame, S. (1959) *I re di Roma nella leggenda e nella storia*, Naples

Adam, R. and Briquel, D. (1982) 'Le miroir prénestin de l'antiquario comunale de Rome et la légende des jumeaux divins en milieu latin à la fin du IVe siècle av. J.C.', *Mélanges de l'Ecole française de Rome (Antiquité)* 94: 33–65

Alföldi, A. (1965) *Early Rome and the Latins* (Jerome Lectures seventh series), Ann Arbor

  (1973) 'La struttura politica di Roma nei suoi primordi', *Rendiconti dell'Accademia nazionale dei Lincei* ser. 8.27: 307–33

  (1974) *Die Struktur des voretruskischen Römerstaates* (Bibliothek der klassischen Altertumswissenschaften, n.F 1.5), Heidelberg

Altheim, F. (1938) 'The First Roman Silver Coinage', in *Transactions of the International Numismatic Congress in London, 1936* (London), 137–50

Ampolo, C. (1987) 'Roma arcaica tra Latini ed Etruschi: aspetti politici e istituzionali', in M. Cristofani (ed.), *Etruria e Lazio arcaica* (Quaderni del Centro di studio per l'archeologia etrusco-italica 15, Rome), 75–87

  (1988) 'La nascita della città', in *Storia di Roma* i: *Roma in Italia*, Turin, 153–80

Ampolo, C. and Manfredini, M. (1988) *Plutarco: le vite de Teseo e Romolo* (Scrittori greci et latini), Milan

André, J. (1967) *Les noms d'oiseaux en latin* (Etudes et commentaires 66), Paris

Atkinson, D. (1916) *The Romano-British Site on Lowbury Hill in Berkshire*, Reading

Austin, R. G. (1952) *M. Tulli Ciceronis pro M. Caelio oratio* (ed. 2), Oxford

Barnes, T. D. (1981) *Constantine and Eusebius*, Harvard

Bayet, J. (1920) 'Les origines de l'arcadisme romain', *Mélanges de l'Ecole française de Rome* 38: 64–143

Beard, M. (1990) 'Priesthood in the Roman Republic', in M. Beard and J. North (eds.), *Pagan Priests: Religion and Power in the Ancient World* (London), 17–48

(1993) 'Looking (harder) for Roman myth: Dumézil, declamation and the problems of definition', in F. Graf (ed.), *Mythos in mythenloser Gesellschaft: das Paradigma Roms* (Colloquia Raurica 3, Stuttgart), 44–64

Beaujeu, J. (1974) 'Le frère de Quirinus (à propos de Virgile, *Eneide* I, 292, et de Properce IV, 1, 9)', in *Mélanges de philosophie, de littérature et d'histoire ancienne offerts à Pierre Boyancé* (Collection de l'Ecole française de Rome 22, Rome), 57–72

Belier, W. W. (1991) *Decayed Gods: Origin and Development of Georges Dumézil's 'Idéologie tripartie'* (Studies in Greek and Roman Religion 7), Leiden

Berczelly, L. (1978) 'A sepulchral monument from Via Portuense and the origin of the Roman biographical cycle', *Acta ad archaeologiam et artium historiam pertinentia* 8: 49–74

Bickerman, E. J. (1952) 'Origines Gentium', *Classical Philology* 47: 65–81

Billows, R. (1989) 'Legal fiction and political reform at Rome in the early second century B.C.', *Phoenix* 43: 112–33

Binder, G. (1964) *Die Aussetzung des Königskindes* (Beiträge zur klassische Philologie 10), Meisenheim am Glan

Bömer, F. (1958) *P. Ovidius Naso: Die Fasten* II, Heidelberg

Borgeaud, P. (1988) *The Cult of Pan in Ancient Greece* (tr. K. Atlass and J. Redfield), Chicago

Bowie, E. L. (1993) 'Lies, fiction and slander in early Greek poetry', in C. Gill and T. P. Wiseman (eds.), *Lies and Fiction in the Ancient World* (Exeter), 1–37

Braund, D. C. (1980) 'The Aedui, Troy, and the *Apocolocyntosis*', *Classical Quarterly* 30: 420–5

Brelich, A. (1976) *Tre variazioni romane sul tema delle origini* (ed. 2), Rome

Bremmer, J. N. (1987a) 'Romulus, Remus and the foundation of Rome', in J. N. Bremmer and N. M. Horsfall, *Roman Myth and Mythography* (Institute of Classical Studies Bulletin Supplement 52, London), 25–48

(1987b) 'Caeculus and the foundation of Praeneste', ibid. 49–59

(1987c) 'Slow Cybele's arrival', ibid. 105–11

Briquel, D. (1976a) 'Les jumeaux à la louve, et les jumeaux à la chèvre, à la jument, à la chienne, à la vache', in R. Bloch (ed.), *Recherches sur les religions de l'Italie antique* (Hautes études du monde gréco-romain 7, Geneva and Paris), 73–97

(1976b) 'Les enterrés vivants de Brindes', *Mélanges offerts à Jacques*

Heurgon: l'Italie préromaine et la Rome républicaine I (Collection de l'Ecole française de Rome 27, Rome), 65–88

(1977) 'Perspectives comparatives sur la tradition relative à la disparition de Romulus', *Latomus* 36: 253–82

(1980) 'Trois études sur Romulus', in R. Bloch (ed.), *Recherches sur les religions de l'antiquité classique* (Hautes études du monde gréco-romaine 10, Geneva and Paris), 267–346

(1984) *Les Pélasges en Italie: recherches sur l'histoire de la légende* (Bibliothèque des Ecoles françaises d'Athènes et de Rome 252), Rome

(1986) 'A propos d'un oracle de Préneste', *La divination dans le monde étrusco-italique* II (Caesarodunum Supplement 54, Tours), 114–20

(1991) *L'origine lydienne des Etrusques: histoire de la doctrine dans l'antiquité* (Collection de l'Ecole française de Rome 139), Rome

Brize, P. (1980) *Die Geryoneis des Stesichorus und die frühe griechische Kunst* (Beiträge zur Archäologie 12), Würzburg

Brommer, F. (1956) 'Pan', in *Paulys Realencyclopädie der classischen Altertumswissenschaft* Supplementband VIII (Stuttgart), 949–1008

Brouwer, H. H. J. (1989) *Bona Dea: The Sources and a Description of the Cult* (Etudes préliminaires aux religions orientales dans l'empire romain 110), Leiden

Brown, P. (1978) *The Making of Late Antiquity* (Carl Newell Jackson Lectures), Harvard

Bruit Zaidman, L. and Schmitt Pantel, P. (1992) *Religion in the Ancient Greek City* (tr. P. Cartledge), Cambridge

Brunt, P. A. (1988) *The Fall of the Roman Republic and Related Essays*, Oxford

Burkert, W. (1962) 'Caesar und Romulus-Quirinus', *Historia* 11: 356–76

(1983) *Homo Necans: the Anthropology of Ancient Greek Sacrificial Ritual and Myth* (tr. P. Bing), Berkeley

(1992) *The Orientalizing Revolution: Near Eastern Influence on Greek Culture in the Early Archaic Age* (trans. M. E. Pinder and W. Burkert), Harvard

Cairns, F. (1979) *Tibullus: a Hellenistic Poet at Rome*, Cambridge

Cameron, A. (1993) *The Greek Anthology from Meleager to Planudes*, Oxford

Capponi, F. (1977) 'Avifauna nella divinazione e nel mito', *Latomus* 36: 440–56

Carcopino, J. (1925) *La louve du Capitole*, Paris

Carettoni, G. (1983) *Das Haus des Augustus auf dem Palatin*, Mainz

Classen, C. J. (1963) 'Zur Herkunft der Sage von Romulus und Remus', *Historia* 12: 447–57

(1965) 'Die Königszeit im Spiegel del Literatur der römischen Republik', *Historia* 14: 385–403

(1971) Review of Strasburger 1968, *Gnomon* 43: 479–84

Coarelli, F. (1983) *Il foro romano: periodo arcaico*, Rome

(1985) *Il foro romano: periodo repubblicano e augusteo*, Rome

(1987) *I santuari del Lazio in età repubblicana* (Studi NIS archeologia 7), Rome

(1988) 'I santuari, il fiume, gli empori', in *Storia di Roma* I: *Roma in Italia* (Turin), 127–51

Cornell, T. J. (1975) 'Aeneas and the twins: the development of the Roman foundation legend', *Proceedings of the Cambridge Philological Society* n.s. 21: 1–32

(1986) 'The value of the literary tradition concerning archaic Rome', in K. A. Raaflaub (ed.), *Social Struggles in Archaic Rome: New Perspectives on the Conflict of the Orders* (Berkeley), 52–76

(1989) 'Rome and Latium to 390 B.C.' and 'The recovery of Rome', in *The Cambridge Ancient History* VII.2 (ed. 2, Cambridge), 243–350

Cornell, T. (1991) 'The tyranny of the evidence: a discussion of the possible uses of literacy in Etruria and Latium in the archaic age', in *Literacy and the Roman World* (*JRA* Supplementary series 3, Ann Arbor), 7–33

Courtney, E. (1993) *The Fragmentary Latin Poets*, Oxford

Crawford, M. H. (1974) *Roman Republican Coinage*, Cambridge

(1985) *Coinage and Money under the Roman Republic: Italy and the Mediterranean Economy*, London

Cristofani, M. (1985) *I bronzi degli Etruschi*, Novara

De Sanctis, G. (1907) *Storia dei Romani* I, Turin

(1956) *Storia dei Romani* (ed. 2), Florence

De Simone, C. (1975) 'Etruskischer Literaturbericht: neuveröffentlichte Inschriften 1970–1973', *Glotta* 53: 125–81

Degrassi, A. (1963) *Inscriptiones Italiae* XIII.2, Rome

Derow, P. S. and Forrest, W. G. (1982) 'An inscription from Chios', *Annual of the British School at Athens* 77: 79–92

Dorcey, P. F. (1992) *The Cult of Silvanus: a Study in Roman Folk Religion* (Columbia Studies in the Classical Tradition 20), Leiden

Drossart, P. (1972) 'La mort de Rémus chez Ovide', *Revue des études Latines* 50: 187–204

Drummond, A. (1989) 'Rome in the fifth century I: the social and economic framework', in *The Cambridge Ancient History* VII.2 (ed. 2, Cambridge), 113–242

Dulière, C. (1979) *Lupa Romana: recherches d'iconographie et essai d'interprétation* (Etudes de philologie, d'archéologie et d'histoire publiées par l'Institut Historique Belge de Rome 18), Brussels and Rome

Dumézil, G. (1968) *Mythe et Epopée* I: *L'idéologie des trois fonctions dans les épopées des peuples indo-européens*, Paris
(1970) *Archaic Roman Religion* (trans. Philip Krapp), Chicago
(1973) *From Myth to Fiction* (trans. Derek Coltman), Chicago
(1974) *La religion romaine archaique* (ed. 2), Paris

Eames, J. D. (1975) *The MGM Story*, London

Eliade, M. (1954) *The Myth of the Eternal Return*, Princeton
(1982) *A History of Religious Ideas* II: *From Gautama Buddha to the Triumph of Christianity*, Chicago

Faraone, C. A. (1992) *Talismans and Trojan Horses: Guardian Statues in Ancient Greek Myth and Ritual*, New York

Fay, E. W. (1914) 'Varroniana: De Lingua Latina, Part II', *American Journal of Philology* 35: 245–67

Feeney, D. C. (1991) *The Gods in Epic: Poets and Critics of the Classical Tradition*, Oxford

Finley, M. I. (1983) *Politics in the Ancient World*, Cambridge

Fontenrose, J. (1978) *The Delphic Oracle: its Responses and Operations*, Berkeley and Los Angeles

Fox, M. (1993) 'History and rhetoric in Dionysius of Halicarnassus', *Journal of Roman Studies* 83: 31–47

Fraschetti, A. (1981) 'Le sepolture rituali del Foro Boario', in *Le délit religieux dans la cité antique* (Collection de l'Ecole française de Rome 48, ed. J. Scheid, Rome), 51–115

Gabba, E. (1960) 'Studi su Dionigi di Alicarnasso: 1. La constituzione di Romolo', *Athenaeum* 38: 175–225
(1967) 'Considerazioni sulla tradizione letteraria sulle origini della Repubblica', in *Les origines de la République romaine* (Fondation Hardt Entretiens 13, Geneva), 135–69
(1974) 'Storiografica greca e imperialismo romano', *Rivista storica italiana* 86: 625–42
(1976) 'Sulla valorizzazione politica della leggenda delle origini troiane di Roma fra III et II secolo a.C.', in M. Sordi (ed.), *I canali della propaganda nel mondo antico* (Contributi dell'Istituto di storia antica 4, Milan) 84–101
(1991) *Dionysius and The History of Archaic Rome* (Sather Classical Lectures 56), Berkeley and Los Angeles

Gell, Sir W. (1834) *The Topography of Rome and its Vicinity*, London

Gigon, O. (1954) 'Zur Geschichtsschreibung der römischen Republik', in *Sprachgeschichte und Wortbedeutung: Festschrift Albert Debrunner gewidmet* (Bern), 151–69

Gisinger, F. (1957) 'Promathos', *Paulys Realencyclopädie der classischen Altertumswissenschaft* XXIII.1 (Stuttgart), 1285–6

Gottschalk, H. B. (1980) *Heraclides of Pontus*, Oxford

Grant, M. (1971) *Roman Myths*, London

Gratwick, A. S. (1982) 'The origins of Roman drama', in E. J. Kenney and W. V. Clausen (eds.), *The Cambridge History of Classical Literature* II: *Latin Literature* (Cambridge), 77–93

Gronewald, M. (1983) 'Ein neues Fragment der Laudatio funebris des Augustus auf Agrippa', *Zeitschrift für Papyrologie und Epigraphik* 52: 61–2

Gruen, E. S. (1990) *Studies in Greek Culture and Roman Policy* (Cincinnati Classical Studies 7), Leiden

(1992) *Culture and National Identity in Republican Rome*, Cornell

Güntert, H. (1923) *Der arische Weltkönig und Heiland*, Halle

Hanson, J. A. (1959) *Roman Theater-Temples* (Princeton Monographs in Art and Archaeology 33), Princeton

Harris, J. R. (1906) *The Cult of the Heavenly Twins*, Cambridge

(1913) *Boanerges*, Cambridge

(1927) *Was Rome a Twin-Town?* (Woodbrooke Essays 8), Cambridge

Harris, W. V. (1979) *War and Imperialism in Republican Rome 327–70 B.C.*, Oxford

Hartwig, P. (1904) 'Ein roemisches Monument der Kaizerseits mit einer Darstellung des Tempels des Quirinus', *Mitteilungen des deutschen archaeologischen Instituts, roemische Abteilung* 19: 23–37

Haskell, F. (1993) *History and its Images: Art and the Interpretation of the Past*, Yale

Herbert-Brown, G. (1994) *Ovid and the Fasti: a Historical Study*, Oxford

Herder, J. G. (1787) *Ideen zur Philosophie der Geschichte der Menschheit*, dritter Teil, Riga and Leipzig

(1909) *Sämtliche Werke* XIV (ed. B. Suphan), Berlin

Heurgon, J. (1961) *La vie quotidienne chez les Etrusques*, Paris

Hölkeskamp, K.-J. (1987) *Die Entstehung der Nobilität: Studien zur sozialen und politischen Geschichte der römischen Republik im 4. Jhdt. v. Chr.*, Stuttgart

Holleman, A. W. J. (1974) *Pope Gelasius I and the Lupercalia*, Amsterdam

Holloway, R. R. (1994) *The Archaeology of Early Rome and Latium*, London

Hölscher, T. (1978) 'Die Anfänge römischer Repräsentationskunst', *Mitteilungen des deutschen archaeologischen Instituts, roemische Abteilung* 85: 315–57

Holzinger, K. von (1912) 'Diokles von Peparethos als Quelle des Fabius Pictor', *Wiener Studien* 34: 175–202

Horsfall, N. (1979) 'Stesichorus at Bovillae?' *Journal of Hellenic Studies* 99: 26–48

Horsfall, N. M. (1987) 'Myth and mythography at Rome', in N. M. Horsfall and J. N. Bremmer (eds.), *Roman Myth and Mythography* (Institute of Classical Studies Bulletin Supplement 52, London), 1–11

How, W. W. and Wells, J. (1912) *A Commentary on Herodotus*, Oxford

Hübinger, U. (1992) 'The cult in the "Sanctuary of Pan" on the slopes of Mount Lykaon', in R. Hägg (ed.), *The Iconography of Greek Cult in the Archaic and Classical Periods (Kernos* Supplement 1, Liège), 189–212

Hughes, D. D. (1991) *Human Sacrifice in Ancient Greece*, London

Humphrey, J. H. (1986) *Roman Circuses: Arenas for Chariot-Racing*, London

Jacks, P. (1993) *The Antiquarian and the Myth of Antiquity: the Origins of Rome in Renaissance Thought*, Cambridge

Jacoby, F. (1955) *Die Fragmente der griechische Historiker*, dritter Teil, Kommentar vol. (b), Leiden

Jocelyn, H. D. (1971) 'VRBS AVGVRIO AVGVSTO CONDITA: Ennius ap. Cic. *Diu.* 1.107 (= *Ann.* 77–96 V²)', *Proceedings of the Cambridge Philological Society* n.s. 17: 44–74

Jones, A. H. M. (1948) *Constantine and the Conversion of Europe* (Teach Yourself History Library), London

Jordan, H. (1885) *Quaestiones Ennianae* (Academia Albertensis Regimontii), Königsberg

Jurgeit, F. (1980) 'Aussetzung des Caeculus – Entrückung der Ariadne', in H. A. von Cahn and E. Simon (eds.), *Tainia: Roland Hampe zum 70. Geburtstag am 2. Dezember 1978 dargebracht* (Mainz), 269–79

Kearns, E. (1989) *The Heroes of Attica* (Institute of Classical Studies Bulletin Supplement 57), London

Klügmann, K. (1879) 'Due specchi di Bolsena e di Talamone', *Annali dell'Istituto di corrispondenza archeologica* 51: 38–53

Koeppel, G. H. (1980) 'Fragments from a Domitianic monument in Ann Arbor and Rome', *Bulletin of the Museum of Art and Archaeology, Ann Arbor* 3: 15–29

Krämer, H. J. (1965) 'Die Sage von Romulus und Remus in der lateinischer Literatur', in H. Flashar and K. Gaiser (eds.), *Synusia: Festgabe für Wolfgang Schadewaldt zum 15 März 1965* (Pfullingen), 355–402

Krampf, F. (1913) *Die Quellen der römischen Gründungssage* (Inaugural-Dissertation), Leipzig

Krappe, A. H. (1930) *Mythologie universelle*, Paris
(1933) 'Notes sur la légende de la fondation de Rome', *Revue des études latines* 35: 146–52

Kraus, C. S. (1994) *Livy Ab urbe condita Book VI* (Cambridge Greek and Latin Classics) Cambridge

Kretschmer, P. (1909) 'Remus und Romulus', *Glotta* 1: 288–303

Lamberton, R. (1988) *Hesiod* (Hermes Books), New Haven

Last, H. (1928) 'The founding of Rome', in *The Cambridge Ancient History* VII (Cambridge), 333–69

Levick, B. (1976) *Tiberius the Politician*, London

(1978) 'Concordia at Rome', in R. G. A. Carson and C. M. Kraay (eds.), *Scripta Nummaria Romana: Essays Presented to Humphrey Sutherland* (London), 217–33

Lewis, Sir G. C. (1855) *An Enquiry into the Credibility of Early Roman History*, London

Lincoln, B. (1975–6) 'The Indo-European myth of creation', *History of Religions* 15: 121–45

Linderski, J. (1986) 'The Augural Law', in H. Temporini and W. Haase (eds.), *Aufstieg und Niedergang der römischen Welt* II.16.3 (Berlin), 2146–312

Lommel, H. (1950) 'Vedische Einzelstudien', *Zeitschrift der deutschen morgenländischen Gesellschaft* 99: 223–57

Macaulay, T. B. (1842) *Lays of Ancient Rome*, London

MacKendrick, P. (1989) *The Philosophical Books of Cicero*, London

Malcovati, H. (1955) *Oratorum Romanorum fragmenta* (ed. 2), Turin

Maltby, R. (1991) *A Lexicon of Latin Etymologies* (ARCA 25), Leeds

Manganaro, G. (1976) 'Una biblioteca storica nel ginnasio a Tauromenion nel II sec. a.C.', in A. Alföldi, *Römische Frühgeschichte: Kritik und Forschung seit 1964* (Bibliothek der klassischen Altertumswissenschaften, n.F 1.6, Heidelberg), 83–96

Martin, P. M. (1971) 'A propos d'une notice de Dénys d'Halicarnasse (*A.R.* 1, 73, 3)', *Latomus* 30: 22–44

Mattingly, H. B. (1993) 'L. Porcius Licinus and the beginning of Latin poetry', in H. D. Jocelyn and H. Hurt (eds.), *Tria Lustra: Essays and Notes Presented to John Pinsent* (Liverpool Classical Papers 3, Liverpool), 163–8

Mayer, D. (1994) *Playing out the Empire: Ben-Hur and other Toga Plays: a Critical Anthology*, Oxford

Mazzarino, S. (1960) 'Antiche leggende sulle origini di Roma', *Studi romani* 8: 385–92

(1966) *Il pensiero storico classico* (ed. 2), Bari

Meates, G. W. (1979) *The Roman Villa at Lullingstone, Kent*, Chichester

Meiggs, R. (1982) *Trees and Timber in the Ancient Mediterranean World*, Oxford

Mele, A. (1979) *Il commercio greco arcaico: prexis ed emporie* (Cahiers du Centre Jean Bérard 4), Naples

(1987) 'Aristodemo, Cuma e il Lazio', in M. Cristofani (ed.), *Etruria e Lazio arcaico* (Quaderni del Centro per l'archeologia etrusco-italica 15, Rome), 155–77

Menichetti, M. (1988) 'Le aristocrazie tirreniche: aspetti iconografici' in *Storia di Roma* I: *Roma in Italia* (Turin), 75–124

Mesk, J. (1914) 'Die römische Gründungssage und Naevius', *Wiener Studien* 36: 1–35

Michels, A. K. (1955) 'The topography and interpretation of the Lupercalia', *Transactions of the American Philological Association* 84: 35–59

Millar, F. (1989) 'Political power in mid-Republican Rome: curia or comitium?', *Journal of Roman Studies* 79: 138–50

Momigliano, A. (1957) 'Perizonius, Niebuhr and the character of the early Roman tradition', *Journal of Roman Studies* 47: 104–14

(1960) *Secondo contributo alla storia degli studi classici* (Edizioni di storia e letteratura 77), Rome

(1975) *Quinto contributo alla storia degli studi classici e del mondo antico* (Edizioni di storia e letteratura 135–6), Rome

(1977a) *Essays in Ancient and Modern Historiography*, Oxford

(1977b) Review of Alföldi 1974, *Rivista storica italiana* 89: 160–2

(1980) *Sesto contributo alla storia degli studi classici e del mondo antico* (Edizioni di storia e letteratura 149–50), Rome

(1982) *New Paths of Classicism in the Nineteenth Century* (History and Theory Beiheft 21), Middletown Conn.

(1984a) 'Georges Dumézil and the trifunctional approach to Roman civilization', *History and Theory* 33: 312–30

(1984b) *Settimo contributo alla storia degli studi classici e del mondo antico* (Edizioni di storia e letteratura 161), Rome

(1985) *Tra storia e storicismo* (Biblioteca di scienze dell'uomo 1), Pisa

(1987) *Ottavo contributo alla storia degli studi classici e del monto antico* (Edizioni di storia e letteratura 169), Rome

(1989) 'The origins of Rome', in *Cambridge Ancient History* VII.2 (ed. 2, Cambridge), 52–112

Mommsen, T. (1845) 'De comitio Romano curiis Ianique templo', *Annali dell'Istituto di corrispondenza archeologica* 16: 288–318

(1864) *Römische Forschungen* I, Berlin

(1879) *Römische Forschungen* II, Berlin

(1881) 'Die Remuslegende', *Hermes* 16: 1–23

(1886) 'Die Tatius-legende', *Hermes* 21: 570–87

(1887) *Römisches Staatsrecht* II (ed. 3), Leipzig

(1906) *Gesammelte Schriften* IV, Berlin

(1908) *Gesammelte Schriften* V, Berlin

Montanari, E. (1976) *Roma: momenti di una presa di coscienza sociale* (Chi siamo 3), Rome

Moretti, L. (1980) 'Chio e la lupa Capitolina', *Rivista di filologia e di istruzione classica* 108: 33–54

Much, R. (1967) *Die Germania des Tacitus*, Heidelberg

Müllenhoff, K. (1900) *Deutsche Altertumskunde* IV: *Die Germania des Tacitus*, Berlin

Münzer, F. (1920) *Römische Adelsparteien und Adelsfamilien*, Stuttgart

Nash, E. (1968) *Pictorial Dictionary of Ancient Rome*, London

Nicolet, C. (1980) *The World of the Citizen in Republican Rome* (tr. P. S. Falla), London

Niebuhr, B. G. (1811) *Römische Geschichte* I, Berlin
  (1828) *The History of Rome* I (trans. J. C. Hare and C. Thirlwall), Cambridge
  (1849) *Lectures on Roman History* (trans. H. le M. Chepmell and F. C. F. Demmler), London

Niese, B. (1888) 'Die Sagen von der Gründung Roms', *Historische Zeitschrift* 59: 481–506

Nisbet, R. G. M. (1984) 'Horace's *Epodes* and history', in T. Woodman and D. West (eds.), *Poetry and Politics in the Age of Augustus* (Cambridge), 1–18

Nisbet, R. G. M. and Hubbard, M. (1970) *A Commentary on Horace Odes Book I*, Oxford
  (1978) *A Commentary on Horace Odes Book II*, Oxford

North, J. A. (1989a) 'The Roman counter-revolution', *Journal of Roman Studies* 79: 151–6
  (1989b) 'Religion in Republican Rome', in *The Cambridge Ancient History* VII.2 (ed. 2, Cambridge), 573–624

Ogilvie, R. M. (1965) *A Commentary on Livy Books 1–5*, Oxford

Otto, W. F. (1913) 'Die Luperci und die Feier der Lupercalien', *Philologus* 26: 161–95

Page, D. (1973) 'Stesichorus: *The Geryoneis*', *Journal of Hellenic Studies* 93: 138–54

Pairault Massa, F.-H. (1992a) 'Aspetti e problemi della società prenestina tra IV e III sec. a.C.', in *La necropoli di Praeneste: periodi orientalizzante e medio-repubblicana* (Atti del secondo convegno di studi archeologici, Palestrina), 109–45
  (1992b) *Iconologia e politica nell'Italia antica* (Biblioteca di archeologia 18), Milan

Pais, E. (1913) *Storia critica di Roma durante i primi cinque secoli* I, Rome

Pallottino, M. (1957) 'Promathos', *Paulys Realencyclopädie der classischen Altertumswissenschaft* 23: 1285–6

(1981) *Genti e culture dell'Italia preromana* (Guide allo studio della civiltà romana 1.2), Rome

(1991) *A History of Earliest Italy* (tr. M. Ryle and K. Soper), London

Palmer, R. E. A. (1970) *The Archaic Community of the Romans*, Cambridge

(1976) 'Jupiter Blaze, gods of the hills, and the Roman topography of *CIL* VI 377', *American Journal of Archaeology* 80: 43–56

Paris, R. (1988) 'Propaganda e iconografia: una lettura del frontone del tempio di Quirino sul frammento del "rilievo Hartwig" nel Museo Nazionale romano', *Bollettino d'arte* 52: 27–38

Pasquali, G. (1949) 'L'idea di Roma: antichità, scrittori greci', *Enciclopedia italiana* 29: 906–15

Peek, W. (1968–75) *Lexikon zu den Dionysiaka des Nonnos*, Hildesheim

Penn, W. S. (1960) 'Springhead: Temples III and IV', *Archaeologica Cantiana* 74: 113–40

Pensabene, P. (1988) 'Scavi nell'area del tempio della Vittoria e del santuario della Magna Mater sul Palatino', *Quaderni del Centro di studi per l'archeologia etrusco-italica* 16: 54–67

(1990) 'L'area sud-ovest del Palatino', in M. Cristofani (ed.), *La grande Roma dei Tarquinii* (Rome), 86–90

Perret, J. (1942) *Les origines de la légende troyenne de Rome (281–31)*, Paris

Peter, R., (1886) 'Faustulus', in W. H. Roscher (ed.), *Ausführliches Lexikon der griechischen und römischen Mythologie* 1.5 (Leipzig), 1461–9

Phillips, E. D. (1953) 'Odysseus in Italy', *Journal of Hellenic Studies* 73: 53–67

Pinsent, J. (1975) *Military Tribunes and Plebeian Consuls: the Fasti from 444V to 342V* (*Historia* Einzelschriften 24), Wiesbaden

Pokorny, J. (1959) *Indogermanisches Etymologisches Wörterbuch*, Bern

Pontone, A. G. (1986) *Fratricide as the Founding Myth of Rome: the Roman Historiographical Perspective* (Ph.D. thesis, New York University)

Pötscher, W. (1984) 'Die Lupercalia – eine Strukturanalyse', *Grazer Beiträge* 11: 221–49

Poucet, J. (1985) *Les origines de Rome: tradition et histoire* (Publications des facultés universitaires Saint-Louis 38), Brussels

Poultney, J. W. (1953) 'Latin *parra*, Umbrian *parfa*', in *Studies Presented to David Moore Robinson* II (St Louis), 469–76

Powell, J. G. F. (1988) *Cicero, Cato maior de senectute* (Cambridge Classical Texts and Commentaries 28), Cambridge

Preller, L. (1883) *Römische Mythologie* (ed. 3 by H. Jordan), Berlin

Price, S. R. F. (1984) *Rituals and Power: the Roman Imperial Cult in Asia Minor*, Cambridge

Prinz, F. (1979) *Gründungsmythen und Sagenchronologie* (Zetemata 72), Munich

Puhvel, J. (1970) 'Aspects of equine functionality', in J. Puhvel, ed., *Myth and Law among the Indo-Europeans: Studies in Indo-European Comparative Mythology* (Berkeley and Los Angeles), 159–72

(1975–6) 'Remus et frater', *History of Religions* 15: 146–57

(1987) *Comparative Mythology*, Baltimore

Raaflaub, K. A. (1986), 'From protection and defense to offense and participation: stages in the conflict of the orders', in K. A. Raaflaub (ed.), *Social Struggles in Archaic Rome: New Perspectives on the Conflict of the Orders* (Berkeley), 198–243

Raaflaub, K. A. and Toher, M. (eds.) (1990) *Between Republic and Empire: Interpretations of Augustus and his Principate*, Berkeley and Los Angeles

Rathje, A. (1983) 'A banquet service from the Latin city of Ficana', *Analecta Romana* 12: 7–29

(1990) 'The adoption of the Homeric banquet in central Italy in the orientalizing period', in O. Murray (ed.), *Sympotica: a Symposium on the Symposion* (Oxford), 279–88

Rawson, E. (1981) 'Chariot-racing in the Roman Republic', *Papers of the British School at Rome* 49: 1–16

(1991) *Roman Culture and Society: Collected Papers*, Oxford

Reid, J. S. (1912) 'Human sacrifices at Rome and other notes on Roman religion', *Journal of Roman Studies* 2: 34–52

Reinhold, M. (1979) 'Eighteenth-century American political thought', in R. R. Bolgar (ed.), *Classical Influences on Western Thought AD 1650–1870* (Cambridge), 222–43

Ridgway, D. (1988) 'The Etruscans', in *Cambridge Ancient History* IV (ed. 2, Cambridge), 634–75

Rix, H. (1989) 'Dichtersprachliche Traditionen aus vorliterarischer Zeit?', in G. Vogt-Spira (ed.), *Studien zur vorliterarischen Periode im frühen Rom* (ScriptOralia 12, Tübingen), 29–39

Rosenberg, A. (1914a) 'Remus', *Paulys Realencyclopädie der classischen Altertumswissenschaft*, zweiter Reihe I (Stuttgart), 597–8

(1914b) 'Romulus', ibid. 1074–104

Rösler, W. (1990) '*Mnemosyne* in the *Symposion*', in O. Murray (ed.), *Sympotica: a Symposium on the Symposion* (Oxford), 230–7

Rubinsohn, W. Z. (1987) *Spartacus' Uprising and Soviet Historical Writing* (tr. J. G. Griffith), Oxford

Sartori, P. (1898) 'Ueber das Bauopfer', *Zeitschrift für Ethnologie* 13: 1–54

Scardigli, B. (1991) *I trattati romano-cartaginesi* (Relazioni interstatali nel mondo antico, fonti e studi 5), Pisa

Schilling, R. (1960) 'Les "Castores" romains à la lumière des traditions indo-européennes', in *Hommages à Georges Dumézil* (Collection Latomus 45, Brussels), 177–92

(1979) *Rites, cultes, dieux de Rome* (Etudes et commentaires 92), Paris

Schmidt, P. L. (1989) 'Postquam ludus in artem paulatim verterat: Varro und die Frühgeschichte des römischen Theaters', in G. Vogt-Spira (ed.), *Studien zur vorliterarischen Periode im frühen Rom* (ScriptOralia 12, Tübingen), 77–134

Schröder, W. A. (1971) *M. Porcius Cato, das erste Buch der Origines: Ausgabe und Erklärung der Fragmente* (Beiträge zur klassichen Philologie 41), Meisenheim am Glan

Schultz, W. (1916) 'Tages', in W. H. Roscher (ed.), *Ausfürliches Lexikon der griechischen und römischen Mythologie* v.1 (Leipzig), 4–5

Schulze, W. (1904) *Zur Geschichte lateinischer Eigennamen* (Abhandlungen der königlichen Gesellschaft der Wissenschaften zu Göttingen, phil.-hist. Kl. n.f. 5.5), Berlin

Schumacher, W. N. (1968–9) 'Antikes und Christliches in der Auspeitschung der Elia Afanacia', *Jahrbuch für Antike und Christentum* 11–12: 65–75

Schur, W. (1921) 'Griechische Traditionen von der Gründung Roms', *Klio* 17: 137–52

Schwegler, A. (1853) *Römische Geschichte* i, Tübingen

Scullard, H. H. (1981) *Festivals and Ceremonies of the Roman Republic*, London

Seaford, R. (1981) 'The Mysteries of Dionysus at Pompeii', in H. W. Stubbs (ed.), *Pegasus: Classical Essays from the University of Exeter* (Exeter), 52–68.

(1994) *Reciprocity and Ritual: Homer and Tragedy in the Developing City-State*, Oxford

Severyns, A. (1963) *Recherches sur la Chrestomathie de Proclos* iv: *La vita Homeri et les sommaires du cycle* (Bibliothèque de la Faculté de Philosophie et Lettres de l'Université de Liège 170), Paris

Skutsch, O. (1961) 'Enniana iv: *Condendae urbis auspicia*', *Classical Quarterly* 55: 252–67

(1968) *Studia Enniana*, London

(1985) *The Annals of Q. Ennius* Oxford

Small, J. P. (1982) *Cacus and Marsyas in Etrusco-Roman Legend* (Princeton Monographs in Art and Archaeology 44), Princeton

Smits, E. C. H. (1946) *Faunus*, Leiden

Solin, H. (1983) 'Varia onomastica, v', *Zeitschrift für Papyrologie und Epigraphik* 51: 180–2

Soltau, W. (1909) 'Die Entstehung der Romuluslegende', *Archiv für Religionswissenschaft* 12: 101–25

Sommella Mura, A. (1981) 'L'area sacra del Foro Boario: il tempio arcaico', in *Enea nel Lazio: archeologia e mito* (Rome), 115–23

Sorlin, P. (1980) *The Film in History: Restaging the Past*, Oxford

Steinby, E. M. (ed.) (1993) *Lexicon Topographicum Urbis Romae I A-C*, Rome

Strasburger, H. (1968) *Zur Sage von der Gründung Roms* (Sitzungsberichte der Heidelberger Akademie der Wissenschaften, phil.-hist. Kl. 1968.5), Heidelberg

(1982) *Studien zur alten Geschichte* 2 (Collectanea 42.2, Hildesheim and New York), 1017–55

Strøm, I. (1971) *Problems Concerning the Origin and Early Development of the Etruscan Orientalizing Style* (Odense University Classical Studies 2), Odense

Sutherland, J. (1975) *The Oxford Book of Literary Anecdotes*, Oxford

Syme, R. (1978) *History in Ovid*, Oxford

Tabeling, E. (1932) *Mater Larum: zum Wesen der Larenreligion* (Frankfurter Studien zur Religion und Kultur der Antike 1), Frankfurt

Taplin, O. (1993) *Comic Angels and Other Approaches to Greek Drama through Vase-Paintings*, Oxford

Taylor, L. R. (1960) *The Voting Districts of the Roman Republic* (Papers and Monographs of the American Academy in Rome 20), Rome

Thomas, R. (1992) *Literacy and Orality in Ancient Greece*, Cambridge

Thomsen, R. (1980) *King Servius Tullius: a Historical Synthesis* (Humanitas 5), Cophenhagen

Timpe, D. (1988) 'Mündlichkeit und Schriftlichkeit als Basis der frührömischen Überlieferung', in J. von Ungern-Sternberg and H. Reinau (eds.), *Vergangenheit in mündlicher Überlieferung* (Colloquium Rauricum 1, Stuttgart), 266–86

Tirelli, M. (1981) 'La rappresentazione del sole nell'arte etrusca', *Studi etruschi* 49: 41–50

Torelli, M. (1982) *Typology and Structure of Roman Historical Reliefs*, Ann Arbor

(1984) *Lavinio e Roma: riti iniziatici e matrimonio tra archeologia e storia*, Rome

(1989) 'Archaic Rome between Latium and Etruria', in *Cambridge Ancient History* VII.2 (ed. 2, Cambridge), 30–51

Trieber, C. (1888) 'Die Romulussage', *Rheinisches Museum* 43: 569–82

Ulf, C. (1982) *Das römische Lupercalienfest* (Impulse der Forschung 38), Darmstadt

Ungern-Sternberg, J. von (1988) 'Überlegungen zur frühen römischen Überlieferung im Lichte der Oral-Tradition-Forschung', in J. von Ungern-Sternberg and H. Reinau (eds.), *Vergangenheit in mündlicher Überlieferung* (Colloquium Rauricum 1, Stuttgart), 237–65

Vaahtera, J. (1993) 'The origin of Latin *suffragium*', *Glotta* 70: 1–15

Vaglieri, D. (1907) 'Regione x: scoperte al Palatino', *Notizie degli scavi* 1907: 185–205

Vance, W. L. (1989) *America's Rome*, Yale

Versnel, H. S. (1976) Review of Alföldi 1974, *Biblioteca Orientalis* 33: 391–401

Veyne, P. (1960) 'Iconographie de la "transvectio equitum" et des Lupercales', *Revue des études anciennes* 62: 100–10

Visser, M. (1982) 'Worship your enemy: aspects of the cult of heroes in ancient Greece', *Harvard Theological Review* 75: 403–28

Wachter, R. (1987) *Altlateinische Inschriften: sprachliche und epigraphische Untersuchungen zu den Documenten bis etwa 150 v. Chr.*, Bern

Wagenvoort, H. (1956) *Studies in Roman Literature, Culture and Religion*, Leiden

Walbank, F. W. (1957) *A Historical Commentary on Polybius* 1, Oxford
    (1960) 'History and tragedy', *Historia* 9: 216–34
    (1985) *Selected Papers: Studies in Greek and Roman History and Historiography*, Cambridge

Walker, A. D. (1993) '*Enargeia* and the spectator in Greek historiography', *Transactions of the American Philological Association* 123: 353–77

Ward, D. (1968) *The Divine Twins: an Indo-European Myth in Germanic Tradition* (Folklore Studies 19), Berkeley and Los Angeles

Weigel, R. (1992) 'Lupa Romana', *Lexicon Iconographicum Mythologiae Classicae* vi.1: 292–6

Weinstock, S. (1946) 'Martianus Capella and the cosmic system of the Etruscans', *Journal of Roman Studies* 36: 101–29
    (1950) 'C. Fonteius Capito and the *Libri Tagetici*', *Papers of the British School at Rome* 18: 44–9
    (1971) *Divus Julius*, Oxford

West, M. L. (1966) *Hesiod: Theogony*, Oxford
    (1985) *The Hesiodic Catalogue of Women: Its Nature, Structure, and Origins*, Oxford
    (1988) 'The rise of the Greek epic', *Journal of Hellenic Studies* 108: 151–72

West, S. (1984) 'Lycophron italicised?', *Journal of Hellenic Studies* 104: 127–51

White, K. D. (1967) *Agricultural Implements of the Roman World*, Cambridge

White, P. (1993) *Promised Verse: Poets in the Society of Augustan Rome*, Harvard

Wiseman, T. P. (1974) 'Legendary genealogies in Late-Republican Rome', *Greece and Rome* 21: 207–18

(1979) 'Topography and rhetoric: the trial of Manlius', *Historia* 28: 32–50

(1981) 'The temple of Victory on the Palatine', *Antiquaries Journal* 61: 35–52

(1986) 'Monuments and the Roman annalists', in I. S. Moxon, J. D. Smart and A. J. Woodman (eds.), *Past Perspectives: Studies in Greek and Roman Historical Writing* (Cambridge), 87–100

(1987) *Roman Studies Literary and Historical*, Liverpool

(1988) 'Satyrs in Rome? The background to Horace's *Ars Poetica*', *Journal of Roman Studies* 78: 1–13

(1989) 'Roman legend and oral tradition', *Journal of Roman Studies* 79: 129–37

(1991) 'Democracy and myth: the life and death of Remus', *Liverpool Classical Monthly* 16.8: 115–24

(1992) 'Lucretius, Catiline and the survival of prophecy', *Ostraka* 1.2: 7–18

(1993) 'Rome and the resplendent Aemilii', in H. D. Jocelyn and H. Hurt (eds.), *Tria Lustra: Essays and Notes presented to John Pinsent* (Liverpool Classical Papers 3, Liverpool), 181–92

(1994) *Historiography and Imagination: Eight Essays on Roman Culture* (Exeter Studies in History 33), Exeter

(1995) 'The god of the Lupercal', *Journal of Roman Studies* 85

Wood, H. G. (ed.) (1933) *Amicitiae Corolla: a Volume of Essays Presented to James Rendel Harris, D.Litt., on the Occasion of his Eightieth Birthday*, London

Wood, M. (1975) *America in the Movies, or 'Santa Maria, it had slipped my mind'*, New York

Zanker, P. (1988) *The Power of Images in the Age of Augustus* (trans. Alan Shapiro), Ann Arbor

Zetzel, J. E. G. (1994) 'Looking backward: past and present in the late Roman Republic', *Pegasus* 37: 20–32

Zevi, F. (1970) 'Considerazioni sull'elogio di Scipione Barbato', *Studi miscellanei* 15: 63–73

Zorzetti, N. (1990) 'The *Carmina Convivalia*', in O. Murray (ed.), *Sympotica: a Symposium on the Symposion* (Oxford), 289–307

Index

236